WAYSIDE SCHOOL
GETS A LITTLE STRANGER

WAYSIDE SCHOOL
CLOSED
FOR REPAIR

LOUIS SACHAR
ILLUSTRATED BY TIM HEITZ

Long tail Books

To Carla and Sherre, with love

1. EXPLANATION

For two hundred and forty-three days, a lonely **sign** hung on the front of the old school building.

On some days a child would come, look at the sign, then sadly walk away.

Or else a child would come, look at the sign, stand on her

head, then sadly walk away.

Louis watched them come and go.

But he never said "Hi!" to them. He hid when they came.

It was his job to repair the school.

Louis used to be the **yard** teacher at Wayside School. He passed out the balls and played with the kids at **recess** and lunch.

When the school closed, the children were sent to other schools. **Horrible** schools. No two kids were sent to the same school.

Louis was afraid he'd cry if he talked to them.

But he worked hard. For two hundred and forty-two days, he pushed and pulled, **shovel**ed and **mop**ped. He never left the building. At night he slept on the **couch** in the teachers' **lounge** on the twelfth floor.

Some days it seemed **hopeless**. The worst part was the smell. He often had to run and **stick** his head **out** a window to get a breath of fresh air. But whenever he felt like quitting, he thought about those poor kids, stuck in those horrible schools, and he just worked harder.

And at last, two hundred and forty-three days later, the school was ready to open.

Well, almost ready. There was one little problem.

Suddenly, from somewhere inside the building, or maybe just inside his head, Louis heard a loud "**moo**."

He put his hands over his ears and said, "I don't hear it, I don't hear it, I don't hear it," until the mooing stopped.

He had **scrub**bed and **polish**ed **every inch** of Wayside School. There were no cows anywhere. He was sure of it! Still, every once in a while, he heard something go "moo." Or at least he thought he did.

He took the sign off the door.

But before you enter, you should know something about Wayside School.

Wayside School is a thirty-**story** building with one room on each floor, except there is no nineteenth story.

Mrs. Jewls teaches the class on the thirtieth story.

Miss Zarves teaches the class on the nineteenth story. There is no Miss Zarves.

Understand?

Good; explain it to me.

"*Louis!*" someone shouted.

He turned to see a red and blue **overcoat** running toward him. "Hi, Sharie!" he said. He couldn't see her face, but he knew she had to be somewhere inside the coat.

Sharie jumped into his arms.

"I **bet** you're glad to be back," said Louis.

"**You bet!**" said Sharie. "Now I can finally get some sleep!"

All around the **playground**, old friends were getting back together.

"Hi, old **pal**!" said John.

"Hey, good **buddy**," said Joe.

"Bebe!" **yell**ed Calvin from one side of the playground.

"Calvin!" shouted Bebe from the other.

They ran and **smash**ed into each other.

"Hi, Eric, good to see you," said Eric.

"Hey, good to see you too," said Eric. "Oh, look. There's Eric!"

"Hi, Eric! Hi, Eric!"

"Hi, Eric."

"Hi, Eric."

Even Kathy said hello to everybody.

"Hey, Big Ears!" she said to Myron as she **slap**ped him on the back. "What's happ'nin', Smelly?" she asked Dameon. "You didn't take a bath for two hundred and forty-three days, did you? Hi, Allison. Did you get uglier while you were away, or were you always this ugly and I just forgot?"

"That's a nice sweater, Kathy," said Allison, who always tried to say something nice.

Kathy **moved on** to Terrence. "I'm sure glad to see you, Terrence!" she said.

"You are?" asked Terrence.

"Yes," said Kathy. "I thought you'd be in **jail** by now."

Todd came running across the playground.

"Hi, Todd!" shouted Sharie, right in Louis's ear.

Todd kept running.

"Hey, Todd!" called Jason. "Good to see you!"

"Hi, Todd!" called Myron and D.J.

But Todd didn't answer. He just kept running until he reached the school building.

Then he kissed Wayside School.

Out of all the schools, Todd had been sent to the very worst one. It was **awful**! The first thing he had to do every morning was—

Wait a second. I don't have to tell you. You already know.

Todd was sent to your school.

2. A MESSAGE FROM THE PRINCIPAL

Dameon hurried up the stairs. He couldn't wait to see Mrs. Jewls, his favorite teacher in the whole world.

But the thirtieth floor was a lot higher up than he remembered, even if there was no nineteenth.

By the time he got up there, his legs hurt, his **side ached**, and he had a **blister** on the back of his **ankle** where it **rub**bed against his **sneaker**.

He **stumbled** into the room and **collapsed** on the floor. "Hi, Mrs. Jewls," he **gasp**ed.

"Hi, Dameon, welcome back!" said Mrs. Jewls.

Dameon looked up at her. Something seemed different about her, but he wasn't sure what it was.

"Oh, Dameon, would you do me a **favor**?" she asked.

"Sure," said Dameon.

"I left my pencil in the office," said Mrs. Jewls. "Would you mind going down and getting it for me?"

"No problem," said Dameon.

"It's yellow," said Mrs. Jewls. "It has a **point** at one end and a red **erase**r at the other."

Dameon **got to his feet** and headed down the stairs.

One by one the other children **stagger**ed into the classroom, **huff**ing **and puff**ing. They were all **out of shape**.

Still, they were very excited to be back in Mrs. Jewls's class. Shouts of joy could be heard from every corner of the room.

Mrs. Jewls held up two fingers.

All the children became quiet. Joy stopped shouting.

Mrs. Jewls told the children to sit at their old desks. "So, did anyone learn anything at your other schools?" she asked.

Mac raised his hand. "Oooh! Oooh!" he **grunt**ed.

"Yes, Mac," said Mrs. Jewls.

"**Civilization!**" **declare**d Mac.

"What about civilization?" asked Mrs. Jewls.

"We learned it," said Mac.

"That's very **impress**ive," said Mrs. Jewls. "Would you like to tell the class something about civilization?"

Mac thought a moment. "I don't remember," he said. "But I know we learned it."

"That's good, Mac," said Mrs. Jewls. "Anyone else learn anything?"

Rondi raised her hand. "**Evaporation**," she said.

"Good," said Mrs. Jewls. "What is evaporation?"

"I don't know," said Rondi.

Dana raised her hand. "I learned about **exaggeration**," she said. "It was all my teacher ever talked about. We had like ten thousand tests on it, and the teacher would kill you if you didn't **spell** it right."

"That's very good, Dana!" said Mrs. Jewls. "You learned your lesson well."

"I did?" asked Dana.

Mrs. Jewls **shrugg**ed. "Well, I guess we'll just continue where we **left off**."

Just then Mr. Kidswatter's voice came over the P.A. system.[1] "Good morning, boys and girls."

Mr. Kidswatter was the **principal**. He **pause**d a moment because he thought every kid in school was saying "Good morning, Mr. Kidswatter" back to him.

Nobody said it.

Sharie **buried** her head in her huge coat, closed her eyes, and went to sleep.

---

1 P.A. system (= Public Address System) 큰 건물이나 넓은 장소에 설치된 확성 장치. 많은 사람들에게 음성이나 음악을 전달하기 위해 사용한다.

"Welcome back to Wayside School!" said Mr. Kidswatter. "I know I'm sure glad to be back. It was wonderful to see all your bright and **chipper** faces this morning. I missed every single one of you.

"And welcome back to Miss Mush, too. Today's lunch menu will be **bake**d **liver**[2] in purple sauce. Miss Mush actually cooked this before the school was closed, but she **assures** me it is still as **tasty** as ever!"

"I'm sure it is," said Myron.

"A safety **reminder**. Now, it has been a while since you've had to **rush** up and down the stairs, and I want to make sure there are no accidents. So remember this simple rule. When you go up the stairs, stay to your right. When you go down the stairs, stay to your left. That way, there should be no problems.

"Okay, let's all have a good day. And remember, I'm your friend. And you're my friends. And if you ever need a friend, you can always come to me."

"Isn't that nice," said Mrs. Jewls.

"What a **bunch** of **baloney**! There I was, lying on a beach in Jamaica, when suddenly I get a fax that the **dumb** school was back open. Well, those kids better not **bother** me. My friends? That's a joke! Like I would really want to be friends with those

---

2 baked liver 구운 간 요리.

little snot-nose[3]—*What?* Don't tell me to shut up! You shut up! What's on? You mean they're hearing what I'm saying right this very second? Well, how do you turn it off? What button? I don't see a red button. There is no red button. Oh, here it

---

3   snot-nose 건방진 녀석.

3. POETRY

Mrs. Jewls told everyone to pick a color and write a **poem** about it.

"Huh?" said Joy.

"For example," said Mrs. Jewls, "if brown was your favorite color, you might write: 'At the **circus** I saw a **clown**. On his face was a great big **frown**. His sad eyes were big and brown.'"

"Could you repeat that just a little bit slower?" asked Joy.

Mrs. Jewls repeated it for her.

"Ooh, I'm going to do purple!" said Rondi. Rondi loved anything purple.

15

"You can't do purple," said Allison. "I'm doing it."

"So?" said Rondi. "Mrs. Jewls didn't say two people couldn't do the same color."

"But purple is my favorite color in the world," said Allison.

Rondi and Allison were best friends, but Allison always **got her way**.

Rondi **switch**ed to blue.

Joe raised his hand. "I don't know what **rhyme**s with red," he said.

Mrs. Jewls gave him a few **suggestion**s. "Bed, led, wed. Think of words that end in 'e-d.'"

"Oh, I **get it**!" said Joe. He set to work.

Rondi tried to think of words that rhymed with blue. She raised her hand. "Mrs. Jewls!" she said. "I chose blue. Can I rhyme that with zoo?"

"Yes, that would be a good rhyme," agreed Mrs. Jewls.

"How about **glue**?" asked Rondi.

"Yes, that rhymes too," said Mrs. Jewls.

"Oh, I know!" said Rondi. "How about stew?[1]"

"Just pick one and get started," said Mrs. Jewls.

Rondi smiled. "This is fun," she told Allison. "There are lots of words that rhyme with blue."

Allison **grunt**ed.

---

1 stew 스튜. 고기를 큼직하게 썰어서 버터로 볶다가, 양파, 감자, 당근 등을 차례로 넣고 물을 부어 푹 끓인 음식.

Nothing rhymed with purple. In her mind, Allison had **gone through** every letter of the **alphabet:** *aurple, burple, curple, durple* . . . **all the way** to *zurple.*

But after **making a** big **stink** over it with Rondi, she couldn't switch colors now.

Rondi was just about to start her poem when she got an even better idea: Love That's True. "Poets are always writing about Love That's True, aren't they, Mrs. Jewls?"

"Sometimes," said Mrs. Jewls.

Rondi smiled. Except she really didn't know much about true love.

"Morning **dew**!" she said. "Poets write about morning dew too, don't they, Mrs. Jewls?"

"I believe so," said Mrs. Jewls.

Dana walked to Mrs. Jewls's desk. "I can't think of anything that rhymes with pink," she **complain**ed.

"I'm sure you'll *think* of something," said Mrs. Jewls. She **wink**ed at her.

"I can't think," said Dana. "My mind's **on the blink**. I'm no good at poetry. I **stink**!"

"Just keep trying," said Mrs. Jewls.

Dana returned to her seat. She started to put her name on her paper, but her pen wouldn't write. "Great!" she complained. "Now my pen's out of ink!"

"Hey, Dana," whispered John. "Do you want to borrow my pen?"

"Sure," said Dana.

"Too bad, I'm using it," said John. Then he and Joe **cracked up**.

Meanwhile, Allison was going through the alphabet for the tenth time. . . . *Murple, nurple, ourple, qurple,* . . . she thought.

"My left shoe!" **exclaim**ed Rondi.

"You better choose something, Rondi, and get started," advised Mrs. Jewls.

"I got it!" said Rondi. "A Bird That Flew!"

At the end of the day, the children **turn**ed **in** their poems.

Yellow

by Kathy

I don't feel too well, oh

I don't know who to tell, oh

I'm sick and I smell, oh

*My **barf** is yellow*

Green

by Stephen

The swimming pool has lots of chlorine.[2]

It turned my hair green.

---

2 chlorine 염소. 자극적인 냄새가 나는 녹황색의 기체로 살균제나 표백제를 만들 때 주로 사용한다.

Brown

by Joy

At the circus I saw a clown.

On his face was a great big frown.

His sad eyes were big and brown.

Red

by Joe

*The **fire truck** is red!*

It hurried!

*The **siren wail**ed!*

The house burned!

*The **firemen** saved*

The baby who screamed.

Pink

by Dana

My favorite color is pink.

John is a ratfink![3]

Purple

by Allison

The baby won't stop crying.

---

3   ratfink 보기 싫은 녀석, 비열한 사람.

His face is turning purple.

Will anything make him feel better?

I bet a burp'll.

Blue

by Rondi

That was as far as she got.

4. DOCTOR PICKLE

Actually his name was Doctor Pickell, with the **accent** on the second **syllable**. But that wasn't why everyone called him Dr. Pickle.

Dr. Pickle was a **psychiatrist**. He had thick **eyebrow**s and wore tiny glasses. He had a small **beard** on the **tip** of his **pointed chin**.

A psychiatrist is a doctor who doesn't **cure** people with sick bodies. He cures people with sick minds.

Although Dr. Pickle had a pretty sick mind himself.

One day a woman came into his office. She **smoke**d too much, and she wanted him to help her quit.

"I know that smoking is no good for me," she said as she **puff**ed on her **cigarette**. "It's bad for my heart. It fills my **lungs** with **gunk**. And my husband won't kiss me because my breath **stinks**. But I can't quit!"

She finished her cigarette, **smush**ed it out in an **ashtray**, then **immediate**ly **lit** another one.

"Have a seat," said Dr. Pickle.

She sat down on the **couch**.

"Look into my eyes," said Dr. Pickle.

The woman **stared** into his deep, **penetrating** eyes.

Dr. Pickle held up a gold chain. At the end of the chain was a green stone that was almost **transparent**, but not quite. It looked l ike a pickle.[1]

Hence, his name.

"Watch the pickle," he said, as he gently moved the chain.

The pickle went **back and forth**, back and forth, back and forth.

The woman's eyes went back and forth, back and forth, back and forth.

"Put down your cigarette," Dr. Pickle said in a strong but gentle voice.

The woman set her cigarette in the ashtray as she continued

---

1 **pickle** 피클. 오이와 양파 등의 채소를 식초, 설탕, 소금, 향신료를 섞어 만든 액체에 담아 절여서 만든다.

to stare at the pickle.

"You are getting sleepy," said Dr. Pickle. "Your **eyelid**s are getting heavy."

The woman **blink**ed her eyes.

"When I **count** to three," said Dr. Pickle, "you will fall into a deep, deep sleep. One . . . two . . . three."

The woman's eyes closed.

Dr. Pickle put down the pickle. "Can you hear me?" he asked.

"Yes," said the woman, in a low voice from deep inside her.

"You will do what I say," said Dr. Pickle.

"I - will - do - what - you - say," the woman repeated.

"I am going to count to five," said Dr. Pickle. "And then you will wake up. And, as usual, you will want to smoke a cigarette."

"I - will - want - to - smoke - a - cigarette," the woman repeated.

"But when you put the cigarette in your mouth," said Dr. Pickle, "it will feel just like a **worm**. A **wiggling**, **slimy** worm."

"A - **yucky** - **icky** - worm," repeated the woman.

"Good," said Dr. Pickle. "Now just one more thing." He **rub**bed his beard and smiled. "Whenever your husband says the word 'potato,' you will **slap** him across the face."

"When - Fred - says - 'potato' - I - will - slap - his - face."

"Good," said Dr. Pickle. He counted to five.

The woman woke up.

"So do you think you can help me?" she asked in her normal voice, as she reached for her cigarette.

Dr. Pickle **shrug**ged.

She put her cigarette in her mouth, then screamed as she pulled it out.

She looked at the cigarette, **puzzle**d. "Hm?" she said. She placed it back in her mouth, then **spit** it out onto the floor.

"I'm sorry," she said, a little **confuse**d. She picked up the cigarette and put it in the ashtray.

"That's all right," said Dr. Pickle.

She took out a new cigarette from her pack, but as soon as she put that in her mouth, she spit it out too.

"I'm sorry," she said again. "I don't know what's **come over** me."

She walked out of his office shaking her head. She dropped her pack of cigarettes in the **trash**.

She never smoked again.

It was an interesting thing about the word "potato." Whenever Fred said it, she slapped him. And he'd ask her why she slapped him, but she never remembered slapping him, so they'd get in a big fight, each calling the other crazy. Then they'd kiss and **make up**, which was nice because her breath didn't stink.

They never **figure**d **out** it had anything to do with saying "potato." How could they?

But deep down they both must have realized it somehow, because while they used to eat lots of potatoes, they **gradual**ly ate fewer and fewer, until they finally stopped eating them **altogether**.

24

Dr. Pickle was a good doctor, but he kept playing those kinds of jokes on people. There was a woman who **quack**ed like a duck whenever she saw a **freight** train with more than twenty cars. There was a man who took off his shoe anytime someone said "parking meter.[2]"

Eventually Dr. Pickle was caught, and he was no longer allowed to **practice psychiatry**. So he had to find another job.

He became a **counselor** at an **elementary school**.

---

2 parking meter 주차 요금 징수기. 길 위에 주차된 차에 대해 요금을 징수하는 기계.

5. A STORY WITH A DISAPPOINTING ENDING

Paul's father was a **security guard** at a museum. The museum had a very famous painting.

It was painted by Leonardo da Vinci.[1] It was called the *Mona Lisa*.[2]

Next to the painting was a **sign**.

---

1 Leonardo da Vinci 레오나르도 다 빈치. 르네상스 시대의 이탈리아를 대표하는 천재적
  인 미술가.
2 Mona Lisa 모나리자. 레오나르도 다 빈치가 피렌체의 부호 프란체스코 델 조콘다의 부
  인을 그린 초상화.

DO NOT TOUCH!

All day Paul's father made sure nobody touched the painting.

At night, after the museum closed, Paul's father was alone. Just him and the *Mona Lisa*.

And the sign. Do not touch! Do not touch! Do not . . .

He was dying to touch it. The **tips** of his fingers **tingle**d with **desire**.

But this story isn't about Paul's father. It's about Paul.

Paul was a student in Mrs. Jewls's class. He sat behind Leslie.

Leslie had two long brown **pigtail**s that reached down to her **waist**. They just hung there, all day, right in front of Paul's face.

The Mona Leslie.

Do not touch! Do not touch! Do not . . .

Paul reached out, **grab**bed, and **yank**ed!

"Yaaaaaaaahhhhhhhhh!" screamed Leslie.

Mrs. Jewls sent Paul to the **counselor**'s office.

The counselor's office was on the fourth floor. Paul had never been there before.

Like every student in Wayside School, he was afraid of the counselor. The counselor had a very **scary** face, with big, **bushy eyebrow**s and a little **beard** on his **pointed chin**.

Paul **knock**ed on the door.

"Come in," said the counselor.

Paul entered and sat down on the **couch**.

"What's the problem?" asked the counselor.

"I pulled Leslie's pigtails again," said Paul. "I know it's wrong, but I just can't help myself."

"Watch the pickle," said the counselor.

Paul's eyes went **back and forth** as he **stared** at the **sway**ing pickle.

"You are getting sleepy," said the counselor. "Your **eyelids** are getting heavy."

Paul suddenly felt very tired. He could **hardly** keep his eyes open.

"When I **count** to three," said the counselor, "you will fall into a deep, deep sleep. One . . . two . . . three."

Paul closed his eyes. He wasn't **exactly** asleep. He felt like he was living in a dream. But it was a very **pleasant** dream. He felt happy and safe.

"Can you hear me?" asked the counselor.

"Yes," said Paul. He was no longer afraid of the counselor. In fact, he liked him a lot.

"You will do what I say," said the counselor.

"I - will - do - what - you - say," Paul repeated.

"I am going to count to five," said the counselor. "And then you will wake up. You will return to your classroom. You will take your seat behind Leslie. You will want to pull one of her pigtails. But when you reach for it, it will **turn into** a **rattlesnake**."

"Leslie's - pigtails - are - rattlesnakes," said Paul.

"Very good," said the counselor. "Now just one more thing." He rubbed his beard and smiled.

"When Leslie says the word 'pencil,' her ears will turn into candy. The most delicious candy in the world. The candy of your dreams."

Paul **lick**ed his lips. He could almost taste the rich chocolate and **chewy** caramel.

"And you will try to eat the candy."

"When - Leslie - says - 'pencil' - I - will - eat - her - ears," said Paul.

The counselor counted to five.

Paul's eyes **blink**ed open.

"You may go back to class now," said the counselor.

"I'm not in trouble?" asked Paul.

"No," said the counselor.

Paul shrugged. He returned to class. As he passed Leslie, she **stuck out** her **tongue** at him.

He sat down behind her.

"What'd the counselor do to you?" asked Eric Fry.

"Nothing," said Paul. "He's a nice man."

He looked at Leslie's pigtails. He had pulled the one on the left. But he still wanted to pull the one on the right.

He **lunge**d for it.

It **hiss**ed at him. Its tail **rattle**d.

He screamed and fell back over in his chair.

Everyone laughed.

"Paul, are you all right?" asked Mrs. Jewls.

"Uh, I guess so," said Paul, getting back up.

He didn't feel much like pulling Leslie's pigtails anymore.

It was just a short while later that Leslie's pencil **point** broke.

"Oh, great!" she **complain**ed.

"What's the matter?" asked Jenny, who sat next to Leslie.

Leslie showed her the broken pencil point.

"You want to borrow mine?" asked Eric Fry, who sat behind Jenny.

"No, I'll just go **sharpen** it," said Leslie. She went to the back of the room and sharpened her pencil.

She returned to her seat. She set the pencil on her desk, but it **roll**ed off when she sat down.

"Hey, where'd it go?" she asked, turning around.

"Where'd what go?" asked Paul.

"There it is," said Jenny. "Under Paul's desk."

"What's under my desk?" asked Paul.

"I'll get it," said Eric Fry. He reached under Paul's desk, picked up the pencil, and handed it to Leslie.

She thanked him and everyone returned to work.

30

6. PET DAY

All the kids in Mrs. Jewls's class brought a **pet** to school. The room was very **noisy**. Dogs **bark**ed. Cats **meow**ed. A frog **croak**ed. A pig **squeal**ed. A cow **moo**ed. Birds **tweet**ed.

Mrs. Jewls held up two fingers.

All the animals became quiet.

Stephen didn't have a pet. So he brought an orange. He kept it in a **cage** on his desk so it couldn't escape.

Todd brought Ralphie, his baby brother.

"Todd?" said Mrs. Jewls.

Todd barked.

"You cannot have a pet human," said Mrs. Jewls.

"He doesn't **bite**," Todd **assured** her.

Joy told Todd to sit and be quiet.

Mrs. Jewls got a large piece of poster board[1] from the **supply closet**. "Let's make a **chart**," she said.

Across the top of her chart she wrote, "Name of Kid," "Kind of Pet," "Name of Pet."

She started with Deedee. She wrote "Deedee" under "Name of Kid." "And you have a dog," she said.

"Cat," said Deedee.

"Cat?" asked Mrs. Jewls.

Deedee **nod**ded as she petted her dog.

Mrs. Jewls **moved on** to Ron. "Ron, I see you have a cat."

"Dog," said Ron, as he **stroke**d the cat on his **lap**.

Mrs. Jewls shrugged. "Okay," she said.

"He's my dog," said D.J.

"Ron has your dog?" asked Mrs. Jewls.

"Ron has a cat," said D.J.

"That's what I thought," said Mrs. Jewls. "But what—"

"What's a dog," said Jenny.

Mrs. Jewls covered her ears and shook her head. "Let's start all over again," said Mrs. Jewls. She got a new piece of poster board from the supply closet.

---

1 **poster board** 포스터를 만드는 데 주로 쓰이는 두꺼운 판지.

"Mac, what's your dog's name?"

"What's my dog's name," said Jenny.

"I'm not talking to you, Jenny. I'm talking to Mac."

"He can't talk," said Mac.

"Who can't talk?" asked Mrs. Jewls.

"Mac," said Mac.

Billy barked at Mac.

Mac barked at Billy.

Todd barked at both of them.

Joy made Todd lie down by her feet.

Mrs. Jewls moved on. "What's your pet, Myron?" she asked.

"Your pet's a **turtle**," said Sharie.

"What?" asked Mrs. Jewls.

"What is Jenny's pet," said Sharie.

"Jenny's pet is a dog!" said Mrs. Jewls. "What's his name, Jenny?"

Jenny nodded. Her dog sat up straight and tall and seemed to smile at Mrs. Jewls.

"He's handsome," said Mrs. Jewls.

"My mouse is handsome," said Benjamin. Benjamin had a little white mouse in a cage on his desk.

"If you like mice," said Dana, **making a face**.

"Mrs. Jewls likes mice," said Calvin. "She eats them."

"**Gross!**" said Dana.

"He won't come when you call him," said Kathy. "He doesn't

know his name."

Billy meowed.

"Will Mrs. Jewls eat yogurt[2]?" asked John.

"**No way!**" said Calvin.

"I will too," said Mrs. Jewls. "I like yogurt. I like strawberry best."

Maurecia **beamed**. "Mrs. Jewls likes strawberry best," she **bragged**.

"You shouldn't pick favorites," complained Dana.

"Do you like crackers,[3] Mrs. Jewls?" asked Rondi.

"Don't worry," said Calvin. "Mrs. Jewls won't eat crackers."

"How do you know what I'll eat, Calvin?" asked Mrs. Jewls, a little **annoy**ed. "I like eating crackers with cheese on top."

"Oh, gross!" said Myron.

"He won't come when you call him," Kathy said again.

"Mac! Keep Mac away from my socks!" shouted Allison.

"Wait," said Jason. "Now you've got my socks, and I've got your socks."

"I can tell the difference between my socks and your socks, Jason," said Allison.

Mrs. Jewls covered her ears and shook her head. She moved on. "What's your pet, Dameon?" she asked.

"I already told you he was a turtle," said Sharie.

---

2 yogurt 요구르트. 우유의 유산균 발효에 의해 만들어진 유제품으로 약간 시큼한 맛과 걸쭉한 상태가 특징이다.

3 cracker 밀가루를 주재료로 하여 얇고 딱딱하게 구운 과자.

"I wasn't talking to you, Sharie," said Mrs. Jewls. "I was talking to Dameon."

"Your nose a ferret,[4]" said Dameon.

"My nose a ferret?" asked Mrs. Jewls.

"My nose a hamster,[5]" said Joe.

Billy **bleat**ed.

Mrs. Jewls **lick**ed her leg.

"Hey, Paul," said Leslie. "I like your **pigtail**s."

"Thanks," said Paul. "May I touch your **pajamas?**"

"Go ahead," said Bebe, who was already petting Leslie's pajamas. "She won't **scratch** you."

"This is crazy!" shouted Terrence.

"He's cute," said Dana.

---

4   ferret 페럿. 족제비과의 애완동물.
5   hamster 햄스터. 비단털쥐과의 포유류이며 애완동물로 널리 기른다.

Name of Kid	Kind of Pet	Name of Pet
Deedee	Dog	Cat
Ron	Cat	Dog
D.J.	Dog	O.K.
Jenny	Dog	What
Mac	Dog	Mac
Joy	Dog	Todd
Sharie	Turtle	Yorpet
Benjamin	Mouse	Handsome
Calvin	Cat	Mrs. Jewls
Kathy	Skunk	Gross
John	Frog	Yogurt
Maurecia	Cat	Strawberry
Rondi	Bird	Crackers
Myron	Chipmunk	Cheese
Allison	Cat	Socks
Jason	Cat	Socks
Dameon	Ferret	Yorno
Joe	Hamster	Mino
Paul	Pig	Tails
Leslie	Cat	Pajamas
Terrence	Dog	Crazy
Eric Fry	**Kid** (Goat)	Billy
Eric Bacon	Dog	Billy
Eric Ovens	Cat	Billy
Dana	Dog	Pugsy
Bebe	Bird	Picasso
Todd	Kid (Human)	Ralphie
Stephen	Orange	Fido

7. A BAD WORD

Early in the morning, a white **limousine** drove up to Wayside School.

Just like always.

The **chauffeur** got out of the car, then opened the **passenger** door.

Just like always.

Mr. Kidswatter stepped out of the car. "Thank you, James," he said.

"My name is David," said the chauffeur.

Just like always.

Mr. Kidswatter entered the school building.

"Good morning, Mr. Kidswatter," said Mrs. Day, the school secretary. She handed him a cup of hot coffee.

Just like always.

"Thank you, Miss Night," said Mr. Kidswatter.

He walked into his office.

Except his office door was closed.

He smashed into it, spilling coffee all over his green suit.

"Who closed my door?" he demanded.

"Why didn't you just open it?" asked Mrs. Day.

"It's *always* open in the morning," said Mr. Kidswatter. "How was I supposed to know it was closed *this time?*"

Up on the thirtieth story, Mrs. Jewls took roll.

Todd was absent.

"Oh dear, I hope Todd is all right," said Mrs. Jewls.

"Todd's never all right!" said Joy.

She and Maurecia laughed.

Dameon looked at Mrs. Jewls. Ever since he returned to Wayside School, he'd thought there was something *different* about her, but he still couldn't figure out what it was.

Mr. Kidswatter's voice came over the P.A. system. "Good morning, boys and girls."

There was the usual pause.

"Today I want to talk about doors," said Mr. Kidswatter.

38

"This should be interesting," said Mrs. Jewls.

"Do you know how many doors there are in this school building?" asked Mr. Kidswatter.

Mrs. Jewls shook her head.

"Well, there are a lot! Over thirty! And some of you probably have doors at home too. Maybe more than one. All those doors. Think about it."

"Well, Mr. Kidswatter has certainly given us something to think about this morning," said Mrs. Jewls.

"So remember," said Mr. Kidswatter. "And please be careful! Always check to see if a door is open before going through it. And if it's not open, open it. If you can't open it yourself, ask someone to open it for you. This may not **make** a lot of **sense** to you now, but someday you'll thank me."

Mrs. Jewls looked around the class. "That's good advice," she said. "I think most of you already knew it, but at least it's nice to know we have a **principal** who cares."

"I hate doors!" shouted Mr. Kidswatter. "It's a **dumb** word. Door. Door. Door. Who **made up** that word, anyway?"

Mrs. Jewls waited a little longer, but Mr. Kidswatter seemed to be finished. "Some people just don't like doors," she said.

"I have made a new rule!" declared Mr. Kidswatter. "You may no longer say that word. You know what word I mean— but don't say it! Instead, I have made up a new word for you: 'Goozack.' Open the goozack. Shut the goozack. **Lock** the goozack. Don't you think that's a better word? I do. **From now on**, that other word is a bad word. I have made my decision."

Everyone turned around and looked at the goozack.

Suddenly it opened.

Todd entered. "I'm sorry I'm late," he said.

"That's okay," said Mrs. Jewls. "I'm just glad you're not sick or hurt."

"My dad locked his keys in the car," Todd explained. "We had to use a **coat hanger** to unlock the door."

Everyone **gasp**ed.

Mrs. Jewls made Todd write his name on the **blackboard** under the word **DISCIPLINE**.

8. SANTA CLAUS

'Twas[1] the last day of school
Before winter vacation,
And the children were having
*A small **celebration**.*

*Their **artwork** was hung*
*By the **blackboards** with **pride**:*
Snowmen, and mooses,[2]

---

1 'Twas 'It was'의 축약형.
2 moose 무스. 현존하는 가장 큰 사슴으로, 몸집이 말보다 크다.

*And a **joyful sleigh** ride.*

*They ate **homemade** cookies,*
  (Red and green ones, of course.)
When Kathy declared,
  "I don't believe in Santa Claus!"

She just opened her mouth,
  And said what she said.
"Santa Claus isn't real,
  *And **besides** that, he's dead!*

*"So you **bet** I will **pout**,*
  And you bet I will cry.
"You bet I will shout,
  I'm telling you why . . . ."

Stephen covered his ears. "No, you're wrong!" he shouted. "It's not true. There is a Santa Claus. I know there is!"

"Ho, ho, ho," laughed Kathy.

"Kathy is just saying that because she never gets any presents," said Jason.

"All she ever gets is a **lump** of **coal**!" said Rondi.

"Wrong!" said Kathy. "I get lots of presents. My parents buy them for me. They have lots of money. They buy me anything I want."

She **bit** off the head of a **reindeer** cookie. "The only thing that matters is how rich your parents are. If they have lots of money, then you'll get lots of good presents. If they're poor, then you'll just get a few **crummy** presents."

Everyone tried to argue with her, but Kathy just asked them all the old questions, like "How does a fat man **fit** down a **skinny chimney?**" or "How could he visit everyone's house in the whole world in one night?"

And of course nobody knew the answers. Nobody ever has.

"Only Santa knows the answers to those questions," said Rondi.

"Don't you even like Christmas?" asked Stephen.

"Sure," said Kathy.

"I get lots of presents,
And I don't have to work."
*Then she stuck out her **tongue***
*and called Stephen a **jerk**.*

*Poor Stephen **sputtered***
As his face turned quite blue,
"If you don't believe in Santa,
He won't believe in you!"

*But Kathy just **yelped**.*

"You know that it's true!
Do you still believe in the Easter bunny,[3]
The tooth fairy,[4] and Miss Zarves too?"

"Let's ask Mrs. Jewls!" said Maurecia.
*"She's a teacher who's **wise**.*
Let's ask Mrs. Jewls.
She never lies!"

The children crowded round
Their wise teacher's desk
And asked her the question
Never found on a test.

"Is there a Santa?
*You're a teacher with **smarts**!*
Is Santa Claus real?"
They asked with pure hearts.

And oh, Mrs. Jewls,
That teacher so wise,

---

3 **Easter bunny** 부활절에 아이들에게 부활절 달걀 등의 선물이 담긴 바구니를 가져온다는
토끼.

4 **tooth fairy** 밤에 어린아이가 자신의 침대 머리맡에 빠진 이를 놓아두면 이것을 가져가고
그 대신에 동전을 놓아둔다는 상상 속의 존재.

Looked at their faces
　　*And bright, **eager** eyes.*

She had to say something.
　　It was her job to reply.
"Tell them," yelped Kathy.
　　"That reindeer can't fly!"

Outside the window
　　***Snowflakes** were falling. . . .*
Inside the window
　　*Mrs. Jewls was **stalling**. . . .*

*"Are our parents all **liars?**"*
　　*"Is it all just a **trick***
To make us be good
　　For fear of St. Nick?[5]"

"Tell us the truth;
　　*Don't try to **fake** it.*
Is there a Santa?
　　*Let us know; we can **take it**."*

---

5 St. Nick 성 니콜라우스(Saint Nicholas). 산타클로스의 유래가 된 성직자로 산타클로스를 부르는 다른 이름이다.

Mrs. Jewls cleared **her throat,**
Then she cleared it again.
She put down her pencil.
She picked up her pen.

"Hey, look!" shouted Leslie.
"Look there! Who's that?
Someone is coming in
Through the goozack!"

Sure enough, the door opened.
It had to open quite wide!
As a strange-looking stranger
Stepped **sideways** inside.

He wore a red **suit**
And had a white, **fluffy beard.**
And even for Wayside
He looked pretty **weird!**

His fat **belly** shook
Like a **bowl** full of Jell-O.[6]
There was no **doubt** about it.

---

6 Jell-O 젤로. 과일의 맛이 나는 젤리.

It was Louis, the **yard** teacher.

"What are you doing in that stupid suit, Louis?" asked Sharie. "Aren't you hot?"

"Why are you wearing a fake beard?" asked Todd.

"Is that a **pillow** under your jacket?" asked Jason.

Kathy was **delight**ed. "See!" she said. "That proves there's no Santa Claus! If there was, Louis wouldn't have to **dress up** like a **fool** and pretend to be him."

"I'm not Louis," said Louis. "I'm Santa Claus. Ho! Ho—"

"You're lying to us, Louis," said John. "Everyone is always lying to us. Kathy's right. Christmas is nothing but a dirty, **stink**ing lie!"

"I was just trying to bring a little holiday cheer," said Louis.

"Go home, Jerome," said Terrence.

"Now, that's no way to talk to Louis," said Mrs. Jewls. "Louis is one of Santa's special helpers."

"Really, Louis?" asked Deedee.

Louis looked at Mrs. Jewls. "That's right," he said.

The children were all very **impress**ed.

"Have you ever met him?" **demand**ed Kathy.

"Well, no, not **exact**ly," Louis admitted.

"See!" said Kathy. "It's just another lie."

"You don't have to meet Santa to be one of his special helpers," said Mrs. Jewls.

"Then how do you know what he wants you to do?" asked John.

"That's easy," said Mrs. Jewls. "You just have to be nice to other people. Whenever you give someone a present or sing a holiday song, you're helping Santa Claus. To me, that's what Christmas is all about. Helping Santa Claus!"

"Can I be one of his helpers?" asked Dameon.

"**You bet**," said Mrs. Jewls.

"Hey, everybody," shouted Dameon. "I'm one of Santa's helpers!"

"Me too," said Allison.

"There must be a Santa Claus!" cheered Stephen. "Because it feels so good to help him."

So the children all helped Santa,
In every way they could,
By singing songs and giving gifts
And just by being good.

"But there is no Santa Claus!"
Kathy continued to yelp.
"Well, if that's the case," said Mrs. Jewls.
"He must really need our help."

9. SOMETHING DIFFERENT
ABOUT MRS. JEWLS

The children returned from Christmas vacation. On each desk were two **knit**ting **needle**s and a **hunk** of **yarn**.

"Today we are going to learn how to knit," said Mrs. Jewls.

She showed the class how it was done. "See, you stick this needle through here, then **wrap** this around this like this, stick this through this, pull this like this, and then you stick this here. Any questions?"

Everyone **stared** at her.

"Good," said Mrs. Jewls. "I want everybody to make socks. Okay, get started."

Dameon looked at his knitting needles. He didn't have a **clue**.

He looked back at Mrs. Jewls. Now, more than ever, he was sure she was somehow *different*.

She was sitting at her desk, knitting and eating Baloneos. Dameon couldn't remember Mrs. Jewls ever eating a Baloneo before.

A Baloneo was an Oreo[1] cookie, except instead of the white part, there was a round hunk of baloney.[2]

Miss Mush **invent**ed them.

"Hey, Mac," whispered Dameon. "Does Mrs. Jewls seem different to you?"

"She's fat," said Mac.

"That's not a nice thing to say," said Dameon.

"I didn't say it to Mrs. Jewls," said Mac. "I didn't go, 'Hey, Mrs. Jewls. You're fat!' "

Mrs. Jewls **clear**ed **her throat** as she stood up. She walked around the room. "Very nice, D.J.," she said. "You're doing fine, Rondi."

She stopped at Joe's desk.

"Oh, Joe!" she **gush**ed. "Look, everybody, I want you to see Joe's sock!" She held it up. "Isn't it the most beautiful sock you ever saw?"

It was a great sock. Everybody **ooh**ed **and aah**ed.

Joe was as surprised as anyone. He didn't know he knew

---

1 Oreo 오레오. 원형의 초콜릿 비스킷 사이에 크림이 들어있는 쿠키.
2 baloney 볼로냐 소시지. 이탈리아 도시 볼로냐(Bologna)에서 유래했다.

how to make socks. But the boy was born to knit.

Mrs. Jewls started to cry. "I love this sock," she **sob**bed.

"Uh-oh," said Kathy. "I think she's finally **flip**ped **out!**"

"I love you, Kathy," said Mrs. Jewls. She looked around the room. "I love all of you."

She put her hand on Kathy's desk. "I love this desk," she said. "I love the blackboard. I love the clock on the wall."

There was a **ruler** on the floor.

Mrs. Jewls picked it up. "I love this ruler," she **declare**d.

"Hey, that's mine!" said Dana. "But, uh, that's okay, Mrs. Jewls. You can have it."

"I don't want your ruler, Dana," said Mrs. Jewls, handing it to her.

"You want my pair of **scissors**?" offered Sharie.

"Don't give her anything sharp!" warned Kathy.

Mrs. Jewls **wipe**d away her tears and smiled at the class. "I'm going to miss all of you very much," she said.

"Are you going away?" asked Dameon.

"Yeah, to the loony bin,[3]" whispered Kathy.

"Are you sick?" asked Eric Ovens.

"No, I'm not sick," said Mrs. Jewls. "In fact, I'm better than I've ever been." She **beam**ed. "I'm going to have a baby!"

Everyone gasped.

3　loony bin 정신병원.

Dameon couldn't believe it! He was so happy he jumped out of his seat and hugged Mrs. Jewls.

She was soon surrounded by all her students, even Kathy, wanting to hug her.

"Today is my last day here," Mrs. Jewls told her students. "My doctor doesn't want me walking up and down thirty **flights of stairs** every day. I wasn't even supposed to come today, but I just had to say good-bye."

"I thought you were getting fat," said Mac. "But I didn't want to say anything."

"Thank you, Mac," said Mrs. Jewls. "You are very **considerate**."

"Can I touch your **stomach**?" asked Stephen.

Mrs. Jewls laughed. "Sure," she said.

The children **took turns** touching her stomach.

"What are you going to name your baby?" asked Allison.

"I don't know yet," said Mrs. Jewls. "What do you think?"

"Well, if she's a girl," said Allison, "I think you should name her Rainbow Sunshine."

"That's a nice name," said Mrs. Jewls. "And if he's a boy?"

"Bucket Head,[4]" said Allison. She didn't like boys.

"If he's a boy, you should name him Jet Rocket!" said Joe.

"Jet Rocket Jewls," **mused** Mrs. Jewls. "That **has a** nice **ring to it**. And what if she's a girl?"

---

4 bucket head 바보, 멍청이.

"**Cootie** Face,[5]" said Joe.

Mrs. Jewls laughed. "So let me **get** this **straight**," she said. "If he's a boy, I'll name him Bucket Head."

"Right," said Allison and Rondi.

"And if she's a girl, I'll name her Cootie Face."

"Right," said Joe and John.

Dameon laughed. He knew Mrs. Jewls was only joking. At least he hoped she was.

Terrence placed his **palm** flat against Mrs. Jewls's stomach. "Hey," he **exclaim**ed. "The **dude** kicked me!"

Suddenly Dameon felt very sad. He was going to miss her a lot! He wiped a tear from his eye. "It's unfair!" he shouted. "We finally come back to Wayside School after being gone for so long. And now you're leaving us!"

"I have to," said Mrs. Jewls.

"I know," **whine**d Dameon. "You have to make sure that you and your baby are healthy. But it still isn't fair!"

"I think you'll like your **substitute** teacher," said Mrs. Jewls. "I spoke to him over the vacation. He seems like a very nice man."

"A man?" asked Dameon. "Cool!"

They all thought it was pretty **neat** to have a man teacher.

"Yes," said Mrs. Jewls. "His name is Mr. Gorf."

---

5   cootie face 'cootie(이)'라는 단어로 유추해 보면 '지저분한 녀석'이라는 의미로 쓰였다.

10. MR. GORF

"Mr. Gorf," muttered Joy as she walked down the stairs to recess. "Did she say Mr. Gorf?"

Maurecia nodded.

Leslie caught up to them. "Did she say Mr. Gorf?"

"I think so," said Maurecia.

"Do you think—?" Leslie asked.

"I don't know," said Maurecia.

"I hope not," said Joy.

Before Mrs. Jewls ever came to Wayside School, the children had a teacher named Mrs. Gorf. She wasn't very nice.

Even Myron was worried. And Myron had never gotten in trouble in his whole life.

"Mr. Gorf might be a good teacher," said Eric Bacon. "Just because he has the same last name as Mrs. Gorf doesn't mean he'll be **horrible**."

"That's right," said Eric Ovens. "People with the same name can be different."

"I agree," said Eric Fry.

"There are probably lots of people named Gorf," Dameon said **hopeful**ly. "I bet if you looked in the phone book, you'd find ten whole pages of Gorfs."

"Well, I don't know about you, but I'm not coming to school tomorrow," said Joy.

"Me neither," Maurecia agreed.

But the next morning their parents made them all go to school.

Everyone arrived **on time**. Nobody **dare**d to be late.

But there was no teacher.

Deedee sat down next to Myron. "Is he here?" she whispered.

"Sh!" whispered Myron. He folded his hands on his desk and stared straight ahead.

One by one, the children entered the classroom and quietly sat down at their desks.

They couldn't **take** any **chances**. Mr. Gorf might walk through the door any moment. Or maybe he was already there, hiding in the coat **closet**, just waiting for someone to do something wrong.

"I didn't want to come today," whispered Calvin. "But my parents made me."

"Sh!" said Bebe. "He might hear you."

Mr. Kidswatter's voice came over the P.A. system. "**Good morning, boys and girls.**"

"Good morning, Mr. Kidswatter," the children all answered together, like good little boys and girls.

They listened **attentive**ly to their principal. Then, when Mr. Kidswatter was finished, they took out their **arithmetic** books and started working.

After that, they did **social studies**, reading, and **spelling**.

When the recess bell rang, the children put their books **neatly** in their desks, quietly **lined up**, and walked out of the room and down the stairs.

"So how's your **substitute** teacher?" asked Louis, out on the **playground**.

"**Tough!**" said Bebe. "I've never worked so hard in my life."

"I did more work before ten o'clock than most people do in a day," said Calvin.

"But he's very fair," Myron quickly added, **just in case** Mr. Gorf was listening. He might have been hiding in the **bush**es.

"Yes, he's nice and fair and a very good teacher," said Jenny.

"Very smart too," said Deedee. "We're lucky to have him."

Louis **twist**ed the end of his **mustache** between his fingers.

After recess the children returned to class and worked until

56

lunchtime. At lunch they ate all the food Miss Mush **served** them. Their manners were perfect.

Mr. Gorf might have been hiding under the table.

After lunch they returned to class and **practiced** their **handwriting.**

Myron looked around. All of a sudden he got a **terrible urge** to do something. Anything!

"Ugga bugga," he said.

Jenny put her finger to her lips.

"Biff. Boff. Boof!" said Myron, a little louder.

"Sh!" said Jenny.

Myron stood up. "No!" he shouted. "I don't have to be quiet!"

Everyone tried to get Myron to **hush** up.

Myron climbed on top of his desk. "Look around, **folks!** There's no teacher! We're doing all this work for nothing!"

"Get down!" whispered Allison. "Do you want to get us all in trouble?"

Myron jumped on top of Allison's desk. "Hi, Allison!" he said. Then he **hop**ped over to Deedee's desk, then Ron's, then Maurecia's.

"Please, Myron," said Maurecia.

"This is fun!" said Myron. He made a great **leap** and **land**ed on top of the teacher's desk.

Mrs. Jewls had always kept a coffee can full of Tootsie Roll Pops[1] on her desk. It was still there.

"Hey, anyone want a Tootsie Roll Pop?"[1] asked Myron.

Everyone stared at him.

Myron took one for himself. He sat in the teacher's chair, with his feet up on the teacher's desk, and **suck**ed on it.

"Please stop, Myron!" **beg**ged Jenny. "What if he's hiding in the closet?"

"**Get real!**" said Myron. "Why would he hide in the closet?"

"What if Mr. Gorf was married to Mrs. Gorf?" asked Allison.

Myron laughed. "Who would ever want to marry Mrs. Gorf?" he asked.

"Somebody had to marry her," said Rondi. "Or else she wouldn't have been a Mrs."

"What if he loved her very much?" asked Allison. "And then one day she didn't come home from work. And he never saw her again. And he didn't know what happened to her. But he knew she used to teach this class! So he might be hiding in the closet to try to find out if we're the ones who **got rid of** her."

"If I was married to Mrs. Gorf," said Jason, "I'd be glad she never came home. He should thank us."

"Nice going, Jason!" said Jenny. "If he *is* hiding in the closet, you just told him we're the ones who got rid of his wife."

"Well, if I didn't, you just did," said Jason.

"It doesn't matter!" shouted Myron. "Because Mr. Gorf is

---

1 Tootsie Roll Pop 툿시 롤 팝. 초콜릿 캔디의 이름.

not hiding in the closet!"

Myron went to the back of the room and opened the closet door.

A man stepped out. "Thank you," he said. "I **accidental**ly **lock**ed myself in here this morning, and I've been waiting for someone to open the door."

Myron **swallow**ed his Tootsie Roll Pop, stick **and all**.

11. VOICES

"My name is Mr. Gorf," said the man who stepped out of the **closet**.

And, surprising as it may seem, the children weren't afraid.

It was his voice. His voice was full of **comfort** and **wisdom**, like an old **leather** chair in a **dusty** library. It didn't matter what he said. It felt good just to listen to him.

He was a handsome man, with neatly **comb**ed brown hair and clean **fingernail**s. He carried a brown **briefcase**.

Nobody even noticed that his nose had three **nostril**s.

"Since I am going to be your teacher for the next few months, let me tell you a bit about myself. I was born in the Himalayan Mountains[1] in a town called Katmandu.[2]"

"Cat Man Do," said Terrence. "Cool."

Everyone laughed. They weren't laughing at Terrence. There was just something about the name of that city and the way Terrence said it.

Terrence's voice was like a **rusty drainpipe**.

"Have you ever been married?" asked Allison. Allison's voice was like a cat walking across a piano.

"No, I'm a **bachelor**," said Mr. Gorf.

Allison smiled, greatly **relieve**d.

"Well, that's enough about me," said Mr. Gorf. "How about some of you telling me about yourselves?"

"My name is Mac," said Mac, without raising his hand. Mac's voice was like a **freight** train. "I built the biggest snowman you ever saw. Man, it was huge. I had to stand on a **ladder** to put the hat on his head. It was a stovepipe hat,[3] like Abraham Lincoln[4] wore, but I don't know why they call it that. We have a microwave oven.[5] Have you ever put a bag of marshmallows in a microwave oven? Man, it's like—"

---

1 Himalayan Mountains 히말라야 산맥. 인도 대륙 북쪽에서 중앙아시아 고원 남쪽을 동서로 길게 연결하는 만년설의 산맥.
2 Katmandu 네팔의 수도 카트만두.
3 stovepipe hat 높이가 18센티미터 정도 되는 길고 높은 예장용 모자.
4 Abraham Lincoln 에이브러햄 링컨. 미국의 제16대 대통령으로 남북 전쟁에서 북군을 지도하여 점진적인 노예 해방을 이루었다.
5 microwave oven 전자레인지. 마이크로파를 이용하여 음식물을 가열하는 장치.

Mr. Gorf's nose **flared**.

His right nostril flared to the right. His left nostril flared to the left. And the hole in the middle seemed to get larger.

Mac **cough**ed. He tried to speak, but no words came out.

"Thank you, Mac," said Mr. Gorf. "Anyone else?"

Deedee raised her hand.

"Yes, young lady," said Mr. Gorf.

Deedee **giggle**d. She liked the way he said "young lady." "My name is Deedee," she said. Her voice was small, but full of energy, like a superball. "I like soccer and Ninja Turtles.[6] My favorite—"

Mr. Gorf's nose flared.

Deedee lost her voice too.

"Who's next?" asked Mr. Gorf. "Yes, the girl in the **polka-dot** shirt."

"My name's Maurecia," said Maurecia. "I have two brothers and one sister."

Maurecia's voice was like a pineapple milkshake.

Mr. Gorf **suck**ed it up through his nose.

"Hey, what's going—," said Todd.

Todd was silent.

"Look at his nose!" shouted Eric Bacon. "It has—"

Eric Bacon had nothing else to say.

"Nobody say anyth—," Jenny tried to warn. Her voice disappeared

---

6 Ninja Turtles 닌자 거북이. 돌연변이 반응을 일으킨 거북이 4마리가 팀을 이루어서 여러 모험을 한다는 이야기를 다룬 애니메이션.

up Mr. Gorf's nose.

Soon the class was quiet.

Mr. Gorf's middle nostril had snorted all of their voices.

Except for Allison. She remained silent. She knew she'd only get one chance to speak, and she had to wait for just the right moment.

"What good little boys and girls you are," said Mr. Gorf. "So nice and quiet." He laughed.

"Of course, this isn't my real voice," he said. "I stole this voice from a gentleman I met in Scotland."

He touched the tip of his nose.

"This is my voice!" he squawked.

If a donkey could talk, and if the donkey had a sore throat, and if it spoke with a French accent—that was what Mr. Gorf's voice sounded like.

But what he said next was even more horrible than his voice.

"Mrs. Gorf was my mommy."

The children sat frozen in their chairs, too scared to move.

Suddenly there was a knock on the door.

Mr. Gorf touched his nose. "Who is it?" he asked in the pleasant voice he stole from the Scottish gentleman.

"Miss Mush," said Miss Mush from the other side of the door. "I just came up to say hello and welcome you to Wayside School."

"That's very nice of you, Miss Mush," said Mr. Gorf. "But

we're very busy right now. Maybe we can get together for tea and crumpets[7] sometime."

Miss Mush giggled. "That sounds lovely," she said. "By the way, Mr. Gorf, are you married?"

"No, I'm single," said Mr. Gorf.

"So am I," said Miss Mush.

"Miss Mush!" shouted Allison. "Help! Mr. Gorf is taking—"

Mr. Gorf's nose flared.

"Did you say something, Allison?" asked Miss Mush.

Mr. Gorf touched his nose. Then he spoke, this time using Allison's voice. "Mr. Gorf is taking us on a **field** trip next week. But he might need help. Do you want to come with us?"

"Maybe," said Miss Mush. "Thank you, Allison."

"Oh, don't thank me," said Allison's voice. "Thank Mr. Gorf. He's the best teacher in the whole world!"

"I'm glad," said Miss Mush. "He sounds very **charming**."

"And so do you," said Mr. Gorf, speaking like the gentleman from Scotland. He touched his nose.

"See you later, Miss Mush," said the voice of Eric Ovens.

"Take care," said Calvin's voice.

"Have a nice day," said Kathy's voice.

---

7 crumpet 크럼펫. 애프터눈 티타임에 곁들여 내는 영국 전통 팬케이크. 윗면에 작은 구멍들이 있는 동글납작한 형태로 버터와 함께 먹는다.

12. NOSE

Mr. Gorf locked the door. "I don't want any more **interrupt**ions," he said.

Very quietly, Leslie **slip**ped a piece of paper out of her desk. Then she **felt around** for a pencil.

Mr. Gorf returned to the teacher's desk. He opened the top **drawer** and took out the class list. It had the names of all the children in the class, their parents' names, and their parents' home and work phone numbers.

"Let's play a game!" he said, speaking in his own, normal, French-**donkey**-with-a-**sore**-throat voice. "The name of the game is Who Am I Now?"

Leslie found a pencil. She held the piece of paper on her **lap**, where Mr. Gorf couldn't see it, and wrote HELP in big letters. She had to get it to Louis, the **yard** teacher.

Mr. Gorf touched the **tip** of his nose. "Who am I now?" he asked.

It was a girl's voice, soft and warm, with just a little bit of a **giggle** in it.

Everyone looked at Rondi.

"Rondi," said Mr. Gorf. He opened his **briefcase** and **removed** a **portable** phone. He **dial**ed Rondi's home number.

"Hello, Mommy," Mr. Gorf said into the phone, using Rondi's voice. "No, nothing's wrong. I just called to say I hate you! You're the worst mommy in the whole world. You're ugly and you smell bad! It's not fair! Out of all the mommies in the world, I got stuck with you!"

He **hung up** the phone.

Rondi sat crying in her chair.

Mr. Gorf touched his nose. "Isn't this a good game?" he asked, sounding very much like a sick French donkey. "Rondi is crying. And at home, her mother is crying too." He laughed. "Too bad you won't ever be able to tell her you're sorry, Rondi."

Leslie carefully folded the piece of paper into a paper airplane. There was one open window, next to Sharie's desk.

Mr. Gorf touched his nose. "Who am I now?" he asked.

Everyone tried not to look at Joe.

Mr. Gorf called Joe's mother at work. "Hello, Mommy," he said. "I hate you! I wish you'd go away forever! Then maybe Daddy will marry somebody good this time."

Leslie knew she'd only have one chance. It would take a perfect throw. She tossed the paper airplane toward the window.

Mr. Gorf saw it. "Hey!" he shouted.

The airplane sailed closer . . . closer . . . but then at the last second it made a sudden turn, hit the wall, and landed on the floor.

Mr. Gorf laughed. He picked up the airplane and unfolded it. "Help," he sneered. "No one can help you now! You took my mommy away from me. And I'm going to take your mommies away from you!"

He touched his nose.

"Who am I now?" he asked.

It was Leslie's voice.

He started to dial her home phone number but was interrupted by a knock on the door.

"Oh, Mr. Gorf!" sang Miss Mush.

"Yes," said Mr. Gorf, still in Leslie's voice. He touched his nose and cleared his throat. "I mean, yes?" This time he sounded like a donkey with tonsillitis.[1] He touched his nose again. "Yes?" he asked

---

1   tonsillitis 편도염. 편도에 염증이 생기는 질환을 통칭하는 말.

in the pleasant voice he took from the Scottish gentleman.

"It's me again," said Miss Mush. Miss Mush's voice was like two **boots slosh**ing through mud. "I **baked** you a pie, Mr. Gorf. To welcome you to Wayside School."

Mr. Gorf **sigh**ed. "You are very kind, Miss Mush," he said. "But we are all quite busy at the moment. Perhaps another—"

"It's best to eat it while it's still warm," said Miss Mush. "You probably don't get fresh pies very often. Being a **bachelor and all**."

"I really hate to **disturb** the class," said Mr. Gorf. "**I'll tell you what**. I'll just come outside a moment, and you can hand it to me."

He **glare**d at the class, **daring** them to move. Then he opened the door.

"I hope you like **pepper** pie," said Miss Mush. She **smash**ed it in his face.

Mr. Gorf turned around. His face was covered with a thick pepper cream. He **sneeze**d.

Calvin laughed.

"Hey, my voice is back!" said Calvin. "Wait a second. This isn't my voice. I sound like Bebe!"

Mr. Gorf sneezed again.

"I can talk!" shouted Jenny. "But who am I?"

Mr. Gorf sneezed.

"You're Maurecia!" said Jason. Jason sounded like the gentleman from Scotland.

Mr. Gorf kept sneezing.

"Who might I be, sonny?[2]" Paul **cackle**d. He sounded like somebody's grandmother.

Todd **bark**ed.

"AAAACHOOOO!!!!!!"

Mr. Gorf sneezed so hard his nose flew off his face. He screamed like a donkey, then ran noseless out of the room.

"Oh, **gross**!" said Jason. "Now I sound like Allison."

Bebe said something in Italian.

"Nobody **panic**," said Miss Mush. "Your voices are **bouncing** around, trying to find where they **belong**. It might take a while, but soon you will be back to normal."

"How do you know?" asked Leslie, although she sounded like Paul. "And how'd you know to smash a pepper pie in Mr. Gorf's face?"

"I wasn't **exact**ly sure," explained Miss Mush. "But when I came up the first time, I heard Kathy say 'Have a nice day.' So, either Kathy had decided to be nice to me, or Mr. Gorf was a mean teacher who sucked children's voices up his nose." She **shrug**ged. "I just didn't think Kathy would be nice."

"Maybe if you learned to brush your teeth," **mutter**ed Kathy.

Mr. Gorf's nose lay on the floor. Miss Mush picked it up and

2　sonny 애야, 자네.

put it in her **apron** pocket. "It will go good in spaghetti sauce," she said.

Soon all the children had their real voices back. Rondi and Joe called their mothers on Mr. Gorf's portable phone and told them they loved them.

While far away, in a small village in Scotland, a man who hadn't spoken for twenty years turned to his wife and said, "Top of the morning to you,[3] Tilly."

---

3   **top of the morning to you** '안녕하세요'라는 뜻의 아침 인사.

13. THE NEW TEACHER

The new teacher entered the classroom carrying a big blue notebook **stuff**ed with papers. She had white hair and wore glasses. She was a lot older than anyone else in the class.

She took a big breath. "My,[1] it's tiring walking up all those stairs, isn't it?" she said.

Nobody said anything. They just **stared** at her.

She set her notebook on the teacher's desk. "My name is Mrs. Drazil," she said. "And I'm not from Brazil." She smiled at her

---

1 my 이런, 어머나. 놀라움이나 낭패를 나타내는 표현.

little joke.

Nobody else smiled. After Mrs. and Mr. Gorf, they didn't trust teachers.

Drazil, thought Deedee. *Where have I heard that name before?*

"Where are you from?" asked Leslie.

"Actually, I was born not too far from here," said Mrs. Drazil.

"Then why'd you say you came from Brazil?" asked Benjamin.

"No, I said I wasn't from Brazil," said Mrs. Drazil.

"Have you ever been to Brazil?" asked Eric Fry.

"No," explained Mrs. Drazil. "It was just a little joke. Brazil rhymes with Drazil. I thought it might help you remember my name."

Terrence laughed. "Drazil—Brazil!" he shouted. "That's funny!"

Several other kids laughed too.

But not Deedee. She had heard of Mrs. Drazil somewhere. She was sure of it. And whatever she had heard, she was sure it wasn't good.

"What's a Brazil?" asked Eric Ovens.

"Brazil is the largest country in South America," said Mrs. Drazil.

"Oh," said Eric Ovens. "I thought it was one of those things that, you know, women wear, you know, on their **bosom**."

Several kids laughed.

"No, that's a **brassiere**," said Mrs. Drazil.

There was more **laughter**.

Stephen was shocked. "She said 'brassiere'!" he whispered.

"Right in class!"

"I know, I heard her!" said Jason.

But Deedee still didn't trust her, even if she did say "brassiere" right out loud.

There was a television show that Deedee liked to watch. It was about real **criminals**. At the end of the show, they always asked the viewers to call the police if they knew where any of the criminals were.

Deedee wondered if she had seen Mrs. Drazil on that show.

"Does anybody have any questions they'd like to ask me?" asked Mrs. Drazil.

Ron raised his hand.

Mrs. Drazil pointed to him.

"How old are you?" asked Ron.

Dana **gasp**ed. "You're not supposed to ask someone *that!*" she said.

"Especially someone as old as Mrs. Drazil!" said Mac.

Mrs. Drazil smiled. "I don't mind," she said. "I'm sixty-six years old. You can ask me anything you want."

"*Anything?*" asked Joy.

"I'm a teacher," said Mrs. Drazil. "That's what I'm here for."

Paul raised his hand. "How much do you **weigh**?" he asked.

"One hundred and twenty-four pounds,[2]" said Mrs. Drazil.

---

2 **pound** 무게의 단위 파운드. 124파운드는 약 56.2킬로그램이다.

"How much money do you make?" asked Eric Bacon.

"I'm a substitute teacher," explained Mrs. Drazil. "So I only make money on days that I teach. Then I make fifty-one dollars and eighteen cents a day."

"What a **rip-off!**" said Jenny. "You should make at least two hundred!"

"That would be nice," said Mrs. Drazil. "But I'm a teacher because I love to teach. I love to see young children learn."

Joy raised her hand. "How many men have you kissed in your whole life?"

Mrs. Drazil thought a moment as she appeared to be **count**ing on her fingers. "Thirty-one," she said.

Everyone gasped.

Deedee raised her hand.

Mrs. Drazil smiled at her. "Yes, the girl in the pretty flowered T-shirt."

"Have you ever been in **jail?**" asked Deedee.

"No," said Mrs. Drazil.

"Are the police after you?"

"No," said Mrs. Drazil.

Deedee still didn't trust her.

"Okay," said Mrs. Drazil. "Before we get started I want to say one more thing. I enjoy teaching so much that sometimes I **get** a little **carried away.** I talk too much. So if I start to get **boring,** will somebody please raise your hand and tell me."

"**For real?**" asked Todd. "You want us to tell you to stop talking?"

"And we won't get in trouble?" asked Bebe.

"No, of course not," said Mrs. Drazil. "You'll be helping me and the rest of your class. You're not going to learn anything if you're bored."

"Cool!" said Terrence.

"Oh, I suppose when I first started teaching, I used to be a little more **strict**," said Mrs. Drazil. "I even worried about things like whether my students had clean **fingernail**s or if their shirts were **tuck**ed in." She laughed. "But times have changed. I've changed. **Besides**, the kids were a lot worse back then. At least *some* of them."

For just a second her sweet face turned **sour** as she looked at her notebook on her desk.

Then she smiled again. "I believe teaching requires **mutual cooperation**. I will cooperate with you, and you need to cooperate with me. If we work together, we will have a very **enjoyable** learning experience."

Her face turned sour again. "But if you **cross** me, you will be very, very sorry." She ran her fingers over her blue notebook. "Oh, maybe not today, maybe not tomorrow, but *someday I will get you!* You can run, but you can't hide."

She smiled. "Okay, let's get started."

14. A LIGHT BULB, A PENCIL SHARPENER, A COFFEEPOT, AND A SACK OF POTATOES

"Galileo[1] was a great scientist," said Mrs. Drazil. "He was born in Italy in 1564 and died in 1642. He was the first person to use a **telescope** to study the stars. And he also helped **figure out** the laws of **gravity**."

"Oh, I know about gravity," said Joe. "Mrs. Jewls pushed a computer out the window. It fell a lot faster than a pencil."

"I don't think so," said Mrs. Drazil. "Galileo proved that all objects fall at the same speed. He **conduct**ed a very famous

---

1   Galileo 갈릴레오 갈릴레이. 이탈리아의 천재 과학자. 진자의 등시성과 관성의 법칙 등을 발견하는 업적을 남겼다.

experiment. He dropped lots of different objects off the **Lean**ing Tower of Pisa.[2] The Leaning Tower of Pisa is in Italy. It was built in—"

Todd raised his hand. "You're getting a little **boring**," he said.

"**Oh, my goodness**, am I?" asked Mrs. Drazil.

Rondi, Leslie, Paul, and Calvin **nod**ded their heads.

"I'm sorry," said Mrs. Drazil. She thought a moment. "I know!" she **exclaim**ed. "Let's do the experiment here!"

The children cheered. They loved experiments.

Mrs. Drazil **rub**bed her hands together. "Let's see. We'll need a **coffeepot**, a pencil **sharpen**er, a **light bulb**, and . . ." She thought a moment. "We need something heavy."

"An elephant's heavy," said Benjamin.

"There are no elephants in Wayside School," said Mrs. Drazil. Everyone laughed.

"How about a **sack** of potatoes?" asked Ron. "I **bet** Miss Mush has one."

"Go see," said Mrs. Drazil.

"There's a coffeepot down in the office," said Stephen.

"Go get it," said Mrs. Drazil.

"If I had a **screwdriver**, I could get the pencil sharpener off the wall," said Eric Fry.

"I've got a screwdriver!" said Jenny.

---

2 Leaning Tower of Pisa 피사의 사탑. 탑의 한쪽 지반이 가라앉으면서 기울어지고 있는 것으로 유명하다.

"Can we use a **fluorescent** light bulb?" asked Bebe. She looked up at the **ceiling**.

"I guess so," said Mrs. Drazil.

"How do I get it?" asked Bebe.

"You're the scientist," said Mrs. Drazil. "You figure it out."

Bebe put her chair on top of her desk and stood on it. She still couldn't reach the ceiling. "Hey, Benjamin, let me have your chair!"

She put Benjamin's chair on top of hers, but she still wasn't tall enough.

Calvin **dump**ed the **wastepaper** basket onto the floor. "Try this," he said.

Bebe turned the **trash** can **upside down** and put it on top of Benjamin's chair. Then she climbed on top, but she still couldn't quite reach.

Leslie brought the class **dictionary**. Jenny and Dana **donate**d their math books. Sharie **grab**bed Mrs. Drazil's old blue notebook.

"Put that down!" **yell**ed Mrs. Drazil. "Right now!"

Sharie dropped the notebook. Mrs. Drazil's kindly old face had suddenly turned mean.

"Don't ever touch that again!" Mrs. Drazil ordered.

Sharie returned, **trembling**, to her seat.

Everyone was staring at Mrs. Drazil. She smiled sweetly. "Go back to what you were doing," she said.

Jason threw Bebe his **lunch box**. She set it on top of the books, then climbed on top. Standing on her **tiptoe**s, she was able to pull the cover off the fluorescent light. She grabbed the light just as the **pile collapse**d beneath her.

She fell to the ground, **triumphant**ly holding the unbroken light bulb high above her head.

Ron returned with a sack of potatoes from Miss Mush.

Stephen returned with Mr. Kidswatter's coffeepot.

Eric Fry un**screw**ed the pencil sharpener from the wall.

Mrs. Drazil wrote "Coffeepot," "Sack of Potatoes," "Pencil Sharpener," and "Light Bulb" on the **blackboard**.

"We're going to drop all four objects out the window at the same time," she said. "How many people think the coffeepot will hit the ground first?"

"Is there coffee in it?" asked John.

"It's about half full," Stephen reported.

Eight kids thought the coffeepot would hit the ground first. Sixteen thought the sack of potatoes would hit the ground first. Three thought the light bulb would be first. Only Terrence thought the pencil sharpener would hit first.

Jason, Jenny, Joe, John, and Joy were the **judge**s. Mrs. Drazil sent them outside.

Stephen held the coffeepot out one window.

Bebe held the light bulb out another.

Eric Fry held the pencil sharpener out another.

And Ron held out the sack of potatoes.

Everyone else crowded around to watch. With everyone on the same side of the classroom, the school leaned a little bit, just like the Leaning Tower of Pisa.

"On your mark. . . . Get set[3] . . . . Let go!" said Mrs. Drazil.

The objects fell through the air and smashed against the **pavement**.

A short while later, the judges returned. Their clothes were **splatter**ed with coffee. Jenny had bits of potatoes in her hair.

"Was the pencil sharpener first?" asked Terrence.

"It happened so fast," said Joe. "They all hit about the same time."

"But the coffeepot made the coolest **explosion**," said Jason.

"I think the light bulb hit the ground last," said John.

"Well, that's possible," said Mrs. Drazil. "Gravity causes all objects to fall at the same **rate**. But air slows them down. That's called air **resist**ance. And that's good. **Otherwise raindrop**s would kill us. Air resistance slows all things down a little bit, but it has a greater effect on very light objects, such as a piece of paper. And of course the shape of the paper is important too. A **crumpled**-up piece of paper will fall faster than—"

"You're getting boring again," said Mac.

Mrs. Drazil stopped talking.

"Now we need a new pencil sharpener," said Leslie.

3　**on your mark, get set** 제자리에! 준비! 경주에서 참가자들에게 자신의 출발 위치에 선 다음 달릴 준비를 하라는 말.

80

Paul **lick**ed her ear.

15. AN ELEPHANT IN WAYSIDE SCHOOL

The bell rang for **recess**, and the children **exploded** out of the building.

Louis, the yard teacher, was ready with a big **pile** of red and green balls.

The kids called, "Hi, Louis!" and "Over here, Louis!" as he **toss**ed the balls to them: over his shoulder, behind his back, through his legs.

Deedee came **charging** out of the building. Usually by the time she got to the **playground**, there were no good balls left, but she could see one red ball by Louis's foot.

She **knock**ed over a kid from the tenth floor and shouted, "Hey, Lou—"

Suddenly she stopped.

She had just remembered where she'd heard of Mrs. Drazil.

It was from Louis! He had once told her about the meanest teacher he'd ever had when he was a kid.

She hurried over to her friends to make sure. "Hey, Todd!" she called.

Todd was playing tetherball[1] with Ron. As he turned to look at Deedee, the ball came around and **bonk**ed him on the head.

"Do you remember when Louis told us about the meanest teacher he ever had?" asked Deedee.

Todd shook his head. After being **conk**ed by the tetherball, he couldn't remember anything.

"I remember," said Jason, who was in line to play. "Whenever Louis got in trouble, the teacher used to put the **wastepaper** basket on his head!"

"That's right!" said Jenny. "And then Louis would have to keep it there the rest of the day. And everyone would laugh at him. And then the teacher would **call on** him to answer questions from the blackboard, but he couldn't see the questions, so she'd give him an F!"

"Do you remember the teacher's name?" asked Deedee.

---

1 tetherball 테더 볼. 기둥에 매단 공을 치고 받는 게임. 이 게임에서 쓰이는 공을 가리키기도 한다.

Her friends shook their heads. Todd couldn't even remember his own name.

"I think it was Mrs. Drazil," said Deedee.

They ran to Louis.

"Hey, Louis!" said Jason. "What was the name of that mean teacher you once had when you were a kid?"

"Which one?" asked Louis.

"The one that put the trash can on your head," said Jenny.

Louis **shudder**ed just thinking about her. "Mrs. Drazil," he whispered.

The kids looked at each other.

"What color hair did she have?" asked Jason.

"Brown," said Louis. "Why?"

"We have a **substitute** teacher," explained Deedee. "She's real nice."

"Good," said Louis.

"Her name is Mrs. Drazil," said Deedee.

"Whoa, I'm getting out of here," said Louis. He started to run, but the kids grabbed him.

"It's okay," said Jenny. "It can't be the same teacher. *Our* teacher is nice."

"And her hair isn't brown," said Jason. "It's white."

Louis relaxed a little bit.

"You want to come up and meet her?" asked Deedee.

"**No way!**" said Louis.

84

"Oh, you're so **silly**, Louis," said Deedee. "She's not the same teacher. And besides, you're a teacher now too."

"Oh, yeah, I forgot," said Louis.

"C'mon, Louis," said Deedee. She held his hand and led him up the stairs.

They entered the classroom.

Mrs. Drazil was putting some of the children's work on the **bulletin board.**

"Mrs. Drazil," said Deedee. "We brought our yard teacher up to meet you."

"It's very nice to meet you," said Mrs. Drazil as she **pin**ned up Joe's **arithmetic** test. "Exercise is so important for young minds and bodies." She turned around.

Louis's face **paled**. "Well, it was nice to meet you," he said very quickly. "I've gotta go. Bye!"

"Stay right where you are, Louis!" ordered Mrs. Drazil.

He **froze.**

Mrs. Drazil slowly walked to her desk. She picked up the old blue notebook.

"*The notebook!*" whispered Louis.

Mrs. Drazil opened it and **flip**ped **through** the pages. "Here we are," she said. She **remove**d a piece of paper and handed it to Louis. "Is this your homework?" she asked.

Louis looked at it.

"You were supposed to copy it over, weren't you?" asked Mrs.

Drazil.

"That was over fifteen years ago," said Louis. "I don't remember."

"I do," said Mrs. Drazil.

"Oh, now I remember!" said Louis. "I was going to copy it over. But then my pencil **point** broke, so I went to **sharpen** it, but the pencil sharpener fell on my foot, so I had to go to the hosp—"

"I don't want any of your famous excuses, Louis," said Mrs. Drazil. "I just want the homework. You may share Deedee's desk."

Louis sat next to Deedee.

"And remember, Louis," said Mrs. Drazil. "I know your **tricks**."

Deedee watched Louis **struggle** with his homework. "Sorry, Louis," she said.

"Don't be sorry," said Mrs. Drazil. "It's for his own good. And I expect **neat**ness, Louis, or else you'll just have to do it again."

He **frown**ed.

Mrs. Drazil stood over him and watched him work. "Your fingernails are **filthy**," she said.

"I'm the yard teacher," Louis tried to explain. "I spend a lot of time outside, in the grass and **dirt** and **stuff**."

"I don't want excuses," said Mrs. Drazil. "I want clean fingernails. And while you're **at it**, **shave** off that **mustache**. It looks like a **hairy caterpillar crawl**ing across your face!"

"Not my mustache," said Louis.

"Unless you want me to **rip** it off for you," said Mrs. Drazil.

Deedee felt **terrible**. "I can't believe Mrs. Drazil still remembers you after all this time," she said.

"An elephant never forgets,[2]" muttered Louis.

"I heard that," said Mrs. Drazil. She put the wastepaper basket on Louis's head.

---

2 An elephant never forgets 코끼리의 기억력이 매우 좋다는 사실에서 유래한 표현으로 기억력이 굉장히 뛰어난 사람을 나타낼 때 쓰인다.

16. MR. POOP

Joy, Maurecia, and Jenny were playing jump rope[1] out on the playground. School hadn't started yet.

Maurecia and Jenny were **twirl**ing. Joy sang as she jumped:

> "My mama wore **pajamas** to the **grocery store**.
> She **smashed** a **bunch** of eggs on the grocery floor.
> One **dozen**, two dozen, four dozen, six.
> She **dumped** a bunch of jelly **jars** into the mix.

---

1   jump rope 줄넘기.

*Grape jelly, **apricot**, don't forget cherry.*
Orange marmalade² and wild strawberry.
*A man walked by and fell in the **glop**.*
*He **slid** next door to the **barber** shop.*
*His **icky-sticky** body got covered in hair.*
*He **tore** a hole in his under—"*

Joy **tripp**ed over the rope. It wasn't her fault. Maurecia had suddenly stopped twirling.

"Hey!" said Joy. "What's the big idea?³"

"Look!" said Maurecia.

A very handsome stranger was walking toward them.

The girls stared at him.

"Good morning, Maurecia," said the stranger. "Jenny. Joy."

"How do you know my name?" Maurecia asked nervously. She wasn't supposed to talk to strangers.

"I've known you a long time," said the stranger. "I see you almost every day."

Maurecia was beginning to feel **scare**d. She looked around for Louis, the **yard** teacher, but didn't see him. "I can scream real loud," she warned.

"Oh my gosh!⁴" said Jenny. "It's Louis!"

---

2 marmalade 마멀레이드. 감귤류의 껍질과 과육에 설탕을 넣어 조린 젤리 모양의 잼.
3 What's the big idea? 어떻게 된 거야? 도대체 어쩔 셈이야?
4 Oh my gosh (= Oh my god) 맙소사! 세상에!

Maurecia looked at the stranger. He did sort of look like Louis.

Except his hair was **comb**ed. His shirt was **tuck**ed in. He was wearing a tie. And there was skin between his nose and mouth.

He had **shaved** off his mustache.

"That's Mr. Louis to you," said Louis. "I'm a teacher, and I expect to be treated with respect."

"You want to play jump rope, uh, Mr. Louis?" asked Maurecia.

Louis was great at jump rope. He could even do it **blindfold**ed. He was the one who taught Joy the song she was singing at the beginning of this story.

"No, thank you, Maurecia," said Louis. "I don't play games. I'm an adult."

"But you're a yard teacher," said Jenny.

"No, I'm a **Professional** Playground **Supervisor**," Louis **correct**ed her. He walked away.

"Wow!" whispered Maurecia. "I never knew Louis was so handsome!"

Jenny **pat**ted her heart. "I think I'm in love," she said.

"I thought he looked kind of **goofy**," said Joy.

Up in class, everyone was talking about the new Louis.

"He looks so **weird** without his mustache," said Calvin.

"He's handsome!" said Bebe.

"He got mad at me for running across the **blacktop**," **complain**ed John. "He made me go **all the way** back to the edge of the blacktop, then walk across it. And I had to call him Mr. Louis."

"I am very proud of Louis," said Mrs. Drazil. "He has always been a **troublemaker**. But I think he is trying to be good. We should all give him a chance."

Joy stared at Mrs. Drazil. *It's your fault,* she thought. *You made him shave off his mustache.*

At recess, Louis refused to pass out the balls.

"I haven't washed them yet," he said.

"You're going to wash the balls?" asked Eric Bacon.

"They're **filthy**," said Louis. "And they all have the wrong amount of air in them."

"I don't care," said Eric Fry.

"I do," said Louis. "Before I can let you play with them, I have to clean them and **pump** them up with the **precise** amount of air as **specified** by POOPS."

"POOPS?" asked Eric Ovens.

"The Professional **Organization** Of Playground Supervisors," explained Louis.

He showed them the POOPS **handbook**.

"Well, what are we supposed to do?" asked Eric Fry.

"Just play and have fun," said Louis. "But remember, **stay off** the grass. No running on the blacktop. No eating. And no **excessive** shouting."

The three Erics walked away. "What a booger brain!⁵" **mutter**ed

---

5 **booger brain** 멍청한 녀석, 바보 같은 녀석.

Eric Bacon.

Louis heard him.

"That's Mr. Booger Brain to you, young man," he said.

The next day, when the kids tried to go outside for recess, they only **made it** down to the fourth floor. The stairs were completely **jam**med with other kids from lower classrooms.

"Hey, what's going on?" shouted Joy.

"Louis won't let anyone outside," somebody shouted back. "He's painting the blacktop!"

"But I have to go to the bathroom!" yelled Stephen.

"Now he's **gone too far!**" said Joy. "Excuse me, out of my way, sorry, **coming through!**" she said as she **squeeze**d in and out of kids, **crawl**ed through legs, climbed over heads, until she **made her way** to the door at the bottom of the stairs.

Louis was **slop**ping black paint across the blacktop. Joy could see him through the glass door. Next to him was a big **bucket** of paint.

"MR. LOUIS!" she shouted so loud that even the kids back up on the fourth floor had to put their hands over their ears.

He came to the door.

"What are you doing?" Joy **demand**ed.

"The blacktop isn't black," explained Louis. "It's gray. A blacktop is supposed to be black. It's right here on page forty-three of the POOPS handbook."

He opened the book and showed page forty-three to Joy.

Joy grabbed the book and threw it out across the graytop. It landed *plop* in the bucket of black paint.

All the kids behind her cheered.

"You're the Poop!⁶" said Joy.

Louis's red face turned even redder. The place where his mustache used to be turned purple.

"That's Mr. Poop to you," he said.

---

6 **poop** 어린 아이의 말로 대변을 나타내는 표현.

17. WHY THE CHILDREN DECIDED THEY HAD TO GET RID OF MRS. DRAZIL

1. SHE WAS NICE.

"I made cookies for everyone this morning," Mrs. Drazil **announced**.

Everyone cheered.

2. SHE THOUGHT UP WAYS TO MAKE LEARNING INTERESTING.

"I made five **dozen** cookies," she said. "There are twelve cookies in a dozen. So, who can tell me how many cookies I made?"

Joe **waved** his arm **back and forth**. "I know! I know!" he said.

"Okay, Joe," said Mrs. Drazil. "How many cookies did I make?"

"Five dozen," Joe said proudly.

3. SHE WAS **PATIENT**.

"Yes, I made five dozen cookies," said Mrs. Drazil. "I told you that. But how many cookies are there?"

"Five dozen," said Joe.

"But how many cookies are in five dozen?" asked Mrs. Drazil.

"Huh?" asked Joe.

"How much is twelve **times** five?" asked Mrs. Drazil.

"Uh, just a second," said Joe. "Can I use pencil and paper?"

"Certainly," said Mrs. Drazil.

Joe took out a piece of paper and a pencil. He wrote the number five on the piece of paper, then **tore** it into twelve pieces. "Sixty!" he said.

Nobody quite understood Joe's **mathematical method**s.

4. SHE WAS FAIR.

"Yes, there are sixty cookies," she said. "And there are twenty-eight children in the class. So, how many cookies should each child get?"

Bebe raised her hand. "A hundred," she said.

"You can't have a hundred cookies," said Mrs. Drazil. "I only made sixty."

"Make some more," said Bebe.

"I made sixty," said Mrs. Drazil. "I'm not making any more."

"Okay," Bebe said with a **sigh**. "I'll take sixty."

"We have to divide them evenly," said Mrs. Drazil. "How

many cookies should each child get, so that every child gets the same amount?"

John raised his hand. "Everyone can have two cookies," he said, "and there will **be** four **left over.**"

"Can I have them?" asked Bebe.

Allison raised her hand. "Everyone can have **exact**ly two and one-seventh cookies," she said.

"Very good, Allison," said Mrs. Drazil. "And John, you were right too." She gave everyone exactly two and one-seventh cookies.

5. SHE WAS A GOOD COOK.

"Best cookies I ever had in my whole life!" said Stephen.

Everyone agreed.

"I got the **recipe** from Miss Mush," said Mrs. Drazil.

"You did?" several kids said together.

"I just added a **pinch** of this and a little of that," said Mrs. Drazil.

6. SHE KNEW WHAT A GOOZACK WAS.

"Jason, would you please open the door?" she said.

Everyone **gasp**ed.

"What's the matter?" she asked.

"You said the D-**word!**" said Dana.

"Door?" asked Mrs. Drazil.

Everyone gasped again.

"You're supposed to call it a goozack," explained Dana.

"Who said so?" asked Mrs. Drazil.

"Mr. Kidswatter," said Dana.

"Mr. Kidswatter is a goozack," said Mrs. Drazil.

Yes, Mrs. Drazil was smart. She was nice. She made learning interesting. She was patient and fair. And she even could make Miss Mush's cookies taste good.

But she made Louis **shave** off his mustache.

And so she had to go.

18. THE BLUE NOTEBOOK

They had a plan. It all **depend**ed **on** Sharie.

Everyone just hoped she wouldn't fall asleep first. Sharie often fell asleep in class.

C'mon, Sharie, thought Deedee. *You can do it.*

Sharie looked out the window. The sky was full of big, **fluffy** clouds. She **yawn**ed. The clouds looked like giant **pillows**.

Sharie imagined herself **wrap**ped up in one of those clouds, soft and **cozy**. She pulled her blue-and-red **overcoat snug**ly over her head.

Her eyes closed. Then they opened wide. "Whazzat?!" she

shouted.

"Sharie?" said Mrs. Drazil.

"Look!" shouted Sharie, pointing out the window. "It's a—Hurry!" Her long **eyelash**es **stuck** straight **out**.

Mrs. Drazil hurried to Sharie's desk. "What is it?"

"A **spaceship**!" said Sharie. "From **outer space**!"

On the other side of the room, Deedee dropped her pencil. She **bent** down to pick it up, then stayed down.

Deedee was part of the plan too. She had a dangerous mission. She had **volunteer**ed for it. She felt it was her **duty**, since she was the one who had brought Louis up to meet Mrs. Drazil **in the first place**.

"You don't have to do it," Ron had told her. "Mrs. Drazil would have seen Louis **sooner or later**."

"No, I'll do it," Deedee had bravely replied.

Now she **crawl**ed across the floor.

Mrs. Drazil looked out the window. "Where?" she asked.

"Wait, it went behind a cloud," said Sharie.

"What did it look like?" asked Mrs. Drazil.

"Like a giant hamburger," said Sharie. "But there was a zizzle stick hanging down from the bottom!"

Deedee crawled to the teacher's desk. She reached up and quietly opened the top **drawer**. She **removed** the blue notebook.

Mrs. Drazil **stared** out the window. "What's a zizzle stick?" she asked.

"I don't know," Sharie said very **mysterious**ly. "They don't have them here on earth."

Deedee crawled safely back to her seat.

At recess everyone crowded around Deedee as she **went through** the blue notebook.

"Louis once put a frog in Mrs. Drazil's shoe," she said.

"Why wasn't her shoe on her foot?" asked Jenny.

"It doesn't say," said Deedee. "There's a whole list of bad things Louis did. And he made it sound like Mrs. Drazil **pick**ed **on** him for no reason!"

"**No wonder** she put a **trash** can on his head!" said Todd.

"What else did he do?" asked Eric Bacon, who was always looking for new ideas.

But Deedee had already turned the page. "There are other kids a lot worse than Louis," she said, **flipping through** the pages.

"What are you looking for?" asked Ron.

"I don't know yet," said Deedee. "But I'll know it when I see it."

She saw it!

It was a note to Mrs. Drazil from a girl named Jane Smith. Deedee read it aloud.

Dear **Lizard** Face,
　　Guess what? I didn't do my homework again! HA HA

HA! And there's nothing you can do about it because you're too stupid and ugly! HA HA HA! My family is moving away tomorrow! And you don't know where! HA HA HA! **Rub** a monkey's **tummy**! By the time you get this letter, I'll be gone. Rub a monkey's tummy with your head!

Love and Kisses,
Jane Smith

Everyone was shocked.

"How old is that letter?" asked Myron.

Deedee checked the date, then did the math in her head. "Jane Smith wrote it twenty-six years ago."

"And look," said Ron, reading over Deedee's shoulder. "Jane didn't do her last twelve homework **assign**ments!"

After recess Sharie saw the UFO[1] again, and Deedee returned the notebook to Mrs. Drazil's desk.

Now all they had to do was find Jane Smith.

---

1 UFO (= Unidentified Flying Object) 미확인 비행 물체. 전문가의 눈이나 전파 탐지로도 정체를 확인할 수 없는 비행체를 말한다.

19. TIME OUT

Miss Zarves taught the class on the nineteenth **story**. There is no nineteenth story. And there is no Miss Zarves.

You already know all that.

But how do you explain the cow in her classroom?

Miss Zarves drew a **triangle** on the **blackboard**. "A triangle has three sides," she said, then pointed to each side. "One, two, three." She drew a **square**. "A square has four sides. One, two, three, four."

She walked around the cow to the other side of the board. She drew a **pentagon**, a **hexagon**, and a perfect **heptagon**. "A heptagon has seven sides," she said.

Miss Zarves was very good at drawing shapes. When most people try to draw heptagons, there is always one side that sticks out funny. But Miss Zarves's heptagon was perfect. Every side was the same length, and every angle the same **degree**.

It was a great **talent**. But nobody **appreciated** her.

Nobody appreciated anything she did. It was like they didn't know she was there.

She **count**ed the sides on the heptagon. "One, two, three, fo—"

"**MOOOOO**," said the cow.

Miss Zarves dropped her **chalk**. She **glare**d at the cow. "I hate this!" she shouted.

It was a brown cow with a white head.

"It's all right, Miss Zarves," said Virginia, her best student. "I'll get the chalk for you."

"No," said Miss Zarves. "Leave it where it is. The cow made me drop the chalk. The cow should pick it up."

Her students **gaped** at her.

"I will not continue," said Miss Zarves, "until that cow picks up the piece of chalk and draws an **octagon** on the board!" She folded her arms across her **chest**, stared at the cow, and waited.

Ray raised his hand.

"Yes, Ray," said Miss Zarves, arms still folded across her chest.

"Uh, cows can't pick up chalk," said Ray.

Miss Zarves sighed. "I know," she said. "And I can't teach with a cow in my classroom!"

No one had ever seen Miss Zarves so upset. She usually had a **pleasant disposition**.

"It's okay, Miss Zarves," said Virginia. "I don't mind the cow."

"You get used to it after a while," said Ray.

"What cow?" asked Nick. "Oh, that one! I forgot it was there."

Miss Zarves smiled. She knew her students were trying to make her feel better.

"Other classrooms have **goldfish** or hamsters," said Virginia. "It's really no different."

"No," said Miss Zarves. "I won't **have it**! All my life I've tried to be **accommodating**. I've never been one to complain. And what has it gotten me? A cow!"

She shook her head. "When I was a little girl, my friends never did what *I* wanted to do," she said. "I always had to do whatever *they* wanted to do.

"And my teacher never **called on** me in class. She always called on the kids who just shouted out without raising their hands, even though she said she wouldn't. She'd say, 'I won't call on you if you don't raise your hand,' but then she always did anyway. But I was a good girl. I never shouted out.

"And she always did things **alphabetically**, so I was always last, if there was time for me at all.

"My parents were too busy for me. They were always **dress**ing up and going out to **fancy** parties. I had to **tuck** myself **in** at night and wish myself sweet dreams."

She took a **tissue** out of her **sleeve** and **wipe**d a tear from her eye.

"Still, I always tried to keep a smile on my face. Well, not anymore! The days of **walk-all-over**-Miss-Zarves are finished!"

She threw open her classroom door. "The **squeaky wheel** gets the **grease!**"

"What are you going to do?" asked Virginia.

"I'm going out there!" said Miss Zarves. "And I'm not coming back until I get some grease!"

She stepped outside. She decided she'd go right to the top! So she headed down the stairs—to the **principal**'s office.

Joy and Maurecia were coming up the stairs.

"Todd is uglier than stupid," said Maurecia.

"You're crazy!" said Joy. "He's stupider than ugly."

"Oooh," **tease**d Maurecia. "I'm going to tell Todd you think he's cute."

Miss Zarves stepped in front of them. "What are you children doing out of class?" she asked.

"I didn't say he was cute," said Joy. "He's just not as ugly as he is stupid."

"That means you think he's handsome," said Maurecia. "Are you going to *marry* him?"

"I asked you a question," said Miss Zarves.

"Ugh, **gross!**" said Joy.

"I'm a teacher," said Miss Zarves. "That means you are supposed to listen to me."

Joy and Maurecia walked right past her.

Miss Zarves sighed, then continued down to Mr. Kidswatter's office. She took a deep breath to **steady** her **nerves**. She was about to **knock** but then changed her mind and just **march**ed right in. "Hey, Kidswatter, I want to talk to you!"

The principal was making a **rubber-band** ball.

"Do you hear me?" asked Miss Zarves.

He opened his desk **drawer** and looked for some more rubber bands.

"If you don't answer me right now," said Miss Zarves, "I'm walking out the door and never coming back!"

Mr. K. **press**ed the **buzzer** on his phone. "Miss Night, you need to order more rubber bands."

"That's it![1]" said Miss Zarves. "I'm leaving. Good-bye. I quit!"

She walked out of the school and took a deep breath of fresh air.

"Please don't go, Miss Zarves," said a voice behind her.

Startled, she turned around.

"We need you," said a **bald**-headed man. He was standing between two other men. Both had black **mustache**s, and one

---

1 that's it 그만해! 더 이상 이 상황을 용납하지 않겠다는 의미이다.

carried a black **attaché case**. The bald man didn't have a mustache.

"Can you see me?" she asked.

"Yes, of course," said the bald man. "And we appreciate all your hard work."

"You do?"

All three **nod**ded very sincerely.

Miss Zarves was **touched**. "I've been teaching for thirty years," she said. "And nobody has ever said that before."

"Well, it's not easy being a teacher," said the bald man.

"I don't get any respect," said Miss Zarves. "People treat me like I'm a nobody."

"It's not easy being a teacher," said the man with the attaché case. "You have to work long hours for very little money."

"I've never gotten paid," said Miss Zarves. "And this is the first time in thirty years I've ever left the building."

"It's not easy being a teacher," agreed the other man with a mustache.

"Even the book I'm reading to my class," said Miss Zarves. "The author **makes fun of** teachers!"

"It's a **tragedy**," said the bald man.

"Then why do it?" asked Miss Zarves. "Why teach anymore? I could quit and nobody would care."

"The children need you," all three men said together.

Miss Zarves sighed. "I like to teach," she said. "I really do. I love the children. It's just—"

She stopped and wiped her eyes.

The man with the attaché case opened it. He took out a **handkerchief** and handed it to Miss Zarves.

"Thank you," she said, **blew her nose**, then gave it back to him.

He placed it back in his attaché case.

"Can you at least get the cow out of my classroom?" she asked.

The bald man smiled. "I'll see what I can do," he said.

Miss Zarves smiled as she slowly shook her head. Then she turned and walked back into the building.

20. ELEVATORS

Mr. Kidswatter's voice came over the **loudspeaker**. "Good morning, boys and girls!"

There was the usual **pause**.

"I have a very important **announce**ment," said Mr. K. "Elevators have been **install**ed in Wayside School!"

For a second, the kids on the thirtieth floor were too **stun**ned to speak. Then everyone went crazy!

"**Yahoooo**!" **yell**ed Sharie.

"Hot diggity dog![1]" shouted Dameon.

Everyone was yelling and jumping.

"Zippity doo dah!" shouted Mrs. Drazil.

Cheers could be heard coming from every classroom in Wayside School. The higher the classroom, the louder the cheers.

"Now, before you all **rush** out and use the elevators," said Mr. Kidswatter, "I want to talk a little bit about elevator safety.

"I don't want the same kind of **chaos** that we have on the stairs every day. I don't know how many times I have to tell you. When you go up the stairs, stay to the right. When you come down the stairs, stay to the left. But still, everyone keeps **bump**ing into each other.

"Well, that won't happen on the elevators. I have **personally** designed a special safety system.

"There are two elevators. One is blue. One is red. When you want to go up, you take the blue elevator. When you want to go down, you take the red elevator. It's that simple. It can't go wrong! The blue one only goes up. And the red one only goes down.

"By the way, has anyone seen my **coffeepot?**"

And so, at last, Wayside School got elevators. A blue one and a red one. They each worked perfectly one time—and never could be used again.

---

1 hot diggity dog 깜짝이야! 이건 좋은데! 기쁨이나 흥분을 나타내는 말.

21. OPEN WIDE

The good news: Jason got to leave school early.

The bad news: He had a **dentist appointment**.

"I'll never ever eat candy again," he promised the Tooth God as he headed down the stairs. "And I'll brush my teeth after every **meal**. I promise. Even if it's just a **snack**. I'll bring my **toothbrush** to school! Just please, *please* don't let her find any **cavities**."

"I've heard that song before," answered a voice inside his head. "Every time you go to the dentist, it's the same thing. But then, a week later, you're eating candy and forgetting to brush your teeth."

"This time I really, really mean it," Jason promised.

"Too late," said the voice.

An hour later Jason was lying on his back in the dentist chair.

"Open," said the dentist.

His dentist was named Dr. Payne. She had long fingers and even longer **fingernail**s.

Jason opened his big mouth. He had the second biggest mouth in his class.

"Wider," said Dr. Payne.

Jason **stretch**ed his mouth until his **cheek**s hurt.

"That's good," said Dr. Payne. "Now just a little bit wider."

The **vein**s in Jason's neck **bulge**d out as he stretched his mouth even wider. His eyes **water**ed. His throat was dry.

"Okay, just hold it like that," said Dr. Payne. She turned on the **suck**ing machine and put a **tube** in Jason's mouth.

The machine made a **gagg**ing noise as it sucked out his last drop of **moisture**.

As Dr. Payne **poke**d around at his teeth she said "**Tsk**, tsk" and "Oh, my!" several times.

"So how do you like school?" she asked.

"Aghaa," said Jason.

"What grade are you in?"

"Aakhalak," said Jason.

"Well, just remember," said Dr. Payne. "It's very important

to always listen to your teachers and do whatever they say."

She poked a tooth with a long, **pointed** dentist **tool**.

"AAAAHhhhhhhhh!" Jason screamed in **agony**.

"Did that hurt?" asked Dr. Payne.

Jason shook his head. If he told her it hurt, she might think it was a cavity. If she couldn't find it herself, he certainly wasn't going to tell her about it.

"Are you sure?" asked Dr. Payne. She poked the same **spot**.

This time Jason didn't make a sound. Tears and **sweat drip**ped down his face.

The **receptionist** came into the room.

"Yes?" said Dr. Payne.

Jason was glad for the break.

"Kendall's mother is on the phone," said the receptionist. "She refuses to pay her **bill**."

"What?!" **exclaim**ed Dr. Payne. "How **dare**—"

"She says you pulled the wrong tooth."

"Give me the phone!" shouted Dr. Payne.

The receptionist handed it to her.

"This is Dr. Payne. What do you mean you're not paying your bill? . . . Well, then, just bring Kendall back in here, and I'll pull that one too. I'll pull them all! But you still have to pay me.

"Your lawyer! I don't care what your lawyer said. You can tell your lawyer to rub a monkey's **tummy**! . . . You heard me! Rub a monkey's tummy with your head!"

She **slam**med down the phone.

Jason looked at the **diploma** hanging on the wall. Before his dentist got married, her name was Jane Smith.

His big mouth opened wider.

22. JANE SMITH

"I found Jane Smith," Jason told Stephen the next morning when he got to school.

"You better tell Deedee," said Stephen.

They hurried across the **playground**.

A **whistle blew**. "No running!" ordered Mr. Louis, the **Professional** Playground **Supervisor**. "Now I want both of you to go back to the edge of the **blacktop**, and *walk* this time."

The boys went back the way they came, then came back the way they went.

Deedee was sitting on a **bench**. She had been benched by Mr.

Louis for **excessive** noisemaking.

"I found Jane Smith," Jason whispered as he walked past her. . . .

. . . Deedee and Jason entered the classroom together. Mrs. Drazil was seated behind her desk. As they passed in front of her, Deedee stopped and said, "Did you have a nice time at the **dentist** yesterday, Jason?"

"Yes, Deedee," said Jason. "It was very nice."

"I wonder if we have the same dentist," said Deedee. "What is your dentist's name?"

"Her name is Dr. Payne," said Jason. "But that hasn't always been her name."

"It hasn't?" asked Deedee.

"Oh, no," said Jason. "Before she was married, her name was Jane Smith."

"Jane Smith?" asked Deedee. "Is that **spell**ed J-A-N-E S-M-I-T-H?"

"Yes, that's how you spell Jane Smith," said Jason. "But like I said, that's not her name anymore. Her name is Dr. Payne. She works at the dentist office at 124 Garden Street."

They took their seats. . . .

. . . Late that afternoon Dr. Payne finished work and walked out of her office. It had been a good day. She had **drill**ed twenty-five teeth.

She made sixty dollars for every tooth she drilled. Twenty-five **times** sixty dollars is $1,500. Not bad for a day's work.

Of course, not all the teeth really had **cavities**, but how would any of her **patient**s find out?

She got into her **fancy** silver-and-black sports car and drove away. She sang along with the radio.

She didn't even notice the old **beat-up** green station wagon[1] in her **rearview mirror**.

She lived in a **mansion** next to the lake. There was a stone wall around the house. She **press**ed a button in her car, and an **iron** gate opened. The gate closed behind her as she headed up the long and **wind**ing **driveway**.

A moment later the old green station wagon stopped and parked next to the gate. A woman got out, walked around to the back, and opened the **tailgate**. She pulled out a **ladder**. She set the ladder up against the wall.

Under her arm she carried an old blue notebook. . . .

. . . Dr. Payne's **butler** handed her a drink. The cook was making dinner.

Dr. Payne's dog, cat, and husband were waiting for her in the **den**. Her dog's name was Brussels, and her cat's name was Sprouts. She **pet**ted them both.

---

1   station wagon 스테이션 왜건. 뒷좌석 뒤에 화물칸을 만들어 사람과 화물을 동시에 운반할 수 있게 제작된 자동차.

Her husband's name was Sham. She petted him too.

"Hi, darling, how was your day?" he asked.

"I made fifteen hundred dollars," said Jane.

They hugged and kissed. They loved each other, but they loved money even more.

Then they had dinner by **candlelight** as they watched the sun set over the lake. After dinner they sat out on the **deck**, under the stars.

Sprouts lay **purr**ing on Jane's **lap**. Brussels sat **faithful**ly by her side.

Life was perfect.

"I love you, darling," she said, petting Sprouts.

"And I love you," said Sham.

"I was talking to the cat," said Jane.

The butler stepped out onto the deck. "Excuse me, madam," he said, "but there's an **elderly** woman out in the **yard**."

Jane's long **fingernail**s **dug** into her cat's neck.

"I wonder how she got past the gate," said Sham.

"I don't know, sir," said the butler. "She's probably hungry. Perhaps I can give her some **left-over**—"

"No!" shouted Jane. "**Get rid of** her!"

"Let me have a look," said Sham. He followed the butler back into the house.

He returned a moment later. "Darling, you'll never guess who's here. One of your former teachers! Isn't that just the sweetest—"

Jane screamed. She jumped to her feet. Sprouts flew off her lap and into the **hot tub**.

"What's wrong?" asked Sham.

"You **idiot**!" shouted Jane. "I told you to get rid of her!" She kicked her dog out of the way, then climbed over the **railing** and jumped off the deck to the ground, fifteen feet^2 below.

Mrs. Drazil came out onto the deck. "You can't **get away** from me, young lady!" she **holler**ed.

Jane hurt her **ankle** pretty badly when she hit the ground. It was either **sprain**ed or broken. She lay on the ground in **agony** as she looked up at her former teacher.

"You have homework to do," said Mrs. Drazil, looking down at her.

Jane's face **twist**ed with pain. "**Rub** a monkey's **tummy**!" she shouted, then **struggle**d to her feet.

She had a **suitcase stash**ed in the **boathouse**, **just in case** this ever happened. She **hobble**d to it, **grab**bed it, then **limp**ed down to the lake, **drag**ging her suitcase behind her.

Mrs. Drazil hurried down the steps on the side of the deck.

Jane **groan**ed as she threw her suitcase into a **motorboat**. Then she pulled herself **aboard** and started the engine.

"Darling, come back!" Sham shouted from the deck as he watched the boat **sputter** across the water.

---

2 **feet** 길이의 단위 피트. 15피트는 약 4.5미터이다.

Mrs. Drazil climbed into an old **rowboat**. "I'll find you, Jane Smith!" she shouted into the darkness. "You can run, but you can't hide!"

Jane's voice **echo**ed back across the black water. "Rub a monkeeee's . . . tumm-mmy . . . with . . . yourrr . . . heaaaaaaaaaa ..."

And neither of them was ever seen again.

23. EARS

Wendy had three. Ears, I mean.

She had one ear on each side of her head, just like most people. But she also had a third ear, which lay flat on top of her head.

You couldn't see it. It was completely covered by her thick, **frizzy** brown hair.

She was an **intelligent** and lovely young woman. She was gentle and kind.

At least, she used to be. Then she met Xavier and became **evil** and **wicked**, but I'll get to that later.

She lived in a small apartment in the big city. She always kept fresh flowers in the **vase** on her kitchen table.

She didn't have any friends. She was afraid someone might find out about her ear. She was very **embarrass**ed by it.

The one on top of her head, I mean. The other two ears were pretty, as ears go.

Actually, the third ear wasn't ugly. In fact, it looked just like her other two.

It was **quantity**, not **quality**, that **bother**ed her.

Then she met Xavier.

It was at a museum. They happened to be standing next to each other looking at the same painting. The *Mona Lisa*.

A **guard** stood by to make sure they didn't touch it.

Xavier was very handsome. But he was **frightful**ly **shy**. He was afraid of women.

"That's a beautiful painting, isn't it?" said Wendy.

Xavier **blush**ed. He wanted to speak, but his mouth **lock**ed shut with fear. It took all his courage just to **nod** his head.

But Wendy knew he liked her.

Because there was something else about her ear I haven't told you yet. The one on top of her head, I mean.

It didn't hear normal sounds. It heard people's brains.

Wendy was able to listen to Xavier's secret thoughts. And this is what she heard.

Yes, the painting is very beautiful. But you are more beautiful than the Mona Lisa. *I wish somebody would paint your picture. I* *would buy it and look at it all day. **Alas, if only I had the courage to talk to you.***

Wendy didn't usually listen to other people's thoughts. She thought it was rude, even though the other people didn't know she was listening.

Besides, most people's thoughts were usually **boring**.

Xavier was getting too nervous standing next to her. He **moved on** to another painting.

Wendy followed him.

She listened to the lonely man's thoughts. They weren't boring at all. Most of his thoughts were about her, but she also learned a few other things. He liked to read. His favorite author was Charles Dickens.[1] He loved animals, especially dogs.

"That painting reminds me of a book," said Wendy. *"A Tale of Two Cities,*[2] by Charles Dickens. Have you read it?"

"Yes!" Xavier **blurt**ed, a little too loudly. "It's my favorite book! I've read everything Dickens has written. Twice. My favorite part is when—"

He suddenly stopped, very embarrassed.

"Please go on," said Wendy.

"No, I don't want to bother you," said Xavier.

---

1 Charles Dickens 찰스 디킨스. 셰익스피어와 더불어 영국을 대표하는 작가. 〈올리버 트 위스트〉, 〈위대한 유산〉 등과 같은 작품을 남겼다.

2 A Tale of Two Cities 찰스 디킨스의 소설 〈두 도시 이야기〉. 프랑스 혁명이라는 역사적 사건을 배경으로 한 소설.

"You're not bothering me," said Wendy. "Charles Dickens is my favorite author. I sometimes read aloud to my dog."

"You have a dog?" asked Xavier.

Wendy nodded.

Xavier **stared** into her dark eyes. "I love dogs," he said, as his brain said, *I love you.*

Wendy and Xavier spent the afternoon together. He could **hardly** stop talking.

It was like a genie[3] had escaped from a bottle. All the love and **emotion** that had been **buried** for so long inside him came **pour**ing out on Wendy.

"I don't even know your name," he suddenly blurted.

"Wendy Nogard," said Wendy.

"I'm Xavier Dalton," said Xavier.

They shook hands and made plans to meet again at the museum the following week.

On her way home, Wendy stopped by the library and **check**ed **out** *A Tale of Two Cities*. Then she went to the **pet** store and bought a dog.

A month later Xavier asked her to marry him.

Wendy didn't know what to say. She loved Xavier. And she knew he loved her. But she still hadn't told him about her ear.

The one on top of her head, I mean.

---

3 genie 지니. 동화와 신화에 나오는 램프 속에 사는 요정.

He knew about the other two. He had **nibble**d on each of them.

"Marriage is a big step," she said. "I'm afraid we haven't known each other long enough."

"I've known you long enough to know I could never be happy without you," said Xavier. "Before I met you, Wendy, I was sad and lonely. But I was used to it. Now I can't imagine living like that again. I don't know what I'd do without you."

He **stroke**d her hair.

"Well, there's one little thing you don't know about me," said Wendy.

His hand **bump**ed into it. "What's this thing?" he asked.

"That's what I was going to tell you about, dear," said Wendy.

Xavier **part**ed Wendy's hair and looked at it. "It's an ear!" he exclaimed.

"Yes, it is," said Wendy. "Some people have two ears. I have three. Now that you know, if you still want to marry me, my answer is yes! Yes, sweetheart, yes!"

"I love you," said Xavier. "That's all that matters to me."

That was what he said. But this is what he was thinking.

Oh, gross! You're disgusting! I never want to touch you again! I can't even stand to look at you! You tricked me, you freak! You monster!

And of course Wendy heard every word.

He stood up. "I'll be right back, sweetheart.[4] I bought you diamond earrings as an **engagement** present. I just need to run back to the jewelry store and buy one more." He hurried out the door.

She never saw him again.

I'm sorry to say this story has a sad ending.

Xavier, thanks to Wendy, **got over** his shyness. He **went out with** lots of women but broke each one's heart. He could never love any of them.

There was a hole in his heart. He was in love with Wendy Nogard, but he didn't know it. And so he could never be happy.

Wendy became a **bitter** and evil person. She was unhappy, and she wanted everyone else to be unhappy too.

Whenever she heard someone thinking happy thoughts, she would listen closely and then do and say just the right thing to make the person feel **rotten**.

She hated children the most. Every time she passed a playground, she heard them laughing and having fun.

So she became a **substitute** teacher.

4　sweetheart 애정을 담아 남을 부르는 호칭.

24. GLUM AND BLAH

Miss Nogard entered the classroom on the thirtieth **story**. She looked at all the bright and **chipper** faces. She knew by the end of the day they would no longer be bright and chipper.

They would be **glum** and **blah**.

She smiled at the class. "Good morning, everybody," she said. "My name is Miss Nogard."

She listened to their brains.

Calvin had **spill**ed orange juice on his **lap** during breakfast and worried that someone might think he had gone to the bathroom in his pants.

Dana had gotten her hair cut yesterday, and she thought it was too short. She was afraid it made her look like a boy. She was especially **sensitive** to this because Dana was sometimes a boy's name.

Jason was mad at his older brother, Justin. Justin was in high school. Justin always got good grades and was a star in everything he did. **Compare**d to Justin, Jason felt like a **loser**. "What's so great about high school?" he had asked this morning. "My school is higher than yours!"

D.J. had heard a song on the radio on his way to school. He hated the song! But it kept playing over and over again in his head.

Bebe had an **itch** on her leg.

Miss Nogard smiled. The bad **stuff** always rose to the top of the brain.

Even if a person was very excited about something wonderful, the person still worried about what could go wrong.

Jenny was going **horseback riding** after school, if it didn't rain. She had never gone horseback riding before. She hoped she wouldn't fall off the horse.

Miss Nogard **clap**ped her hands. "So, who would like to tell me what you've been **work**ing **on**?" she asked.

A few hands went up in the air.

"Oooh! Oooh!" said Mac.

"How about the boy in the orange and purple shirt?" said Miss Nogard.

Everyone looked around.

"The handsome young man sitting right there," said Miss Nogard.

Dana looked at her shirt. It was orange and purple. She pointed at herself and **mouth**ed the word *me?*

"Yes, you," said Miss Nogard.

Dana's face turned red-hot. "I'm a girl," she said.

Everyone laughed.

"Oh, I am so **embarrass**ed!" said Miss Nogard, with her hand over her heart.

"It's not your fault," said Dana. "It's my stupid haircut. I hate it!"

"Oh, no," said Miss Nogard. "You look **adorable**. I see now you're a very pretty girl."

"I'm ugly," **mutter**ed Dana. She **buried** her head under her arms.

"I'd better **call on** someone else," said Miss Nogard.

Suddenly, **out of nowhere**, a brain screamed, *Don't call on me! Whatever you do, please don't call on me!*

It came from Benjamin Nushmutt.

"How about you?" said Miss Nogard, looking right at him.

Just don't ask me my name, thought Benjamin. *I never can say my name in front of people.* He took a breath to **steady** himself. "Well, we've been reading—"

"First tell me your name," Miss Nogard said sweetly.

The **muscles** in Benjamin's face **tighten**ed. He **concentrate**d real hard, then said, "Benjamin Nushmutt."

"I **beg** your **pardon**?" said Miss Nogard.

"Benjamin Nushmutt," he repeated.

"Henderson Schmidt?" asked Miss Nogard.

Benjamin **sigh**ed. "Ben-ja-min Nush! Mutt!" he shouted.

"I'm sorry," said Miss Nogard. "I must have been **distract**ed. What did you say?"

Benjamin **press**ed his lips together. He tried to speak, but his mouth wouldn't open.

"His name is Benjamin," said Jason. "Benjamin Nushmutt."

"Thank you," said Miss Nogard. "That's a very nice name, Benjamin. You shouldn't be **ashamed** of it."

Benjamin covered his red face with his hands.

She turned to Jason. "You look familiar. Do I know you?"

"I don't think so," said Jason.

She stared at him, as if she were trying to remember. "You're Justin, right?"

"I'm Jason. Justin's my older brother."

"So you're Justin's baby brother!" said Miss Nogard.

Everybody laughed.

"I remember Justin. I substituted for his class once. He was the brightest student I ever taught. You must feel very lucky to have such an **exceptional** brother."

His feet stink, thought Jason.

For the rest of the day, Miss Nogard kept **accidentally-on-**

purpose calling Jason "Justin."

One by one, she made every child in the class feel **miserable**. She called Calvin to her desk and asked in a whisper if he had to use the restroom. Whenever she passed D.J., she **hum**med and the song stuck in his head. Whenever Bebe finally stopped thinking about her itch, Miss Nogard would walk by and **scratch** her own leg.

"It looks like it might rain," she said as she stared out the window at the bright blue sky.

Darn,[1] *I'll never get to go horseback riding!* thought Jenny.

"I have a **nephew** who went horseback riding on a day like this," said Miss Nogard. "There wasn't a cloud in the sky. Then suddenly, out of nowhere, it started **thunder**ing and **lightning**. It **spook**ed the horse **terribly**."

"What happened to your nephew?" asked Jenny.

"Oh, he's fine," said Miss Nogard. "He just broke both his arms and legs. He'll be in a **cast** for a year. But he has a very **positive attitude**; that's the important thing. Remember, always keep a positive attitude."

By the end of the day, nobody had a positive attitude. The whole class was glum and blah.

The children walked out of the school building, heads down. Except Jenny, who looked up at the sky, worrying about the weather, although she didn't know if she was more worried about rain or

---

1   darn 'damn' 대신에 쓰는 가벼운 욕설로 '젠장', '빌어먹을'이라는 뜻이다.

sunshine.

Even D.J. was **frown**ing.

"What's the matter?" asked Louis, the yard teacher.

"Nothing," muttered D.J. "I guess I just had a bad day."

"Don't you like your new teacher?" asked Louis.

"She's real nice," said Dana. *It's not her fault I'm the ugliest girl in the world!*

"I like her a lot," said Jason. *It's my brother I hate.*

"Me too," said Benjamin. *I hate myself!*

Louis **rub**bed his upper lip. His **mustache** was beginning to grow back. "What's her name?" he asked.

"Miss Nogard," said Bebe as she scratched the back of her leg **raw**.

"Are you sure?" asked Louis.

"Huh?" asked Bebe.

"I mean," said Louis, "are you sure it's *Miss* Nogard? Not *Mrs.* Nogard?"

"I think," said Bebe. "Why?"

Louis just **shrug**ged.

132

25. GUILTY

Some of the children were working in their **workbook**s. Others were reading in their **reader**s. And still others were **computing** on the computer.

Miss Nogard looked from one to another. *Eenie . . . meenie . . . minie[1] . . . Maurecia!* she thought.

Maurecia was **stamp**ing a stamp.

"Maurecia," said Miss Nogard. "Will you come here, please?"

Maurecia walked to the front of the room. "Yes?" she said

---

1   eenie, meenie, minie 어느 것으로 할까. 여러 가지 중에서 선택을 하거나 술래잡기에서 술래를 정할 때 쓰는 말.

cheerfully.

"Don't 'yes' me, young lady," said Miss Nogard. "You know what you did."

Maurecia looked back at her teacher. *What did I do?* she wondered.

Miss Nogard waited **patiently.** Everyone was **guilty** of something.

I didn't do anything, did I? thought Maurecia. *I've been good, I think. Unless she found out about that* **dictionary** *page I accidentally* **tore.** *No, she couldn't know about that! It happened before she even got here. And I don't think anybody saw me do it.*

"I didn't do anything," she said. *I probably should have told Mrs. Jewls about it,* she realized, *but it wasn't even my fault! I was looking up how to spell '* **journey** *' for my* **journal** *, and the page just* **rip** *ped all by itself.*

"It is one thing to do something wrong, Maurecia," said Miss Nogard. "But when you do, you should admit to it. We all make mistakes. But when you lie about it, you make matters much worse for yourself."

Maurecia **nod**ded as she tried to **figure out** what to do. If Miss Nogard knew she tore the dictionary page, then of course she should admit to it. But there was **no way** Miss Nogard could know! It was impossible.

"I don't know what you mean," she said **innocent**ly. "I didn't do anything wrong." She smiled at her teacher.

Miss Nogard stared at her a long moment, then said, "Will you please bring me the dictionary?"

134

The smile dropped off Maurecia's face and **crash**ed on the floor.

The dictionary lay on top of the bookcase. Maurecia **numb**ly went after it. *How could she know?* she wondered. *It's impossible! Maybe she just wants to look up a word.*

She carried the heavy book back to Miss Nogard.

"Thank you, Maurecia," said Miss Nogard, **flip**ping **through** the pages. "I need to look up 'journey.'"

Maurecia couldn't **take it** any longer. "I ripped it!" she cried out. "I tore the dictionary. I'm sorry. I don't even know how it happened. I was just turning the page, really! Maybe pages only have a certain amount of turns in them. Like, nine hundred and ninety-nine. Then when you turn the page for the thousandth time, it will rip, no matter who turns it."

Miss Nogard sadly shook her head. "I am very disappointed in you," she said. "Not only did you **vandalize** the dictionary. But then you lied about it. I thought I could trust you, Maurecia. I guess I was wrong."

"I'm a **horrible** person," Maurecia agreed. "I'm sorry."

"Don't apologize to me," said Miss Nogard. "It's not my dictionary. It **belongs** to the class."

Maurecia had to stand in front of the class and tell them she was sorry. Then, since nobody would ever be able to use that page again, she had to read it aloud to the class.

She **struggle**d through the difficult words like "**journalism**" and "**judicious**."

"**Speak up**," Miss Nogard had to keep reminding her. "And everyone needs to **pay** close **attention** because there will be a test on it when Maurecia is finished."

"Hey, that's not fair!" **complain**ed Jason. "We didn't rip the dictionary. Why should we be **punished**?"

"It's not punishment," said Miss Nogard. "It is for your own good. Since you can no longer use that page, you need to **memorize** it."

"Thanks a lot, Maurecia!" **grip**ed Jenny.

When Maurecia finished reading it, Miss Nogard made her turn the page over and read the back side of it too.

"But I only ripped the front," said Maurecia. "Not the back."

She finished, then returned to her seat, angry and upset. She wasn't angry at Miss Nogard. Miss Nogard was just being fair, she thought.

But there was only one way Miss Nogard could have known about the torn page, she realized. Somebody in the class must have seen her tear it and then **tattled** on her.

She looked around the room, from Deedee to Todd to Terrence to Joy. She didn't trust any of them.

One of her friends was a **no-good**-dirty-**double-cross**ing-snake-in-the-grass![2]

---

2 snake in the grass '친밀함을 가장한 배신자'라는 뜻으로 숨어있는 적을 가리킬 때 쓰인다.

26. NEVER LAUGH AT A SHOELACE

"This is a **shoelace**," said Mac.

Everybody laughed.

Mac was standing at the front of the room, holding his shoelace in his hand. He felt like a **fool**.

"What a fool!" said Allison.

* * *

It all started a minute earlier, when Miss Nogard asked, "Who has something to share for show-and-tell?[1]"

---

1   show-and-tell 학교 수업 활동의 하나로 학생들이 각자 물건을 가져와서 발표하는 것을 말한다.

But first you should know something about Mac.

Mac's favorite **subject** in the whole world was show-and-tell. He loved it. Especially when he was the one doing the showing and telling.

He often looked through **garbage** cans on his way to school, in search of stuff to show and tell about. Once he found a real **gushy** love letter. It was covered with something that looked like peach **slime**. But that wasn't what made it gushy. The gushy part was what was written in the letter. Mac read it to the class with lots of feeling.

So when Miss Nogard said, "Who has something to share for show-and-tell?" Mac reacted without thinking. His arm shot up like a rocket as he almost jumped out of his seat. "Ooooh! Ooooh!" he **groan**ed.

Then he remembered something. *I didn't bring anything for show-and-tell!*

Miss Nogard heard him. Before he could lower his hand, she called on him.

And that was how he **end**ed **up** with his shoelace **dangling** from his hand like a dead **worm**.

"It came from my **sneaker**," he said. He took off his sneaker and held it up too, next to his shoelace. "See, you stick the laces through the little holes, here. Then tie it in a **bow**. That keeps it from falling off your foot."

"Duh!²" said Dana.

"We know what a shoelace is," said Paul.

"I've been tying my shoes since I was two years old," said Joe.

Calvin and Bebe **boo**ed.

"Sit down," said Jason. "You're boring."

The kids in Mrs. Jewls's class never used to be so mean, but they'd been getting **grumpier** and grumpier ever since Miss Nogard **took over**.

"Put your shoe back on!" said Maurecia. "Your foot **stink**s."

Mac felt terrible.

Miss Nogard smiled. "Go on, Mac," she said. "We're all very interested to hear what you have to say."

He tried to think of some way to make a shoelace interesting. "Uh, shoelaces are real important," he said. "There was once this guy. He was a real fast runner. His name was Howard. Howard Speed! He was the fastest runner in the world! But this was back before shoelaces were **invent**ed. And so, every time Howard **race**d, he ran right out of his shoes!"

Nobody seemed very **impress**ed. But then Rondi asked, "Did it hurt his feet?"

Mac **shrug**ged. "I guess," he said.

"I once **stub**bed my toe on a rock," said Stephen. "It hurt."

"Yeah, and you didn't run as fast as Howard Speed!" said Mac.

---

2 **duh** 흥. 남의 바보 같은 짓이나 말을 탓할 때 사용하는 감탄사.

"He ran so fast that if he kicked a rock, he would break his toe!"

"Did he have **blisters**?" asked Todd.

Mac smiled. "Man, he had the biggest blisters you ever saw in your whole life! **Bleed**ing blisters!"

"Ooooh," Joe and John said together.

"With **pus oozing** out!" said Mac.

"Oh, **gross**!" said Dana, **wide-eyed**.

Everyone was **paying** close **attention** to Mac now.

"Wherever Howard went," said Mac, "he left a **trail** of **bloody footprint**s."

"Cool!" said Terrence.

"And so they had to invent something to keep Howard's sneakers on his feet," said Mac. "First they just tried **nail**ing his shoes to his feet."

"Yowza!³" Bebe **exclaim**ed.

"Why didn't he just use Velcro?⁴" asked Jason.

"Howard lived in Africa," explained Mac. "Velcro trees only grow in Australia. So then they tried **gluing** his shoes to his feet. And that seemed to work. But then, whenever he took off his shoes, like to take a bath or something, he'd **peel** off a **layer** of skin."

"Yuck-ola!⁵" **shriek**ed Allison.

---

3   **yowza** 우와! 와! 놀라움이나 감탄을 나타내는 표현.
4   **Velcro** 벨크로. 한쪽 면에는 갈고리 모양의 작은 돌기가 달려 있고, 다른 한쪽 면에는 올 가미 형태가 달려 있어 양면을 접착하여 고정시키는 여밈 장치.
5   **yuck-ola** 으악! 웩! 경멸이나 혐오감을 나타내는 표현.

"But finally Thomas Edison[6] invented the shoelace, and Howard never ran out of his shoes again."

"Did he win all his races after that?" asked John.

"Well," said Mac, "the next race was for the **championship** of the whole world. Howard **got off** to a real fast start. It looked like he would win for sure. But shoelaces were still a new invention, and Howard wasn't quite used to them yet. Right before he reached the finish line, his shoelace came untied. He **trip**ped over it and fell flat on his face. He broke his nose, lost all his teeth, and had two black eyes![7]"

"Wow," said all three Erics together.

"So remember," said Mac, as he held his shoelace high in the air. "Never laugh at a shoelace!"

Everyone **applaud**ed.

---

6 **Thomas Edison** 토머스 에디슨. 미국의 발명가로 전구를 발명한 것으로 유명하다. 1,000종 이상의 특허를 받아 '발명왕'이라고 불린다.

7 black eye 멍든 눈.

27. WAY-HIGH-UP BALL

Eric Fry, Eric Bacon, and Eric Ovens were playing **way**-high-up ball. They had **made up** the game themselves.

All you needed were two things—a pink **rubber** ball, about the size of a tennis ball, and a real tall school.

Eric Ovens threw the ball way high up. It **bounce**d off the school, just above the third-**story** window.

"Three-pointer,[1]" called Eric Bacon.

They **shove**d and **elbow**ed each other out of the way as they

---

1 three-pointer 농구나 레슬링 등과 같은 스포츠 경기에서 3점을 획득할 만한 가치가 있
   는 플레이를 말한다.

waited for it to come down. At the last second, Eric Fry jumped and caught it.

He got three points. Eric Ovens also got three points since he was the thrower.

Eric Fry threw the ball way high up. It bounced off a window on the fifth floor.

"Five-pointer!" called Eric Ovens.

All three Erics jumped for it. It bounced off their **fingertips** and hit the ground.

The teacher on the fifth story **stuck** her head **out** the window. "Hey, what's going on down there?" she shouted.

The three Erics looked away and **whistled**.

There's one more thing about way-high-up ball I haven't told you. You're not allowed to play it. The Erics had already broken one window.

Eric Bacon looked up, surprised. "Are you talking to us?" he asked.

"Something just **bang**ed against my window," said the teacher.

"Was it a bird?" asked Eric Ovens.

The teacher **stared** at the children a moment longer. Then she pulled her head inside.

Eric Fry threw the ball way high up. It was a six-pointer!

All three fought for position as they waited for it to come down, but at the last second, a **hairy** arm reached above them and caught it.

The arm **belong**ed to Louis, the **yard** teacher.

"Can I play?" asked Louis. His mustache had grown back completely.

"Sure!" all three Erics said together.

"What do I have to do?" asked Louis.

"Just see how high up against the school you can throw it," said Eric Fry.

Louis **grip**ped the ball tightly in his hand. He reached way back, then let it fly.

"Wowww!" the three Erics said together as they watched the ball **soar** up in the air.

It hit up above the eighth-story window; then Louis caught his own **rebound**.

"Sixteen points!" said Eric Bacon.

"Throw it again, Louis," said Eric Ovens.

Now that Louis was playing, lots of kids from all over the **playground** came to play too.

Louis threw the ball way high up. It hit above the eleventh story, then bounced back over everyone's head.

There was a mad **scramble** for the ball. Bebe finally **came up with** it.

"Give it to Louis," said Eric Ovens.

"No, let Bebe throw it," said Louis, who always tried to be fair.

Bebe threw a two-pointer.

144

Jason caught the rebound. "You want to throw it, Louis?" he asked.

"No, you go ahead," said Louis.

Jason threw a glopper.

A glopper is when the ball goes straight up in the air and comes down without touching the building.

Eric Bacon caught it. "Here, Louis," he said.

"No, you throw it," said Louis.

"But you can throw it so much higher," said Eric B.

"We want to see how high you can throw it, Louis," said Leslie.

"C'mon, Louis!" everyone **urged**.

Louis shook his head. "The game is for you kids, not for me."

"Miss Nogard is watching," said Bebe **slyly**.

Louis **glanced** at Miss Nogard, who was standing just outside the front door. "Give me the ball," he said.

The kids cheered.

Louis reached way down, almost to the ground, then **hurled** it up with all his **might**.

The ball reached the fifteenth floor, **halfway** up the school!

"Wow!" everyone said together.

"I got it," called Terrence as he circled under the ball, waiting for it to come down. His knees **wobbled**.

The ball bounced off his face. "Cool," he said as blood **flowed** out of his nose.

"That was a world's record, Louis!" exclaimed Eric Ovens.

Louis smiled proudly. He turned to look at Miss Nogard, but she had already gone inside.

"You like Miss Nogard, don't you?" asked Bebe.

"She seems like a nice person," said Louis.

"She's pretty too," said Eric Bacon as he **nudge**d Louis in the side.

"Well, she is kind of cute," Louis admitted.

"Oooooh," said Joy.

"But do you *love* her?" asked Jenny.

Everyone **giggle**d. Louis's red face got even redder.

"You should **ask** her **out** on a date," said Eric Fry.

"No, I don't think that's a very good idea," said Louis.

"Why not?" asked Eric Ovens. "I think you two would make a real cute couple."

"Bring her flowers," said Dana.

"Buy her candy," said Maurecia.

"Tell her she's got eyes like the moon," said Bebe.

"Eyes like the moon?" asked Louis.

"Girls love it when you tell them that," said Bebe.

"Forget that **gushy stuff**," said Eric Bacon. "Just walk right up to her and say, 'Hey, baby! How about a date?'"

"Just like that?" asked Louis.

"This is what you do," said Terrence. "You take her to a real **scary** movie. And then at the scary part, you put your arm around her."

146

"Ooooh," said Dana and Jenny.

"No, take her dancing," said Myron. "And hold her real close."

"Ooooooh," said the three Erics.

Louis laughed. "You kids are crazy," he said.

"You're **scared** of her, aren't you?" asked Eric Bacon.

"You shouldn't be scared," said Eric Ovens. "You're bigger and stronger and faster than anyone on the playground."

"And you've got the best mustache too," said Eric Fry.

"I'm not afraid of her," Louis tried to explain. "It's just—" He looked up at the very tall school. "Miss Nogard is way-high-up there, and I'm way-down-low here. You'll understand someday when you're older."

He picked up the ball and threw it way high up. It hit somewhere between the eighteenth and twentieth story.

And never came down.

There was no nineteenth story.

28. FLOWERS FOR A VERY SPECIAL PERSON

Of course Miss Nogard knew all about Louis. The children's brains were **buzz**ing about him.

Louis likes Miss Nogard, thought Stephen.

Louis is in love with Miss Nogard, thought Todd.

Louis wants to marry Miss Nogard, thought Sharie.

But even if she couldn't listen to their brains, she would have found out anyway. "Louis, the **yard** teacher, is madly in love with you," said Jenny.

"Oh, really?" said Miss Nogard.

"He dreams about you every night," said Calvin.

"He thinks your eyes are like the moon," said Bebe.

Miss Nogard smiled.

"Do you like him?" asked Jenny.

"He's kind of cute," said Miss Nogard.

"Ooooh," Bebe and Calvin said together.

"What about his **mustache?**" asked Jenny. "Do you like his mustache?"

Miss Nogard thought a moment. "It would probably **tickle** if he kissed me."

The children **gasp**ed as their mouths fell open.

They returned to their desks and told everyone around them what Miss Nogard said.

Miss Nogard smiled. She wondered just how she'd break Louis's heart.

Ever since Xavier broke her heart, she'd become an **expert** at breaking other people's. She listened to men's brains and knew just what to say to make them fall in love with her.

And then she knew just the right thing to say, at just the right moment, to **shatter** their hearts into a million pieces. Even the biggest and strongest man would cry like a baby.

She was **incapable** of love. Her heart was **clogg**ed with **bitter**ness and hate. And **besides**, she knew no one would ever love someone with three ears.

For just a second she felt a **pang** of sadness. Because she really did think Louis was kind of cute. Like a **puppy** dog.

She could almost feel the tickle of his mustache.

"Miss Nogard thinks you're cute," Jenny told Louis at **recess**.

"She's hot for you, Louis!" said Mac.

"She wants to kiss you!" said Bebe.

"C'mon, let's play **kickball**," said Louis.

They played kickball, but it was **weird**. Louis, who was probably the best kickball player ever, did **terribly**. He tripped over the ball when he tried to kick it. And when Terrence kicked a pop-up,[1] Louis tried to catch it, but the ball **bounce**d off his head.

"What's wrong with Louis?" asked Ron. "Is he sick or something?"

"Yes," said Jenny. "He's got a real bad **disease**. And it's **spell**ed L-O-V-E."

The next morning Louis came to school with a **bunch** of flowers in his hand.

Jenny saw him. "Are those for Miss Nogard?" she asked.

"Oh, I don't know," said Louis. "I passed a **field** of **wildflower**s on the way to school. I thought I might give them to someone special." He **wink**ed at her.

He headed toward the school building. Jenny followed.

"*Oooh*, flowers!" said Bebe.

"Are you going to give them to Miss Nogard?" asked Calvin.

---

1 pop-up (= pop fly) 야구에서 타자가 비거리가 짧으면서 높이 날아가는 공을 친 상태나 그 공을 말한다.

"Oh, I don't know," said Louis. "I think she might have a pretty face, I mean **vase**."

Calvin and Bebe followed along with Jenny.

Louis entered the building.

Miss Nogard was in the office. She was getting her mail from her box. Her back was to him.

Louis **froze**.

"Go on, Louis," urged Jenny.

But Louis just stood there. The flowers **rattle**d in his **shaky** hand, and several **petal**s fell to the floor.

Mr. Kidswatter came out of his office. "Good morning, Louis," he said. "What have you got there?"

"Uh, these are for you," said Louis. He **thrust** the flowers into Mr. Kidswatter's hand.

"They're lovely!" said Mr. Kidswatter.

Miss Nogard turned around. "Those are very pretty, Mr. Kidswatter," she said, then headed up the stairs.

Louis watched her go.

"No one's ever brought me flowers before," said Mr. Kidswatter. "You may not believe this, Louis, but I don't have many friends." He put his hand on Louis's shoulder. "You're like a son to me," he said.

"And you're a maggot-**infested**[2] string bean,[3]" **mutter**ed Louis.

---

2   maggot 구더기. 파리의 유충을 말한다.
3   string bean 깍지콩. 새파랗고 기다란 콩깍지를 그대로 요리에 넣어 먹는 콩.

"What?" asked Mr. K.

"I said, you're a **magnificent** human being."

29. STUPID

"Did anyone have any trouble with the homework?" asked Miss Nogard.

They all shook their heads.

Ron shook his head too. *Homework?* he thought. *What homework?*

"Good," said Miss Nogard. "Well, in that case, there won't be any homework tonight."

Everyone cheered.

"Let's just quickly **go over** the answers," she said. "Ron, what was your answer to question one?"

Ron's **stomach flip**ped over. He **fumble**d with his notebook.

"Uh, just a second," he said.

"That's okay, we'll wait," said Miss Nogard.

Ron **flipped through** the pages. "What question are we on?" he asked.

"Question one," said Miss Nogard.

"Um, I couldn't get that one," said Ron.

"Oh," said Miss Nogard. "Well, that's okay, Ron. As long as you tried. Who knows the answer to question one?"

A **handful** of hands went up in the air.

Seven lima beans,[1] thought Jason.

Seven lima beans, thought Rondi.

*Six **cucumbers**,* thought Deedee.

Seven lima beans, thought Stephen.

Miss Nogard **called on** Deedee.

"Six cucumbers," Deedee said proudly.

"No, I'm sorry," said Miss Nogard. "The answer was seven lima beans."

Ooh, I had that! thought Jason.

She should have called on me! thought Rondi.

Deedee is stupid, thought Stephen.

"Okay, question two," said Miss Nogard. "Ron, did you get that one?"

Ron **squirm**ed in his seat. He flipped through his papers. "What

---

1   lima bean 리마콩. 크기가 약간 큰 푸른색 콩이다.

question are we on?" he asked.

"Question two," said Miss Nogard.

"Uh, I couldn't get that one either," said Ron.

Miss Nogard looked at him a moment. "Okay, who knows the answer to question two?"

Abraham Lincoln's hat, thought Todd.

Abraham Lincoln's hat, thought Joy.

Abraham Lincoln's hat, thought Bebe.

George Washington's[2] left shoe, thought Calvin.

"Yes, Calvin," said Miss Nogard.

"George Washington's left shoe!" said Calvin.

"No, I'm sorry," said Miss Nogard. "The answer was Abraham Lincoln's hat."

I knew it! thought Todd.

Calvin's stupid, thought Joy.

"Ron, did you get the answer to number three?" asked Miss Nogard.

Ron shook his sorry little head. He wished he had just told her the truth, but now it was too late.

"Anyone?" asked Miss Nogard.

Chairs and bears, thought Benjamin.

Coats and goats, thought D.J.

Chairs and bears, thought Mac.

---

2 George Washington 조지 워싱턴. 미국의 초대 대통령으로 미국의 독립전쟁을 이끌고 연방헌법을 제정하여 미국 '건국의 아버지'라고 불린다.

Chairs and bears, thought Deedee.

Miss Nogard called on D.J.

"Coats and goats?" he said **hopefully.**

"No, chairs and bears," said Miss Nogard.

What an **idiot***!* thought Benjamin.

"Question four," said Miss Nogard. "Ron?"

. . . And so it went. Miss Nogard **went through** the entire homework **assign**ment, and nobody gave a **correct** answer.

"I'm very disappointed," she said when they were finished. "You **obvious**ly didn't understand it. So I'm afraid I'm going to have to assign homework tonight after all."

Everyone **groan**ed.

"I don't like it any better than you do," said Miss Nogard. "But it's for your own good."

She assigned three pages of homework, plus they had to do yesterday's homework over again as well.

But nobody **blame**d Miss Nogard. They liked her! She didn't even want to give homework.

They blamed each other.

It's not fair! thought Benjamin. *I only missed one problem. But I have to do extra homework because everyone else is so stupid!*

It was the same all around the room. Nobody missed more than two problems. Everyone thought everyone else was stupid!

Miss Nogard smiled as she listened to their thoughts.

I hate Joe! thought John.

156

I hate Calvin! thought Bebe.

I hate Joy! thought Maurecia.

I hate Allison! thought Rondi.

And everyone hated Ron.

30. THE LITTLE STRANGER

Wayside School was no fun anymore.

"Hey, out of my way, buster![1]" said Deedee as she pushed past Ron on her way to her seat.

"Hey, keep your **hairy paws** to yourself!" said Ron.

Nobody had any friends. Everybody hated everybody—except Miss Nogard. They all liked her.

But then a miracle happened.

A new kid came to school.

---

1 buster 야! 임마!

The new kid couldn't talk. She had no teeth. She was almost **bald**.

She was beautiful.

Her name was Mavis Jewls. She was only four days old.

She really was a new kid.

Mrs. Jewls carried her into the classroom.

And when the baby came through the door, all the hate flew out the window.

Louis came in behind them carrying a bassinet,[2] a **diaper** bag, an **assortment** of toys, and a **baby bottle**.

"It's Mrs. Jewls and her baby!" Todd **exclaim**ed.

Louis set the bassinet on Todd's desk. Mrs. Jewls gently laid her baby down in it, on soft yellow **blanket**s.

Everyone crowded around the little stranger.

"Look at her totally tiny toes!" Bebe **squeal**ed. "Aren't those the cutest things you've ever seen in your whole life?"

"**Check out** her nose!" said Myron.

"Oh, she's so beautiful, Mrs. Jewls," said Joy. "Can I touch her?"

"Sure," said Mrs. Jewls.

They **took turns** touching the baby.

"Goo-goo, goo-goo," said Mac as he gently shook Mavis's little hand.

---

2 bassinet 바구니같이 생긴 아기 침대.

"Iggle wiggle poo poo," said Allison, **tapp**ing her on the nose.

"Iggle wiggle poo poo poo," said Rondi, **tickling** her foot.

"Yibble bibble," said Todd.

"Ooh goo boo boo," **coo**ed Joe.

"She's never going to learn to talk around you kids," said Mrs. Jewls with a laugh.

Dana was so happy she cried. She hugged Mrs. Jewls.

They all took turns hugging Mrs. Jewls.

Of course, there was one person who wasn't happy. "May I hold her, Mrs. Jewls?" Miss Nogard asked sweetly.

Mrs. Jewls looked at the **substitute** teacher.

"It's okay," said Allison. "Miss Nogard's a real nice teacher."

"Sure, go ahead," said Mrs. Jewls. "I'm sorry for **interrupt**ing your class like this."

"Oh, that's quite all right," said Miss Nogard, picking up Mrs. Jewls's baby. "She's just **adorable**."

The window by Sharie's desk was wide open. *That's kind of dangerous,* Miss Nogard realized. *Somebody might **accidentally** drop something out the window.*

She slowly moved toward it as she **sway**ed with the baby. "I've heard so much about you, Mrs. Jewls," she said. "The children have missed you."

"I've missed them too," said Mrs. Jewls.

There was a **rubber-band** ball on the floor next to Sharie's desk. Sharie had been making it, although it wasn't nearly as big as the one Mr. Kidswatter had been making.

*If I tripped over that rubber-band ball, something **awful** might happen,* thought Miss Nogard.

She was just about to step on it, when suddenly she became very **curious** about the kind of thoughts babies had. She had never listened to a baby's brain before.

Miss Nogard held Mavis close to her heart and listened. . . .

She **gasp**ed. Her face turned white, and her legs **wobbled** beneath her. As she tried to get her **balance**, she stepped on the rubber-band ball and fell toward the open window.

Louis jumped over Sharie's desk and **grab**bed her **just in time.**

Mrs. Jewls hurried over.

Miss Nogard **tender**ly handed Mrs. Jewls her baby. Then she **faint**ed in Louis's arms.

It is impossible to describe, in words, **exact**ly what Miss Nogard heard when she listened to Mavis's brain.

Babies don't think in words.

Miss Nogard heard pure love. And trust. And faith. With no words to get in the way.

It was a love so strong that it **dissolve**d away all the **bitter**ness that had been **cake**d around her heart.

She opened her eyes.

"Are you all right, Miss Nogard?" asked Stephen.

All the children were very worried about her.

Miss Nogard smiled at Louis, who was still holding her. "I'm fine," she said, then took a couple of steps to **steady** herself. "In fact, I think I'm better than I've been in a long time." She laughed, then hugged Stephen.

"You should feel very proud of your class," she told Mrs. Jewls. "They are bright, **well behaved**, and just a pleasure to teach."

"We are?" asked Maurecia.

Miss Nogard **fluff**ed Maurecia's hair. "Yes, you are," she said. Maurecia smiled up at her.

"I know," said Mrs. Jewls. "As I told my **obstetrician**—"

"Your what?" asked Joy.

"Obstetrician," said Mrs. Jewls. "That's the doctor who helped me have my baby. Then, once a baby is born, she gets a new doctor. That doctor is called a **pediatrician**. That's different from a **podiatrist**, who is a doctor who takes care of people's feet. There are many different kinds of doctors. There's also a—"

Todd raised his hand. "Mrs. Jewls, you're starting to get a little **boring**," he said.

Mrs. Jewls made Todd write his name on the **blackboard** under the word **DISCIPLINE**.

"Hey, Louis!" shouted Mac. "**Ask** Miss Nogard **out** on a date!"

Everyone looked at Louis.

Miss Nogard looked at him too.

"Do it, Louis!" said Leslie.

"I really would like to get to know you better, Miss Nogard," he said.

162

"Ooooh," said Paul and Leslie.

"**Way to go**, Louis!" cheered D.J.

"Call me Wendy," said Wendy Nogard.

"Ooooh," said Bebe and Calvin.

"Okay, Wendy," said Louis. "And you can call me Louis."

"I already do," said Wendy. She smiled at him.

He smiled back. "So what do you say?" he asked. "Would you like to go out sometime?"

Miss Nogard hesitated.

"Say yes, Miss Nogard!" **urge**d Jenny.

Miss Nogard took a deep breath. "I like you, Louis," she said. "But I think there is something you should know about me first."

She **bent** over and **part**ed the hair on top of her head.

Everyone crowded around as they tried to get a good look.

"It's an ear!" shouted Jason.

"Yes, it is an ear," said Miss Nogard.

"Cool!" said Terrence.

"Can I touch it?" asked Dana.

Everyone took turns touching her ear.

The one on top of her head, I mean.

"So, Louis, are you sure you still want to **go out with** me?" she asked.

Louis held her hands in his. "I like you a lot," he said. "It doesn't matter how many ears you have." He **pause**d for a second. "How many ears do you have?"

"Just three," she **assured** him.

"I think your ears are beautiful," said Louis. "I think your nose and **eyebrow**s are beautiful."

Miss Nogard didn't have to read Louis's mind to know he was telling the truth. She could see it in his eyes.

His eyes were like the moon.

She kissed him. His **mustache** tickled.

Everybody oooohed.

WORK BOOK

WAYSIDE SCHOOL
GETS A LITTLE STRANGER

LOUIS SACHAR

ILLUSTRATED BY TIM HEITZ

Contents

'아동 도서계의 노벨상!' 미국 최고 권위의 아동 문학상

뉴베리 상(Newbery Award)은 미국 도서관 협회에서 해마다 미국 아동 문학 발전에 가장 크게 이바지한 작가에게 수여하는 아동 문학상입니다. 1922년에 시작된 이 상은 미국에서 가장 오랜 역사를 지닌 아동 문학상일 뿐 아니라, '아동 도서계의 노벨상'이라 불릴 만큼 최고의 권위를 자랑하고 있습니다.

뉴베리 상은 그 역사와 권위만큼이나 심사기준이 까다롭기로 유명한데, 심사단은 책의 주제의식은 물론 정보의 깊이와 스토리의 정교함, 캐릭터와 문체의 적정성 등을 꼼꼼히 평가하여 수상작을 결정합니다.

그해 최고의 작품으로 선정되면 금색 메달을 수여하기 때문에 '뉴베리 메달 (Newbery Medal)'이라고 부르며, 후보에 올랐던 주목할 만한 작품들은 '뉴베리 아너(Newbery Honor)'라고 하여 은색 마크를 수여합니다.

뉴베리 상을 받게 되면 미국의 모든 도서관에 비치되어 더 많은 독자들을 만나게 되며, 대부분 수십에서 수백만 부가 판매되는 베스트셀러가 됩니다. 뿐만 아니라 뉴베리 상을 수상한 작가는 그만큼 필력과 작품성을 인정받게 되어, 수상작이 아닌 작품들도 수상작 못지않게 커다란 주목과 사랑을 받습니다.

왜 뉴베리 수상작인가?
쉬운 어휘로 쓰인 '검증받은' 영어원서!

'뉴베리 수상작'들은 '검증받은 원서'로 국내 영어 학습자들에게 큰 사랑을 받고 있습니다. '뉴베리 수상작'이 원서 읽기에 좋은 교재인 이유는,
   1. 아동 문학인 만큼 어휘가 어렵지 않습니다.
   2. 어렵지 않은 어휘를 사용하면서도 '문학상'을 수상한 만큼 문장의 깊이가 상당합니다.
   3. 적당한 난이도의 어휘와 깊이 있는 문장으로 구성되어 있기 때문에 초등 고학년부터 성인까지, 영어 초보자부터 실력자까지 모든 영어 학습자들이 읽기에 좋습니다.

실제로 뉴베리 수상작은 강남에서는 엄마표 영어 교재로, 국제중·특목고에서는 입시 필독서로, 대학교에서는 영어 강독 교과서로, 다양하고 폭넓게 활용되고 있습니다. 이런 이유로 뉴베리 수상작은 한국어 번역서보다 오히려 원서의 판매가 훨씬 높은 기현상이 일어날 정도입니다.

'베스트 오브 베스트'만을 엄선한 뉴베리 컬렉션!

「뉴베리 컬렉션」은 뉴베리 메달 및 아너 수상작, 그리고 뉴베리 수상 작가의 유명 작품들을 엄선하여 한국 영어 학습자들을 위한 최적의 교재로 재탄생시킨 영어원서 읽기 시리즈입니다.

1. 영어 수준과 문장 난이도, 분량 등 국내 영어 학습자들에게 적합한 정도를 종합적으로 검토하여 선정하였습니다.
2. 기존 원서 독자들의 인기도까지 감안하여 최적의 작품들을 선별하였습니다.
3. 판형이 좁고 글씨가 작아 읽기 힘들었던 원서 디자인을 대폭 수정하여, 판형을 시원하게 키우고 최적화된 영문 서체를 사용하여 가독성을 극대화하였습니다.
4. 함께 제공되는 워크북은 어려운 어휘를 완벽하게 정리하고 이해력을 점검하는 퀴즈를 덧붙여 독자들이 원서를 보다 쉽고 재미있게 읽을 수 있도록 구성하였습니다.
5. 기존에 높은 가격에 판매되어 구하기 쉽지 않았던 오디오북까지 부록으로 제공하여 리스닝과 소리 내어 읽기에까지 원서를 두루 활용할 수 있도록 했습니다.

루이스 새커(Louis Sachar)는 현재 미국에서 가장 인기 있는 아동 문학 작가 중 한 사람입니다. 그는 1954년 미국 뉴욕에서 태어났으며 초등학교 보조 교사로 일한 경험을 바탕으로 쓴 『웨이사이드 스쿨(Wayside School)』 시리즈로 잘 알려져 있습니다. 그 외에도 그는 『마빈 레드포스트(Marvin Redpost)』 시리즈, 『There's a Boy in the Girls' Bathroom(여자화장실에 남자가 있다고?)』, 『The Boy Who Lost His Face(얼굴을 잃어버린 소년)』 등 20여 권의 어린이책을 썼습니다. 그가 1998년에 발표한 『Holes』는 독자들의 큰 사랑을 받으며 National Book Award 등 많은 상을 수상하였고, 마침내 1999년에는 뉴베리 메달을 수상하였습니다. 2006년에는 『Holes』의 후속편 『Small Steps』를 출간하였습니다.

웨이사이드 스쿨 시리즈는 저자 루이스 새커가 학점 이수를 위해 힐사이드 초등학교(Hillside Elementary School)에서 보조 교사로 일한 경험을 바탕으로 쓴 책입니다. 그곳의 학생들은 루이스를 운동장 선생님(Louis the Yard Teacher)라고 불렀다고 합니다. 이 시리즈의 주인공들은 힐사이드 초등학교에서 루이스가 만난 아이들의 이름에서 따왔고, 저자 자신을 반영한 인물 운동장 선생님 루이스도 등장합니다.

웨이사이드 스쿨은 원래 1층 건물에 30개의 교실을 지을 예정이었지만, 30층 건물에 1층에 1개의 교실이 있는 건물로 지어졌습니다. (학교를 지은 건설업자는 매우 미안하다고 했습니다.) 책의 주인공들은 30층에 있는 학급의 아이들 30명이고, 이들은 모두 별나고 이상합니다.

각 장마다 별나고 이상하며 때로는 초현실적인 일이 일어나는 웨이사이드 스쿨 시리즈는 미국 어린이들의 마음을 사로잡았습니다. 어린이들이 직접 선정하는 IRA-CBC Children's Choice에 선정되었고, 900만 부 이상의 판매를 올렸습니다. 또한 TV 애니메이션 시리즈로도 제작되어 큰 사랑을 받고 있습니다.

원서 본문 텍스트

내용이 담긴 원서 본문입니다.

원어민이 읽는 일반 원서와 같은 텍스트지만, 암기해야 할 중요 어휘들은 볼드체로 표시되어 있습니다. 이 어휘들은 지금 들고 계신 워크북에 챕터별로 정리되어 있습니다.

학습 심리학 연구 결과에 따르면, 한 단어씩 따로 외우는 단어 암기는 거의 효과가 없다고 합니다. 대신 단어를 제대로 외우기 위해서는 문맥(Context) 속에서 단어를 암기해야 하며, 한 단어 당 문맥 속에서 15번 이상 마주칠 때 완벽하게 암기할 수 있다고 합니다.

이 책의 본문은 중요 어휘를 볼드로 강조하여, 문맥 속의 단어들을 더 확실히 인지(Word Cognition in Context)하도록 돕고 있습니다. 또한 대부분의 중요한 단어들은 다른 챕터에서도 반복해서 등장하기 때문에 이 책을 읽는 것만으로도 자연스럽게 어휘력을 향상할 수 있습니다.

또한 본문 아래에는 내용 이해를 돕기 위해 '각주'가 첨가되어 있습니다. 각주는 굳이 암기할 필요는 없지만, 알아두면 도움이 될 만한 정보가 정리되어 있습니다. 각주를 참고하면 스토리를 더 깊이 있게 이해할 수 있어 원서를 읽는 재미가 배가됩니다.

워크북(Workbook)의 구성

Check Your Reading Speed

해당 챕터의 단어 수가 기록되어 있어, 리딩 속도를 측정할 수 있습니다. 특히 리딩 속도를 중시하는 독자들이 유용하게 사용할 수 있습니다.

Build Your Vocabulary

본문에 볼드 표시되어 있던 단어들이 정리되어 있습니다. 리딩 전, 후에 반복해서 보면 원서를 더욱 쉽게 읽을 수 있고, 어휘력도 빠르게 향상 됩니다.

단어는 〈스펠링 - 빈도 - 발음기호 - 품사 - 한글 뜻 - 영문 뜻〉 순서로 표기되어 있으며 빈도 표시(★)가 많을수록 필수 어휘입니다. 반복 등장하는 단어는 빈도 대신 '복습'으로 표기되어 있습니다. 품사는 아래와 같이 표기했습니다.

n. 명사 │ a. 형용사 │ ad. 부사 │ v. 동사

conj. 접속사 │ prep. 전치사 │ int. 감탄사 │ idiom 숙어 및 관용구

Comprehension Quiz

간단한 퀴즈를 통해 읽은 내용에 대한 이해력을 점검해 볼 수 있습니다.

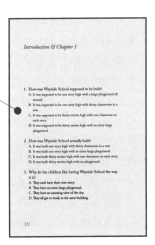

뉴베리 컬렉션, 이렇게 읽어보세요!!

아래와 같이 프리뷰(Preview) → 리딩(Reading) → 리뷰(Review) 세 단계를 거치면서 읽으면, 더욱 효과적으로 영어실력을 향상할 수 있습니다!

1. 프리뷰(Preview) : 오늘 읽을 내용을 먼저 점검한다!

- 워크북을 통해 오늘 읽을 Chapter에 나와 있는 단어들을 쭉 훑어봅니다. 어떤 단어들이 나오는지, 내가 아는 단어와 모르는 단어가 어떤 것들이 있는지 가벼운 마음으로 살펴봅니다.

- 평소처럼 하나하나 쓰면서 암기하려고 하지는 마세요! 그렇게 해서는 원서를 읽기도 전에 지쳐 쓰러져 버릴 것입니다. 익숙하지 않은 단어들을 주의 깊게 보되, 어차피 리딩을 하면서 점차 익숙해질 단어라는 것을 잊지 말고 빠르게 훑어봅니다.

- 뒤 Chapter로 갈수록 '복습'이라고 표시된 단어들이 늘어나는 것을 알 수 있습니다. '복습' 단어인데도 여전히 익숙하지 않다면 더욱 신경을 써서 봐야겠죠? 매일매일 꾸준히 읽는다면, 익숙한 단어들이 점점 많아진다는 것을 몸으로 느낄 수 있습니다.

2. 리딩(Reading) : 내용에 집중하며 빠르게 읽어나가자!

- 프리뷰를 마친 후 바로 리딩을 시작합니다. 방금 살펴봤던 어휘들을 문장 속에서 다시 만나게 되는데 이 과정에서 단어의 쓰임새와 어감을 자연스럽게 익히게 됩니다.

- 모르는 단어, 이해 가지 않는 문장이 나오더라도 멈추지 말고 전체적인 맥락을 잡아가면서 스피디하게 읽어 나가세요. 이해 가지 않는 문장들은 따로 표시를 하되, 일단 넘어가서 계속 읽는 것이 좋습니다. 뒷부분을 읽다 보면 자연히 이해가 되는 경우도 있고, 정 이해가 되지 않는 부분은 리딩을 마친 이후에 따로 리뷰하는 시간을 가지면 됩니다. 문제집을 풀듯이 모든 문장을 분석하면서 원서를 읽는 것이 아니라, 리딩할 때는 리딩에만, 리뷰할 때는 리뷰에만 집중하는 것이 필요합니다.

- 볼드 처리된 단어의 의미가 궁금하더라도, 워크북을 바로 펼치지 마세요. 정 궁금하다면 한 번씩 참고하는 것도 나쁘진 않지만, 워크북과 원서를 번갈아 보면서 읽는 것은 리딩의 흐름을 끊고 단어 하나하나에 집착하는 좋지 않은 리딩 습관을 만들 수 있습니다.

- 같은 맥락에서 번역서를 구해서 원서와 동시에 번갈아 보는 것도 좋은 방법이 아닙니다. 한글 번역을 가지고 있다고 해도 일단 영어로 읽을 때는 영어에만 집중하고 어느 정도 분량을 읽은 후에 번역서와 비교하도록 하세요. 모든

문장을 일일이 번역해서 완벽하게 이해하려는 것은 오히려 좋지 않은 리딩 습관을 심어 주어 장기적으로는 바람직하지 않은 결과를 얻을 수 있습니다. 처음부터 완벽하게 이해하려고 하는 것보다는 빠른 속도로 2~3회 반복해서 읽는 방식이 실력 향상에 더 도움이 됩니다. 만일 반복해서 읽어도 내용 이해가 전혀 되지 않아 곤란하다면 책 선정에 문제가 있다고 할 수 있습니다. 그럴 땐 좀 더 쉬운 책을 골라 실력을 다진 뒤 다시 도전하는 것이 좋습니다.

• 초보자라면 분당 150단어의 리딩 속도를 목표로 잡아서 리딩을 합니다. 분당 150단어는 원어민이 말하는 속도로, 영어 학습자들이 리스닝과 스피킹으로 넘어가기 위해 가장 기초적으로 달성해야 하는 단계입니다. 분당 50~80단어 정도의 낮은 리딩 속도를 가지고 있는 경우는 대부분 영어 실력이 부족해서라기보다 '잘못된 리딩 습관'을 가지고 있어서 그렇습니다. 이해력이 조금 떨어진다고 하더라도 분당 150단어까지는 속도에 대한 긴장감을 놓치지 말고 스피디하게 읽어 나가도록 하세요.

3. 리뷰(Review) : 이해력을 점검하고 꼼꼼하게 다시 살펴보자!

• 해당 Chapter의 Comprehension Quiz를 통해 이해력을 점검해 봅니다.

• 오늘 만난 어휘도 다시 한번 쭉 읊어보면서 복습합니다. 이 때에는 읽으면서 중요하다고 생각했던 단어를 연습장에 써 보면서 꼼꼼하게 외우는 것도 좋습니다.

• 이해가 되지 않는다고 표시해 뒀던 부분도 주의 깊게 분석해 봅니다. 다시 한번 문장을 꼼꼼히 읽고, 어떤 이유에서 이해가 되질 않았는지 생각해 봅니다. 따로 메모를 남기거나 노트를 작성하는 것도 좋은 방법입니다.

• 사실 꼼꼼히 리뷰하는 것은 매우 고된 과정입니다. 원서를 읽고 리뷰하는 시간을 가지는 것은 영어 실력 향상에 많은 도움이 되긴 하나, 이 과정을 철저히 지키려다가 원서 읽기의 재미를 반감시키는 것은 바람직하지 않습니다. 그럴 때는 차라리 리뷰를 가볍게 하는 것이 좋을 수 있습니다. '내용에 빠져서 재미있게', 문제집에서는 상상도 못할 '많은 양'을 읽으면서, 매일매일 조금씩 꾸준히 실력을 키워 가는 것이 원서를 활용하는 기본적인 방법이며, 영어 공부의 왕도입니다. 문제집 풀듯이 원서 읽기를 시도하고 접근해서는 실패할 수밖에 없습니다.

• 이런 방식으로 원서를 끝까지 다 읽었다면, 다시 반복해서 읽거나 오디오북을 활용하는 등 다양한 방식으로 확장이 가능합니다. 더 자세한 원서 활용법은 워크북 말미에 덧붙였으니 참고해 보세요.

Chapters 1 & 2

1. Why was Louis afraid to talk to the children who came to Wayside School while it was closed for repairs?
   A. He was afraid that he would cry.
   B. He was afraid that they would hate him.
   C. He was afraid that they would try to break into the school.
   D. He was afraid that they would yell at him to fix the school faster.

2. What did Louis think of whenever he felt like quitting his repair work on the school?
   A. He thought of the children actually learning things.
   B. He thought of the children stuck in horrible schools.
   C. He thought of retiring and working on a farm instead.
   D. He thought of playing on the playground for a while.

3. What was the little problem that Louis had when the school was ready to open?
   A. He couldn't open the door.
   B. He thought that the school was leaning sideways.
   C. He didn't know who to tell that the school was ready.
   D. He thought he heard a loud 'moo' from inside the building.

4. How did Todd react to the re-opening of Wayside School?
   A. He smashed into Eric.
   B. He jumped into Louis's arms.
   C. He ran and kissed the school.
   D. He slapped Myron on the back.

5. How did the children feel when they got to Mrs. Jewls's classroom?
   A. They were out of shape.
   B. They were well rested.
   C. They were sad to be back in school.
   D. They had forgotten everything they had learned at the other schools.

6. Which of the following was NOT something that the children learned at the other schools?
   A. Civilization
   B. Inspiration
   C. Exaggeration
   D. Evaporation

7. Why did Mr. Kidswatter pause a moment during his announcement?
   A. He had to sneeze.
   B. He thought every kid needed time to pay attention to him.
   C. He thought every kid was saying 'Good morning' back to him.
   D. He thought some kids only understood him when he spoke slowly.

chapter one

Check Your Reading Speed

1분에 몇 단어를 읽는지 리딩 속도를 측정해보세요.

$$\frac{717 \text{ words}}{\text{reading time (} \quad \text{) sec}} \times 60 = (\quad) \text{ WPM}$$

Build Your Vocabulary

sign***
[sain]

n. 표지판, 간판; 징후, 조짐; v. 서명하다; (손으로) 신호를 보내다
A sign is a piece of wood, metal, or plastic with words or pictures on it.

repair**
[ripέər]

n. 수리, 보수; v. 수리하다
A repair is something that you do to mend a machine, building, piece of clothing, or other thing that has been damaged or is not working properly.

yard**
[ja:rd]

n. (학교의) 운동장; 마당, 뜰; 정원
A yard is a flat area of concrete or stone that is next to a building and often has a wall around it.

recess*
[risés]

n. (학교의) 쉬는 시간; (의회·위원회 등의) 휴회 기간; v. 휴회하다, 쉬다
A recess is a break between classes at a school.

horrible**
[hɔ́:rəbl]

a. 지긋지긋한, 끔찍한; 소름끼치는; 불쾌한
If you describe something or someone as horrible, you do not like them at all.

shovel*
[ʃʌ́vəl]

v. 삽질하다, 삽으로 파다; n. 삽
If you shovel earth, coal, or snow, you lift and move it with a shovel.

mop
[map]

v. 대걸레로 닦다; (~에 묻은 액체를) 닦아 내다; n. 대걸레, 자루걸레
If you mop a surface such as a floor, you clean it with a mop.

couch*
[kauʧ]

n. 소파, 긴 의자
A couch is a long, comfortable seat for two or three people.

lounge*
[laundʒ]

n. (호텔·클럽 등의) 휴게실; (공항 등의) 대합실; v. 느긋하게 있다
In a hotel, club, or other public place, a lounge is a room where people can sit and relax.

hopeless*
[hóuplis]

a. 가망 없는, 절망적인; 끔찍한
Someone or something thing that is hopeless is certain to fail or be unsuccessful.

stick out

idiom ~을 내밀다, 튀어나오게 하다
If something is sticking out from a surface or object, it extends up or away from it.

moo
[mu:]

n. 음매(소의 울음소리); v. (소가) 음매 하고 울다
Moo is the noise that cows make.

scrub*
[skrʌb]
v. 문질러 씻다, 청소하다; n. 문질러 씻기
If you scrub something, you rub it hard in order to clean it, using a stiff brush and water.

polish*
[páliʃ]
v. (윤이 나도록) 닦다; 다듬다; n. (광택 나도록) 닦기; 윤
If you polish something, you put polish on it or rub it with a cloth to make it shine.

every inch
idiom 전부 다, 속속들이; 완전히
Every inch of something means the whole surface, distance, or area of it.

story**
[stɔ́:ri]
① n. (= storey) (건물의) 층 ② n. 이야기, 소설; 설명
A story of a building is one of its different levels, which is situated above or below other levels.

overcoat**
[óuvərkòut]
n. 외투, 오버코트
An overcoat is a thick warm coat that you wear in winter.

bet*
[bet]
v. 틀림없다, 분명하다; 돈을 걸다; n. 내기; 짐작
You use expressions such as 'I bet,' 'I'll bet,' and 'you can bet' to indicate that you are sure something is true.

you bet
idiom 물론이지, 바로 그거야
You use 'You bet' to say yes in an emphatic way or to emphasize a reply or statement.

playground*
[pléigràund]
n. (학교의) 운동장; 놀이터
A playground is a piece of land, at school or in a public area, where children can play.

pal*
[pæl]
n. 친구
Your pals are your friends.

buddy*
[bʌ́di]
n. 친구
A buddy is a close friend, usually a male friend of a man.

yell*
[jel]
v. 고함치다, 소리 지르다; n. 고함, 외침
If you yell, you shout loudly, usually because you are excited, angry, or in pain.

smash*
[smæʃ]
v. 부딪치다, 충돌하다; 박살내다; n. 박살내기
If something smashes or is smashed against something solid, it moves very fast and with great force against it.

slap*
[slæp]
v. (손바닥으로) 철썩 때리다; 털썩 놓다; n. (손바닥으로) 철썩 때리기
If you slap someone, you hit them with the palm of your hand.

move on
idiom (새로운 일·주제로) 넘어가다
To move on to something means to start doing or discussing something new.

jail*
[dʒeil]
n. 교도소, 감옥
A jail is a place where criminals are kept in order to punish them, or where people waiting to be tried are kept.

awful**
[ɔ́ːfəl]

a. 끔찍한, 지독한; (정도가) 대단한

If you say that someone or something is awful, you dislike that person or thing or you think that they are not very good.

chapter two

Check Your Reading Speed

1분에 몇 단어를 읽는지 리딩 속도를 측정해 보세요.

$$\frac{736 \text{ words}}{\text{reading time ( ) sec}} \times 60 = (\quad) \text{ WPM}$$

Build Your Vocabulary

side***
[said]

n. (사람 몸통의) 옆구리; (좌우 절반 중 한) 쪽; (아래위나 바닥이 아닌) 옆
Your sides are the parts of your body between your front and your back, from under your arms to your hips.

ache*
[eik]

v. (계속) 아프다; n. (계속적인) 아픔
If you ache or a part of your body aches, you feel a steady, fairly strong pain.

blister
[blístər]

n. 물집, 수포; v. 물집이 생기다
A blister is a painful swelling on the surface of your skin. Blisters contain a clear liquid and are usually caused by heat or by something repeatedly rubbing your skin.

ankle*
[æŋkl]

n. 발목
Your ankle is the joint where your foot joins your leg.

rub**
[rʌb]

v. (표면이) 쓸리다; (손·손수건 등을 대고) 문지르다; n. 문지르기, 비비기
If something you are wearing or holding rubs, it makes you sore because it keeps moving backward and forward against your skin.

sneaker
[sníːkər]

n. (pl.) 고무창을 댄 운동화
Sneakers are casual shoes with rubber soles.

stumble*
[stʌmbl]

v. 비틀거리다; 발이 걸리다, 발을 헛디디다
If you stumble, you put your foot down awkwardly while you are walking or running and nearly fall over.

collapse*
[kəlǽps]

v. 주저앉다; 붕괴되다, 무너지다; n. (건물의) 붕괴
If you collapse onto something, you sit or lie down suddenly because you are very tired.

gasp*
[gæsp]

v. 숨이 턱 막히다, 헉 하고 숨을 쉬다; n. (숨이 막히는 듯) 헉 하는 소리를 냄
When you gasp, you take a short quick breath through your mouth, especially when you are surprised, shocked, or in pain.

favor***
[féivər]

n. 호의, 친절; 지지, 인정; v. 선호하다
If you do someone a favor, you do something for them even though you do not have to.

point***
[pɔint]

n. (사물의 뾰족한) 끝; (말·글에서 제시하는) 의견; 요점; 점수; 점; v. (손가락 등으로) 가리키다
The point of something such as a pin, needle, or knife is the thin, sharp end of it.

erase*
[iréis]

v. (지우개 등으로) 지우다; (완전히) 없애다 (eraser n. 고무 지우개)
An eraser is an object, usually a piece of rubber or plastic, which is used for removing something that has been written using a pencil or a pen.

get to one's feet

idiom 일어서다; 일어나다
If you get to your feet, you stand up.

stagger*
[stǽgər]

v. 비틀거리며 가다; 깜짝 놀라게 하다
If you stagger, you walk very unsteadily, for example because you are ill or drunk.

huff and puff

idiom (몹시 지쳐서) 헉헉거리다
If you huff and puff, you breathe heavily while making a great physical effort.

out of shape

idiom 건강이 안 좋은; 형태가 찌그러진
If you are out of shape, you are unhealthy and unable to do a lot of physical activity without getting tired.

grunt*
[grʌnt]

v. 끙 앓는 소리를 내다; 툴툴거리다; n. (사람이) 끙 하는 소리
If you grunt, you make a low sound, especially because you are annoyed or not interested in something.

civilization*
[sivəlizéiʃən]

n. 문명 사회; 문명
A civilization is a human society with its own social organization and culture.

declare***
[diklɛ́ər]

v. 분명히 말하다; 선언하다, 공표하다
If you declare that something is true, you say that it is true in a firm, deliberate way.

impress*
[imprés]

v. 깊은 인상을 주다, 감동을 주다; (마음·기억 등에) 강하게 남다
(impressive a. 인상적인)
If an object or achievement is impressive, you admire or respect it, usually because it is special, important, or very large.

evaporate*
[ivǽpərèit]

v. (액체가) 증발하다; (차츰) 사라지다 (evaporation n. 증발)
When a liquid evaporates, or is evaporated, it changes from a liquid state to a gas, because its temperature has increased.

exaggerate*
[igzǽdʒərèit]

v. 과장하다 (exaggeration n. 과장)
If you exaggerate, you indicate that something is, for example, worse or more important than it really is.

spell***
[spel]

v. 철자를 맞게 쓰다, 맞춤법에 맞게 글을 쓰다; (어떤 단어의) 철자를 말하다
When you spell a word, you write or speak each letter in the word in the correct order.

shrug*
[ʃrʌg]

v. (두 손바닥을 위로 하고) 어깨를 으쓱하다; n. 어깨를 으쓱하기
If you shrug, you raise your shoulders to show that you are not interested in something or that you do not know or care about something.

leave off

idiom 중단하다
If you leave off something, you stop doing it.

16

principal*
[prínsəpəl]

n. 교장; 학장, 총장; a. 주요한, 주된
The principal of a school or college is the person in charge of the school or college.

pause**
[pɔːz]

v. (말·일을 하다가) 잠시 멈추다; 일시 정지시키다; n. (말·행동 등의) 멈춤
If you pause while you are doing something, you stop for a short period and then continue.

bury**
[béri]

v. (보이지 않게) 묻다; (감정·실수 등을) 감추다
If you bury your head or face in something, you press your head or face against it, often because you are unhappy.

chipper
[ʧípər]

a. 기운찬, 쾌활한; v. 기운을 내다
Chipper means cheerful and lively.

bake**
[beik]

v. (음식을) 굽다; 매우 뜨겁다
If you bake, you spend some time preparing and mixing together ingredients to make bread, cakes, pies, or other food which is cooked in the oven.

liver*
[lívər]

n. (식용하는 짐승의) 간 (요리); (인체의) 간
Liver is the liver of some animals, especially lambs, pigs, and cows, which is cooked and eaten.

assure*
[əʃúər]

v. 장담하다, 확언하다; 확인하다
If you assure someone that something is true or will happen, you tell them that it is definitely true or will definitely happen, often in order to make them less worried.

tasty
[téisti]

a. (풍미가 강하고) 맛있는
If you say that food, especially savory food, is tasty, you mean that it has a fairly strong and pleasant flavor which makes it good to eat.

reminder
[rimáindər]

n. 상기시키는 조언; 생각나게 하는 것
Something that serves as a reminder of another thing makes you think about the other thing.

rush**
[rʌʃ]

v. 급(속)히 움직이다, (너무 급히) 서두르다; n. 혼잡, 분주함
If you rush somewhere, you go there quickly.

bunch*
[bʌnʧ]

n. (양·수가) 많음; 다발, 송이
A bunch of things is a number of things, especially a large number.

baloney
[bəlóuni]

n. 헛소리; 거짓말; 소시지
If you say that an idea or statement is baloney, you disapprove of it and think it is foolish or wrong.

dumb*
[dʌm]

a. 멍청한, 바보 같은; 말을 못 하는
If you say that something is dumb, you think that it is silly and annoying.

bother*
[báðər]

v. 귀찮게 하다, 귀찮게 말을 걸다; 신경 쓰이게 하다; n. 성가심
If someone bothers you, they talk to you when you want to be left alone or interrupt you when you are busy.

Chapters 3 & 4

1. Why did Mrs. Jewls tell everyone in her class to pick a color?

   A. They were writing stories about a color.

   B. They were writing poems about a color.

   C. They were drawing pictures using one crayon.

   D. They were learning how to say a color in a different language.

2. What did Mrs. Jewls tell Joe?

   A. She told him to help Alison choose a color.

   B. She told him to choose a different color.

   C. She told him to think of word that end in 'e-d.'

   D. She told him that many things rhymed with blue.

3. Why could Allison not switch colors with Rondi?

   A. Rondi had chosen purple first.

   B. Rondi had already finished her poem.

   C. Alison was still thinking of a color to choose.

   D. Alison had already switched colors with Rondi.

4. Which of the following was NOT true about Dr. Pickle?

   A. He was a psychiatrist.

   B. He cured people with sick bodies.

   C. His name was actually Doctor Pickell.

   D. He had thick eyebrows and wore tiny glasses.

5. Why did everyone call the psychiatrist Dr. Pickle?

    A. His nose was shaped like a pickle.

    B. He once spilled pickle juice on himself.

    C. He used a gold chain with a green stone like a pickle.

    D. He loved eating pickles more than anything in the world.

6. How did Dr. Pickle help the woman who smoked too much to stop smoking?

    A. He made her think that cigarettes tasted like potatoes.

    B. He made her think that cigarettes smelled like rotten eggs.

    C. He made her think that cigarettes would slap her across the face.

    D. He made her think that cigarettes in her mouth would feel like worms.

7. Why did Dr. Pickle become a counselor at an elementary school?

    A. He wanted to be closer to his own children.

    B. He loved children more than anything in the world.

    C. He got bored and decided to try a new job.

    D. He got caught and was no longer able to practice psychiatry.

chapter three

Check Your Reading Speed

1분에 몇 단어를 읽는지 리딩 속도를 측정해 보세요.

$$\frac{668 \text{ words}}{\text{reading time ( ) sec}} \times 60 = (\quad) \text{ WPM}$$

Build Your Vocabulary

poem**
[póuəm]

n. (한 편의) 시
A poem is a piece of writing in which the words are chosen for their beauty and sound and are carefully arranged, often in short lines which rhyme.

circus*
[sə́:rkəs]

n. 서커스, 곡예
A circus is a group that consists of clowns, acrobats, and animals which travels around to different places and performs shows.

clown*
[klaun]

n. 광대; v. 어릿광대짓을 하다
A clown is a performer in a circus who wears funny clothes and bright make-up, and does silly things in order to make people laugh.

frown*
[fraun]

n. 찡그림, 찌푸림; v. 얼굴을 찌푸리다
A frown is a facial expression that usually shows dislike or displeasure.

get one's way

idiom 생각대로 하다, 제멋대로 하다
If someone gets their way, no one stops them doing what they want to do.

switch*
[switʃ]

v. 전환하다, 바꾸다; n. 스위치
If you switch to something different, for example to a different system, task, or subject of conversation, you change to it from what you were doing or saying before.

rhyme*
[raim]

v. (두 단어나 음절이) 운이 맞다; n. 운(음조가 비슷한 글자)
If one word rhymes with another or if two words rhyme, they have a very similar sound.

suggestion**
[səgdʒésʧən]

n. 제안, 의견; 암시
If you make a suggestion, you put forward an idea or plan for someone to think about.

get it

idiom 이해하다; 야단맞다, 벌 받다
To get it means to understand an argument or the person making it.

glue*
[glu:]

n. 접착제; v. (접착제로) 붙이다
Glue is a sticky substance used for joining things together, often for repairing broken things.

grunt^{복습}
[grʌnt]

v. 꿍 앓는 소리를 내다; 툴툴거리다; n. (사람이) 끙 하는 소리
If you grunt, you make a low sound, especially because you are annoyed or not interested in something.

go through

idiom ~을 살펴보다; ~을 검토하다
If you go through something, you look at, check or examine it closely and carefully, especially in order to find something.

alphabet**
[ǽlfəbèt]

n. 알파벳
An alphabet is a set of letters usually presented in a fixed order which is used for writing the words of a particular language or group of languages.

all the way

idiom 내내, 시종; 완전히
You can use all the way to emphasize that your remark applies to every part of a situation, activity, or period of time.

make a stink

idiom (~에 대해) 소동을 벌이다
If someone makes a stink about something they are angry about, they show their anger in order to make people take notice.

dew*
[dju:]

n. 이슬
Dew is small drops of water that form on the ground and other surfaces outdoors during the night.

complain**
[kəmpléin]

v. 불평하다, 항의하다
If you complain about a situation, you say that you are not satisfied with it.

wink*
[wiŋk]

v. 윙크하다; (빛이) 깜박거리다; a. 윙크
When you wink at someone, you look toward them and close one eye very briefly, usually as a signal that something is a joke or a secret.

on the blink

idiom 더 이상 제대로 작동이 안 되는
If a machine goes on the blink, it stops working properly.

stink
[stiŋk]

v. 아무 쓸모없다; (고약한) 냄새가 나다; n. 악취
If someone or something stinks, they are disgustingly inferior.

crack up

idiom 마구 웃기 시작하다
If you crack up, you start laughing a lot.

meanwhile*
[mí:nwàil]

ad. (다른 일이 일어나고 있는) 그 동안에
Meanwhile means while a particular thing is happening.

exclaim*
[ikskléim]

v. 소리치다, 외치다
If you exclaim, you cry out suddenly in surprise, strong emotion, or pain.

turn in

idiom ~을 제출하다; ~을 돌려주다
If you turn in something such as a piece of written work to someone, you give it to the person who asked you to do it.

barf
[ba:rf]

n. 구토; v. 토하다
If someone barfs, they vomit.

fire truck
[fáiər trʌk]

n. 소방차
A fire truck is a large vehicle which carries fire fighters and equipment for putting out fires.

siren
[sáiərən]

n. (신호·경보 등을 나타내는) 사이렌
A siren is a warning device which makes a long, loud noise. Most fire engines, ambulances, and police cars have sirens.

wail
[weil]

v. (길고 높은) 소리를 내다; 울부짖다, 통곡하다
If something such as a siren or an alarm wails, it makes a long, loud, high-pitched sound.

fireman
[fáiərmən]

n. (pl. firemen) 소방관
A fireman is a person, usually a man, whose job is to put out fires.

bet^{복습}
[bet]

v. 틀림없다, 분명하다; 돈을 걸다; n. 내기; 짐작
You use expressions such as 'I bet,' 'I'll bet,' and 'you can bet' to indicate that you are sure something is true.

burp**
[bə:rp]

n. 트림; v. (아기에게) 트림을 시키다; 트림하다
When someone burps, they make a noise because air from their stomach has been forced up through their throat.

22

chapter four

Check Your Reading Speed

1분에 몇 단어를 읽는지 리딩 속도를 측정해 보세요.

$$\frac{\text{803 words}}{\text{reading time (　) sec}} \times 60 = (\quad) \text{ WPM}$$

Build Your Vocabulary

accent*
[ǽksent]

n. 강세; 억양; 말씨, 악센트; v. (어떤 부분을) 강조하다
An accent is a short line or other mark which is written above certain letters in some languages and which indicates the way those letters are pronounced.

syllable*
[síləbl]

n. 음절
A syllable is a part of a word that contains a single vowel sound and that is pronounced as a unit. So, for example, 'book' has one syllable, and 'reading' has two syllables.

psychiatrist*
[sikáiətrist]

n. 정신과 의사
A psychiatrist is a doctor who treats people suffering from mental illness.

eyebrow*
[áibràu]

n. 눈썹
Your eyebrows are the lines of hair which grow above your eyes.

beard*
[biərd]

n. (턱)수염
A man's beard is the hair that grows on his chin and cheeks.

tip*
[tip]

n. (뾰족한) 끝; v. 기울이다, 젖히다
The tip of something long and narrow is the end of it.

pointed*
[pɔ́intid]

a. (끝이) 뾰족한; (말 등이) 날카로운
Something that is pointed has a point at one end.

chin**
[ʧin]

n. 턱
Your chin is the part of your face that is below your mouth and above your neck.

cure**
[kjuər]

v. (사람·동물을) 낫게 하다; (문제를) 고치다; n. 치유법; 해결책
If doctors or medical treatments cure a person, they make the person well again after an illness or injury.

smoke**
[smouk]

v. (담배를) 피우다; 연기를 내뿜다; n. 연기
When someone smokes a cigarette, cigar, or pipe, they suck the smoke from it into their mouth and blow it out again.

puff*
[pʌf]

v. (담배·파이프 등을) 뻐끔뻐끔 피우다; (연기·김을) 내뿜다; n. (담배·파이프 등을) 피우기
If someone puffs at a cigarette, cigar, or pipe, they smoke it.

cigarette*
[sìgərét]

n. 담배
Cigarettes are small tubes of paper containing tobacco which people smoke.

lung[**] [lʌŋ]

n. 폐, 허파
Your lungs are the two organs inside your chest which fill with air when you breathe in.

gunk [gʌŋk]

n. 끈적끈적한 것, 오물
You use gunk to refer to any soft sticky substance, especially if it is unpleasant.

stink[복습] [stiŋk]

v. (고약한) 냄새가 나다; 아무 쓸모없다; n. 악취
To stink means to smell extremely unpleasant.

smush [smʌʃ]

v. 부수다, 으깨다; 때리다; n. 입
To smush something means to mash or push it down.

ashtray [ǽʃtrèi]

n. 재떨이
An ashtray is a small dish in which smokers can put the ash from their cigarettes and cigars.

immediate[**] [imíːdiət]

a. 즉각적인; 당면한; 아주 가까이에 있는 (immediately ad. 즉시, 즉각)
If something happens immediately, it happens without any delay.

light[***] [lait]

v. (lit/lighted-lit/lighted) 불을 붙이다; (빛을) 비추다; n. 빛
If you light something such as a cigarette or fire, or if it lights, it starts burning.

couch[복습] [kauʧ]

n. 소파, 긴 의자
A couch is a long, comfortable seat for two or three people.

stare[*] [stɛər]

v. 빤히 쳐다보다, 응시하다; n. 빤히 쳐다보기, 응시
If you stare at someone or something, you look at them for a long time.

penetrate[*] [pénətrèit]

v. 꿰뚫어 보다; 관통하다 (penetrating a. 마음속을 꿰뚫어 보는 듯한)
If someone gives you a penetrating look, it makes you think that they know what you are thinking.

transparent[**] [trænspɛ́ərənt]

a. 투명한; 속이 뻔히 들여다보이는
If an object or substance is transparent, you can see through it.

hence[*] [hens]

ad. 이런 이유로
You use hence to indicate that the statement you are about to make is a consequence of what you have just said.

back and forth [bæk ən fɔ́ːrθ]

ad. 앞뒤로; 좌우로; 여기저기에, 왔다갔다
If someone moves back and forth, they repeatedly move in one direction and then in the opposite direction.

eyelid[*] [áilid]

n. 눈꺼풀
Your eyelids are the two pieces of skin which cover your eyes when they are closed.

blink[*] [bliŋk]

v. 눈을 깜박이다; (불빛이) 깜박거리다; n. 눈을 깜박거림
When you blink or when you blink your eyes, you shut your eyes and very quickly open them again.

count[***] [kaunt]

v. (수를) 세다; 계산에 넣다; n. (하나부터 순서대로 세는) 셈; 계산
When you count, you say all the numbers one after another up to a particular number.

24

worm[**]
[wəːrm]

n. 벌레; v. 꿈틀거리며 나아가다
A worm is a small animal with a long thin body, no bones and no legs.

wiggle
[wigl]

v. (좌우·상하로 짧게) 꿈틀꿈틀 움직이다
If you wiggle something or if it wiggles, it moves up and down or from side to side in small quick movements.

slimy
[sláimi]

a. (더럽고) 끈적끈적한, 점액질의
Slimy substances are thick, wet, and unpleasant.

yucky
[jʌ́ki]

a. 역겨운, 구역질나는
Yucky means disgusting, sickening, or nasty.

icky
[íki]

a. (특히 끈적끈적하게) 기분 나쁜
If you describe a substance as icky, you mean that it is disgustingly sticky.

rub[복습]
[rʌb]

v. (손·손수건 등을 대고) 문지르다; (표면이) 쓸리다; n. 문지르기, 비비기
If you rub a part of your body, you move your hand or fingers backward and forward over it while pressing firmly.

slap[복습]
[slæp]

v. (손바닥으로) 철썩 때리다; 털썩 놓다; n. (손바닥으로) 철썩 때리기
If you slap someone, you hit them with the palm of your hand.

shrug[복습]
[ʃrʌg]

v. (두 손바닥을 위로 하고) 어깨를 으쓱하다; n. 어깨를 으쓱하기
If you shrug, you raise your shoulders to show that you are not interested in something or that you do not know or care about something.

puzzle[*]
[pʌzl]

v. 어리둥절하게 하다; n. 퍼즐 (puzzled a. 어리둥절하는, 얼떨떨한)
Someone who is puzzled is confused because they do not understand something.

spit[*]
[spit]

v. (spit/spat-spit/spat) (음식·침 등을) 뱉다; (욕·폭언 등을) 내뱉다; n. 침
If you spit liquid or food somewhere, you force a small amount of it out of your mouth.

confuse[**]
[kənfjúːz]

v. (사람을) 혼란시키다; (주제를) 혼란스럽게 하다 (confused a. 혼란스러워 하는)
If you are confused, you do not know exactly what is happening or what to do.

come over

idiom (어떤 기분이) 갑자기 들다
If a feeling or manner comes over you, it begins to affect you.

trash[*]
[træʃ]

n. 쓰레기; v. 부수다, 엉망으로 만들다; (필요 없는 것을) 버리다
Trash consists of unwanted things or waste material such as used paper, empty containers and bottles, and waste food.

make up

idiom (~와) 화해하다; (이야기 등을) 만들어 내다
If you make up with someone, you end an argument or a disagreement with them.

figure out

idiom (생각한 끝에) ~을 이해하다; (양·비용을) 계산하다
If you figure out someone or something, you come to understand them by thinking carefully.

gradual[*]
[grǽdʒuəl]

a. 점진적인, 서서히 일어나는; (경사가) 완만한 (gradually ad. 서서히)
If something changes or is done gradually, it changes or is done in small stages over a long period of time, rather than suddenly.

altogether[*]
[ɔ:ltəgéðər]

ad. 완전히, 전적으로; 모두 합쳐
You use altogether to emphasize that something has stopped, been done, or finished completely.

quack
[kwæk]

v. (오리가) 꽥꽥거리다; n. (오리가) 꽥꽥 우는 소리
When a duck quacks, it makes the noise that ducks typically make.

freight[*]
[freit]

n. 화물; 화물 운송; v. 화물을 보내다 (freight train n. 화물 열차)
A freight train is a train on which goods are transported.

eventually^{**}
[ivénʧuəli]

ad. 결국, 마침내
Eventually means at the end of a situation or process or as the final result of it.

practice^{***}
[prǽktis]

v. (의사·변호사 등으로) 일하다; 연습하다; n. 실행; 연습
Someone who practices medicine or law works as a doctor or a lawyer.

psychiatry
[sikáiətri]

n. 정신 의학
Psychiatry is the branch of medicine concerned with the treatment of mental illness.

counselor[*]
[káunsələr]

n. (학교의) 학생 상담 교사; 의논 상대자
A counselor is a person whose job is to give advice to people who need it, especially advice on their personal problems.

elementary school[*]
[eləméntəri sku:l]

n. (미국의) 초등학교
An elementary school is a school where children are taught for the first six or sometimes eight years of their education.

Chapters 5 & 6

1. What was Paul's father's job?
   A. A painter who painted copies of the Mona Lisa
   B. A museum guard who guarded the Mona Lisa
   C. A teacher at Wayside School who taught about the Mona Lisa
   D. A museum tour guide who told people about the Mona Lisa

2. Why did Mrs. Jewls send Paul to the counselor's office?
   A. He had pulled Leslie's pigtail.
   B. He needed to deliver a note.
   C. He wanted to meet Dr. Pickle.
   D. His father hadn't let her touch the Mona Lisa.

3. How did Dr. Pickle help Paul?
   A. He made him think Leslie's pigtails were candy.
   B. He made him not be able to see pigtails anymore.
   C. He made him think Leslie's pigtails were rattlesnakes.
   D. He made Paul chew pencils instead of pulling Leslie's pigtails.

4. Why did the story have a disappointing ending?
   A. Paul pulled Leslie's other pigtail.
   B. Paul didn't feel like pulling pigtails anymore.
   C. Leslie never said 'pencil' and Paul didn't try to eat her ears.
   D. Leslie and Paul broke their pencils and were unable to work.

5. How did Mrs. Jewls make the animals in the classroom become quiet?
   A. She held up two fingers.
   B. She barked at them.
   C. She meowed at them.
   D. She turned off the lights.

6. Why was this story so confusing to read?
   A. The story was written backward.
   B. The animal's names were misunderstood.
   C. The animals were talking instead of the children.
   D. The animals all had the exact same name.

7. Why did Myron think that Mrs. Jewls eating crackers with cheese on top was gross?
   A. He thought that she was talking about real food.
   B. He thought that she was talking about Rondi's cat and his dog.
   C. He thought that she was talking about Rondi's bird and his pet chipmunk.
   D. He thought that she was talking about Rondi's pet turtle and his pet chipmunk.

chapter five

Check Your Reading Speed
1분에 몇 단어를 읽는지 리딩 속도를 측정해 보세요.

$$\frac{819 \text{ words}}{\text{reading time ( ) sec}} \times 60 = (\quad) \text{ WPM}$$

Build Your Vocabulary

security[*]
[sikjúərəti]

n. 보안, 경비; 안도감, 안심
Security refers to all the measures that are taken to protect a place, or to ensure that only people with permission enter it or leave it.

guard[**]
[ga:rd]

n. 경비 요원; 보초, 감시; v. 지키다, 보호하다 (security guard n. 경비원)
A security guard is someone whose job is to protect a building or to collect and deliver large amounts of money.

sign[복습]
[sain]

n. 표지판, 간판; 징후, 조짐; v. 서명하다; (손으로) 신호를 보내다
A sign is a piece of wood, metal, or plastic with words or pictures on it. Signs give you information about something, or give you a warning or an instruction.

tip[복습]
[tip]

n. (뾰족한) 끝; v. 기울이다, 젖히다
The tip of something long and narrow is the end of it.

tingle
[tíŋgl]

v. 따끔거리다, 얼얼하다; (어떤 감정이) 마구 일다; n. 따끔거림; 흥분
When a part of your body tingles, you have a slight stinging feeling there.

desire[***]
[dizáiər]

n. 욕구; 바람; 바라는 사람[것]; v. 바라다, 원하다
A desire is a strong wish to do or have something.

pigtail
[pígtèil]

n. (하나 또는 두 갈래로) 땋은 머리
If someone has a pigtail or pigtails, their hair is plaited or braided into one or two lengths.

waist[**]
[weist]

n. 허리
Your waist is the middle part of your body where it narrows slightly above your hips.

grab[*]
[græb]

v. (와락·단단히) 붙잡다; ~을 잡으려고 하다; n. 와락 잡아채려고 함
If you grab something, you take it or pick it up suddenly and roughly.

yank
[jæŋk]

v. 홱 잡아당기다
If you yank someone or something somewhere, you pull them there suddenly and with a lot of force.

counselor[복습]
[káunsələr]

n. (학교의) 학생 상담 교사; 의논 상대자
A counselor is a person whose job is to give advice to people who need it, especially advice on their personal problems.

scary
[skέəri]

a. 무서운, 겁나는
Something that is scary is rather frightening.

bushy
[búʃi]

a. 숱이 많은; 무성한, 우거진
Bushy hair or fur is very thick.

eyebrow^{복습}
[áibràu]

n. 눈썹
Your eyebrows are the lines of hair which grow above your eyes.

beard^{복습}
[biərd]

n. (턱)수염
A man's beard is the hair that grows on his chin and cheeks.

pointed^{복습}
[pɔ́intid]

a. (끝이) 뾰족한; (말 등이) 날카로운
Something that is pointed has a point at one end.

chin^{복습}
[ʧin]

n. 턱
Your chin is the part of your face that is below your mouth and above your neck.

knock**
[nak]

v. (문 등을) 두드리다; (때리거나 타격을 가해) ~한 상태가 되게 만들다;
n. 문 두드리는 소리
If you knock on something such as a door or window, you hit it, usually several times, to attract someone's attention.

couch^{복습}
[kauʧ]

n. 소파, 긴 의자
A couch is a long, comfortable seat for two or three people.

back and forth^{복습}
[bæk ən fɔ́:rθ]

ad. 앞뒤로; 좌우로; 여기저기에, 왔다갔다
Back and forth means moving from one place to another and back again.

stare^{복습}
[stɛər]

v. 빤히 쳐다보다, 응시하다; n. 빤히 쳐다보기, 응시
If you stare at someone or something, you look at them for a long time.

sway*
[swei]

v. (전후·좌우로 천천히) 흔들리다; (마음을) 동요시키다; n. 흔들림
When people or things sway, they lean or swing slowly from one side to the other.

eyelid^{복습}
[áilid]

n. 눈꺼풀
Your eyelids are the two pieces of skin which cover your eyes when they are closed.

hardly***
[háːrdli]

ad. 거의 ~할 수가 없다; 거의 ~아니다; 막 ~하자마자
When you say you can hardly do something, you are emphasizing that it is very difficult for you to do it.

count^{복습}
[kaunt]

v. (수를) 세다; 계산에 넣다; n. (하나부터 순서대로 세는) 셈; 계산
When you count, you say all the numbers one after another up to a particular number.

exact***
[igzǽkt]

a. 정확한, 정밀한; 꼼꼼한, 빈틈없는 (exactly ad. 정확히, 꼭)
You use not exactly to indicate that a meaning or situation is slightly different from what people think or expect.

pleasant**
[plézənt]

a. 쾌적한, 즐거운; 상냥한
Something that is pleasant is nice, enjoyable, or attractive.

turn into

idiom (~에서) ~이 되다, ~으로 변하다
To turn or be turned into something means to become that thing or change into it.

rattlesnake
[rǽtlsneik]

n. [동물] 방울뱀
A rattlesnake is a poisonous American snake which can make a rattling noise with its tail.

lick*
[lik]

v. 핥다; 핥아먹다; n. 한 번 핥기, 핥아먹기
When people or animals lick something, they move their tongue across its surface.

chewy
[ʧúːi]

a. 쫄깃쫄깃한, 꼭꼭 씹어 먹어야 하는
If food is chewy, it needs to be chewed a lot before it becomes soft enough to swallow.

blink^{복습}
[bliŋk]

v. 눈을 깜박이다; (불빛이) 깜박거리다; n. 눈을 깜박거림
When you blink or when you blink your eyes, you shut your eyes and very quickly open them again.

stick out^{복습}

idiom ~을 내밀다, 튀어나오게 하다
If something is sticking out from a surface or object, it extends up or away from it.

tongue**
[tʌŋ]

n. 혀; 언어
Your tongue is the soft movable part inside your mouth which you use for tasting, eating, and speaking.

lunge
[lʌndʒ]

v. 달려들다, 돌진하다; n. 돌진
If you lunge in a particular direction, you move in that direction suddenly and clumsily.

hiss*
[his]

v. 쉬익 하는 소리를 내다; (화난 어조로) 낮게 말하다; n. 쉿 하는 소리
To hiss means to make a sound like a long 's.'

rattle*
[rǽtl]

v. 덜거덕거리다; 당황하게 하다; n. 덜커덕거리는 소리
When something rattles or when you rattle it, it makes short sharp knocking sounds because it is being shaken or it keeps hitting against something hard.

point^{복습}
[pɔint]

n. (사물의 뾰족한) 끝; (말·글에서 제시하는) 의견; 요점; 점수; 점; v. (손가락 등으로) 가리키다
The point of something such as a pin, needle, or knife is the thin, sharp end of it.

complain^{복습}
[kəmpléin]

v. 불평하다, 항의하다
If you complain about a situation, you say that you are not satisfied with it.

sharpen*
[ʃáːrpən]

v. (날카롭게) 깎다; (느낌·감정이) 더 분명해지다
If you sharpen an object, you make its edge very thin or you make its end pointed.

roll**
[roul]

v. 구르다, 굴러가다; n. 통, 두루마리; 명부, 명단
When something rolls or when you roll it, it moves along a surface, turning over many times.

Check Your Reading Speed

1분에 몇 단어를 읽는지 리딩 속도를 측정해 보세요.

$$\frac{667 \text{ words}}{\text{reading time ( ) sec}} \times 60 = (\quad) \text{ WPM}$$

Build Your Vocabulary

pet**
[pet]
n. 애완동물; v. (동물·아이를 다정하게) 어루만지다
A pet is an animal that you keep in your home to give you company and pleasure.

noisy*
[nɔ́izi]
a. (장소가) 시끌벅적한; (사람 등이) 시끄러운
A noisy place is full of a lot of loud or unpleasant noise.

bark*
[baːrk]
v. (개가) 짖다; n. 나무껍질; (개 등이) 짖는 소리
When a dog barks, it makes a short, loud noise, once or several times.

meow
[miáu]
v. (고양이가) 야옹 하고 울다; n. 야옹(고양이 울음소리)
Meow is used to represent the noise that a cat makes.

croak
[krouk]
v. (개구리가) 개굴개굴하다; 목이 쉰 듯 말하다; n. 개굴개굴 우는 소리
When a frog or bird croaks, it makes a harsh, low sound.

squeal
[skwiːl]
v. 꽤액 하는 소리를 내다; n. 끼익 하는 소리
If someone or something squeals, they make a long, high-pitched sound.

moo^{복습}
[muː]
v. (소가) 음매 하고 울다; n. 음매(소의 울음소리)
When cattle, especially cows, moo, they make the long low sound that cattle typically make.

tweet
[twiːt]
v. 짹짹 울다, 지저귀다; n. 짹짹(작은 새가 우는 소리)
When a bird tweets, it makes a weak, chirping sound.

cage*
[keidʒ]
n. 새장, 우리; v. 우리에 가두다
A cage is a structure of wire or metal bars in which birds or animals are kept.

bite**
[bait]
v. (이빨로) 물다, 베어 물다; n. 물기; 한 입
If an animal or person bites you, they use their teeth to hurt or injure you.

assure^{복습}
[əʃúər]
v. 장담하다, 확언하다; 확인하다
If you assure someone that something is true or will happen, you tell them that it is definitely true or will definitely happen, often in order to make them less worried.

supply**
[səplái]
n. 공급품, 비품; 공급(량); v. 공급하다
You can use supplies to refer to food, equipment, and other essential things that people need, especially when these are provided in large quantities.

closet* [klázit]

n. 벽장
A closet is a piece of furniture with doors at the front and shelves inside, which is used for storing things.

chart* [ʧɑːrt]

n. 도표, 차트; v. (과정을) 기록하다
A chart is a diagram, picture, or graph which is intended to make information easier to understand.

nod** [nad]

v. (고개를) 끄덕이다; n. (고개를) 끄덕임
If you nod, you move your head downward and upward to show that you are answering 'yes' to a question, or to show agreement, understanding, or approval.

move on^{복습}

idiom (새로운 일·주제로) 넘어가다
To move on to something means to start doing or discussing something new.

stroke* [strouk]

v. 쓰다듬다, 어루만지다; 달래다; n. 치기, 때리기; (손으로) 쓰다듬기
If you stroke someone or something, you move your hand slowly and gently over them.

lap* [læp]

n. 무릎; (경주에서 트랙의) 한 바퀴
If you have something on your lap when you are sitting down, it is on top of your legs and near to your body.

turtle* [tə:rtl]

n. [동물] (바다) 거북
A turtle is a large reptile which has a thick shell covering its body and which lives in the sea most of the time.

make a face

idiom 얼굴을 찌푸리다, 침울한 표정을 짓다
If you make a face, you show a feeling such as dislike or disgust by putting an exaggerated expression on your face, for example by sticking out your tongue.

gross* [grous]

a. 역겨운; 아주 무례한
If you describe something as gross, you think it is very unpleasant.

no way

idiom 절대로 안 되다; (강한 거절의 의미로) 절대로 안 돼, 싫어
If you say there's no way that something will happen, you are emphasizing that you think it will definitely not happen.

beam* [biːm]

v. 활짝 웃다; 비추다; n. 빛줄기; 기둥
If you say that someone is beaming, you mean that they have a big smile on their face because they are happy, pleased, or proud about something.

brag [bræg]

v. (심하게) 자랑하다
If you brag, you say in a very proud way that you have something or have done something.

annoy** [ənɔ́i]

v. 짜증나게 하다; 귀찮게 하다 (annoyed a. 짜증이 난, 약이 오른)
If you are annoyed, you are fairly angry about something.

bleat [bliːt]

v. (양·염소가) 매애 하고 울다; (약하게) 푸념하다
When a sheep or goat bleats, it makes the sound that sheep and goats typically make.

34

lick^{복습}
[lik]

v. 핥다; 핥아먹다; n. 한 번 핥기, 핥아먹기
When people or animals lick something, they move their tongue across its surface.

pigtail^{복습}
[pígtèil]

n. (하나 또는 두 갈래로) 땋은 머리
If someone has a pigtail or pigtails, their hair is plaited or braided into one or two lengths.

pajamas[*]
[pədʒáːməz]

n. (바지와 상의로 된) 잠옷
A pair of pajamas consists of loose trousers and a loose jacket that people, especially men, wear in bed.

scratch[*]
[skrætʃ]

v. 할퀴다; (가려운 데를) 긁다; n. 긁힌 자국
If a sharp object scratches someone or something, it makes small shallow cuts on their skin or surface.

kid^{**}
[kid]

n. 새끼 염소; 아이; 청소년; v. 농담하다
A kid is a young goat.

Chapters 7 & 8

1. Why did Mr. Kidswatter spill his coffee on his suit?
   A. His office door was closed and he smashed into it.
   B. He tripped on a rubber band ball and dropped his cup.
   C. David drove the limousine over a bumpy road.
   D. The cup was too hot and he dropped it on himself.

2. Which of the following was NOT something that Mr. Kidswatter always did?
   A. He came to school in a white limousine.
   B. He opened the door to his office.
   C. He took a cup of coffee from Mrs. Day.
   D. He called his chauffeur James instead of David.

3. What new rule did Mr. Kidswatter make at Wayside School and why did he make it?
   A. He made a new rule that doors must always be opened, because he walked into a door.
   B. He made a new rule that doors must always be closed, because it kept things private.
   C. He made a new rule that 'door' could no longer be said, because he thought it was a dumb word.
   D. He made a new rule that doors would all be sliding doors, because it was more convenient.

4. Why did Mrs. Jewls make Todd write his name on the blackboard under the word DISCIPLINE?

A. He said 'door.'

B. He came to school late.

C. He broke the door to the classroom.

D. He lost the keys to the classroom.

5. Why did Kathy say that she got a lot of presents for Christmas?

A. She said that she was always a good girl.

B. She said that Santa brought her a lot of presents.

C. She said that her parents had a lot of money and bought her presents.

D. She said that her friends thought she was so nice and bought her presents.

6. What did Mrs. Jewls do when the children asked her if Santa Claus was real?

A. She told them that Santa Claus was real.

B. She told them that Santa Claus was a lie.

C. She told them that Santa Claus was busy.

D. She was stalling and tried not to say anything.

7. How did Mrs. Jewls feel that people could be Santa's helpers?

A. They had to meet Santa Claus in person.

B. They had to dress like Santa Claus.

C. They had to drink milk and eat cookies.

D. They had to be nice to other people.

Check Your Reading Speed

1분에 몇 단어를 읽는지 리딩 속도를 측정해 보세요.

$$\frac{572\ words}{reading\ time\ (\quad)\ sec} \times 60 = (\quad)\ WPM$$

Build Your Vocabulary

limousine
[líməziːn]

n. 리무진(대형 승용차)
A limousine is a large and very comfortable car.

chauffeur
[ʃoufə́ːr]

n. (차를 모는) 기사
The chauffeur of a rich or important person is the man or woman who is employed to look after their car and drive them around in it.

passenger**
[pǽsəndʒər]

n. 승객 (passenger door n. (자동차의) 조수석 문)
A passenger in a vehicle such as a bus, boat, or plane is a person who is travelling in it, but who is not driving it or working on it.

secretary*
[sékrətèri]

n. 비서
A secretary is a person who is employed to do office work, such as typing letters, answering phone calls, and arranging meetings.

smash^{복습}
[smæʃ]

v. 부딪치다, 충돌하나; 박살내다; n. 박살내기
If something smashes or is smashed against something solid, it moves very fast and with great force against it.

spill*
[spil]

v. 흘리다, 쏟다; n. 유출; 흘린 액체
If a liquid spills or if you spill it, it accidentally flows over the edge of a container.

suit**
[suːt]

n. 정장; (특정한 활동 때 입는) 옷; v. (~에게) 편리하다, 맞다; 어울리다
A man's suit consists of a jacket, trousers, and sometimes a waistcoat, all made from the same fabric.

demand***
[dimǽnd]

v. 강력히 묻다, 따지다; 요구하다; n. 요구 (사항)
If you demand something such as information or action, you ask for it in a very forceful way.

story^{복습}
[stɔ́ːri]

① n. (= storey) (건물의) 층 ② n. 이야기, 소설; 설명
A story of a building is one of its different levels, which is situated above or below other levels.

roll^{복습}
[roul]

n. 명부, 명단; 통, 두루마리; v. 구르다, 굴러가다 (take roll idiom 출석을 부르다)
A roll is an official list of people's names.

absent**
[ǽbsənt]

a. 결석한, 결근한; 없는; v. 결석하다, 결근하다
If someone or something is absent from a place or situation where they should be or where they usually are, they are not there.

figure out^{복습}

idiom (생각한 끝에) ~을 이해하다; (양·비용을) 계산하다
If you figure out someone or something, you come to understand them by thinking carefully.

pause^{복습}
[pɔːz]

n. (말·행동 등의) 멈춤; v. (말·일을 하다가) 잠시 멈추다; 일시 정지시키다
A pause is a short period when you stop doing something before continuing.

make sense

idiom 이해가 되다; 타당하다; 이해하기 쉽다
If something makes sense, you can understand it.

principal^{복습}
[prínsəpəl]

n. 교장; 학장, 총장; a. 주요한, 주된
The principal of a school or college is the person in charge of the school or college.

dumb^{복습}
[dʌm]

a. 멍청한, 바보 같은; 말을 못 하는
If you say that something is dumb, you think that it is silly and annoying.

make up^{복습}

idiom (이야기 등을) 만들어 내다; (~와) 화해하다
If you make up something, you invent it, often in order to trick someone.

declare^{복습}
[diklέər]

v. 선언하다, 공표하다; 분명히 말하다
If you declare something, you state officially and formally that it exists or is the case.

lock**
[lak]

v. (자물쇠로) 잠그다; n. 자물쇠 (unlock v. (열쇠로) 열다)
When you lock something such as a door, drawer, or case, you fasten it, usually with a key, so that other people cannot open it.

from now on

idiom 앞으로는 (쭉), 지금부터는
From now on means from this time onward.

coat hanger
[kóut hæŋər]

n. 옷걸이
A coat hanger is a curved piece of wood, metal, or plastic that you hang a piece of clothing on.

gasp^{복습}
[gæsp]

v. 숨이 턱 막히다, 헉 하고 숨을 쉬다; n. (숨이 막히는 듯) 헉 하는 소리를 냄
When you gasp, you take a short quick breath through your mouth, especially when you are surprised, shocked, or in pain.

blackboard*
[blǽkbɔ̀ːrd]

n. 칠판
A blackboard is a dark-colored board that you can write on with chalk.

discipline**
[dísəplin]

n. 규율, 훈육; 단련법, 수련법
Discipline is the practice of making people obey rules or standards of behavior, and punishing them when they do not.

Check Your Reading Speed

1분에 몇 단어를 읽는지 리딩 속도를 측정해 보세요.

$$\frac{926 \text{ words}}{\text{reading time ( ) sec}} \times 60 = (\quad) \text{ WPM}$$

Build Your Vocabulary

celebrate**
[séləbrèit]

v. 기념하다, 축하하다 (celebration n. 기념, 축하)
A celebration is a special enjoyable event that people organize because something pleasant has happened or because it is someone's birthday or anniversary.

artwork
[á:rtwə:rk]

n. (박물관의) 미술품
Artworks are paintings or sculptures which are of high quality.

blackboard**복습
[blǽkbɔ̀:rd]

n. 칠판
A blackboard is a dark-colored board that you can write on with chalk.

pride**
[praid]

n. 자랑스러움, 자부심; 자존심
Pride is a feeling of satisfaction which you have because you or people close to you have done something good or possess something good.

joyful*
[dʒɔifl]

a. 기쁜, 기쁨을 주는; 아주 기뻐하는
Something that is joyful causes happiness and pleasure.

sleigh
[slei]

n. 썰매
A sleigh is a vehicle which can slide over snow. Sleighs are usually pulled by horses.

homemade*
[hóummèid]

a. 집에서 만든, 손으로 만든
Something that is homemade has been made in someone's home, rather than in a shop or factory.

besides**
[bisáidz]

ad. 게다가, 뿐만 아니라; prep. ~외에
Besides is used to emphasize an additional point that you are making, especially one that you consider to be important.

bet복습
[bet]

v. 틀림없다, 분명하다; 돈을 걸다; n. 내기; 짐작
You use expressions such as 'I bet,' 'I'll bet,' and 'you can bet' to indicate that you are sure something is true.

pout
[paut]

v. (짜증이 나서 입술을) 뿌루퉁 내밀다
If someone pouts, they stick out their lips, usually in order to show that they are annoyed or to make themselves sexually attractive.

lump*
[lʌmp]

n. (보통 특정한 형태가 없는) 덩어리
A lump of something is a solid piece of it.

coal*
[koul]

n. 석탄
Coal is a hard black substance that is extracted from the ground and burned as fuel.

bite복습
[bait]

v. (bit-bitten) (이빨로) 물다, 베어 물다; n. 물기; 한 입
If you bite something, you use your teeth to cut into it, for example in order to eat it or break it.

reindeer
[réindìər]

n. [동물] 순록
A reindeer is a deer with large horns called antlers that lives in northern areas of Europe, Asia, and America.

crummy
[krʌ́mi]

a. 형편없는
Something that is crummy is unpleasant, of very poor quality, or not good enough.

fit***
[fit]

v. (모양·크기가) 맞다; (제자리에) 끼우다; a. 적합한, 알맞은
If something fits somewhere, it can be put there or is designed to be put there.

skinny
[skíni]

a. (물건의) 폭이 좁은; 깡마른, 비쩍 여윈
Something that is skinny is having little width and narrow.

chimney*
[tʃímni]

n. 굴뚝
A chimney is a pipe through which smoke goes up into the air, usually through the roof of a building.

tongue복습
[tʌŋ]

n. 혀; 언어
Your tongue is the soft movable part inside your mouth which you use for tasting, eating, and speaking.

jerk*
[dʒəːrk]

n. 얼간이; (갑자기 날카롭게) 홱 움직임; v. 홱 움직이다
If you call someone a jerk, you are insulting them because you think they are stupid or you do not like them.

sputter
[spʌ́tər]

v. (분노·충격으로) 더듬거리며 말하다; (엔진 등이) 털털거리는 소리를 내다
If you sputter, you speak quickly or in a confused way because you are upset or surprised.

yelp
[jelp]

v. 새된 소리를 지르다, 비명을 지르다
If a person or dog yelps, they give a sudden short cry, often because of fear or pain.

wise***
[waiz]

a. 지혜로운, 현명한, 슬기로운
A wise person is able to use their experience and knowledge in order to make sensible decisions and judgments.

smarts
[smaːrts]

n. 머리, 지능
Smarts is an informal way of saying know-how, intelligence, or wits.

eager***
[íːgər]

a. 열렬한, 간절히 바라는, 열심인
If you look or sound eager, you look or sound as if you expect something interesting or enjoyable to happen.

snowflake
[snóuflèik]

n. 눈송이
A snowflake is one of the soft, white bits of frozen water that fall as snow.

stall[star]
[stɔːl]

v. 시간을 끌다; (대답 등을) 피하다; n. (시장의) 가판대, 좌판
If you stall, you try to avoid doing something until later.

liar[star]
[láiər]

n. 거짓말쟁이
If you say that someone is a liar, you mean that they tell lies.

trick[star][star]
[trik]

n. 속임수; v. 속이다, 속임수를 쓰다
A trick is an action that is intended to deceive someone.

fake[star]
[feik]

v. 위조하다; ~인 척하다; a. 가짜의, 거짓된; n. 모조품
If someone fakes something, they try to make it look valuable or genuine, although in fact it is not.

take it

idiom (비난·고통 등을) 견디다, 참다; 이해하다
If you say that you can take it, you mean that you are able to bear or tolerate something difficult or unpleasant such as stress, criticism or pain.

clear one's throat

idiom 목을 가다듬다; 헛기침하다
If you clear your throat, you cough once in order to make it easier to speak or to attract people's attention.

sure enough

idiom 아니나 다를까
You say sure enough, especially when telling a story, to confirm that something was really true or was actually happening.

sideways[star]
[sáidwèiz]

ad. 옆으로; 옆에서
Sideways means in a direction to the left or right, not forward or backward.

suit[복습]
[suːt]

n. 정장; (특정한 활동 때 입는) 옷; v. (~에게) 편리하다, 맞다; 어울리다
A man's suit consists of a jacket, trousers, and sometimes a waistcoat, all made from the same fabric.

fluffy
[flʌ́fi]

a. 솜털의; 푹신해 보이는, 솜털 같은
If you describe something such as a towel or a toy animal as fluffy, you mean that it is very soft.

beard[복습]
[biərd]

n. (턱)수염
A man's beard is the hair that grows on his chin and cheeks.

weird[star]
[wiərd]

a. 기이한, 기묘한; 기괴한, 섬뜩한
If you describe something or someone as weird, you mean that they are strange.

belly[star]
[béli]

n. 배, 복부
The belly of a person or animal is their stomach or abdomen.

bowl[star][star]
[boul]

n. (우묵한) 그릇, 통; 한 그릇(의 양)
A bowl is a round container with a wide uncovered top.

doubt[star][star][star]
[daut]

n. 의심, 의혹; v. 확신하지 못하다, 의심하다
You use no doubt to emphasize that something seems certain or very likely to you.

fellow[star][star]
[félou]

n. 녀석, 친구; 동료; a. 같은 처지에 있는, 동료의
A fellow is a man or boy.

yard^{복습}
[ja:rd]

n. (학교의) 운동장; 마당, 뜰; 정원
A yard is a flat area of concrete or stone that is next to a building and often has a wall around it.

pillow*
[pílou]

n. 베개
A pillow is a rectangular cushion which you rest your head on when you are in bed.

delight*
[diláit]

v. 많은 기쁨을 주다, 아주 즐겁게 하다; n. 기쁨, 즐거움 (delighted a. 아주 기뻐하는)
If you are delighted, you are extremely pleased and excited about something.

dress up

idiom 변장을 하다; 옷을 갖춰 입다
If you dress up like someone else, you put on clothes that make you look like them, for fun.

fool*
[fu:l]

n. 바보; v. 속이다, 기만하다
If you call someone a fool, you are indicating that you think they are not at all sensible and show a lack of good judgment.

stink^{복습}
[stiŋk]

v. (고약한) 냄새가 나다; 아무 쓸모없다; n. 악취 (stinking a. 지독한, 역겨운)
You use stinking to describe something that is unpleasant or bad.

impress^{복습}
[imprés]

v. 깊은 인상을 주다, 감동을 주다; (마음·기억 등에) 강하게 남다
(impressed a. 인상 깊게 생각하는)
If something impresses you, you feel great admiration for it.

demand^{복습}
[dimǽnd]

v. 강력히 묻다, 따지다; 요구하다; n. 요구 (사항)
If you demand something such as information or action, you ask for it in a very forceful way.

exact^{복습}
[igzǽkt]

a. 정확한, 정밀한; 꼼꼼한, 빈틈없는 (exactly ad. 정확히, 꼭)
If you say 'not exactly,' to someone you are telling them politely that they are wrong in part of what they are saying.

you bet^{복습}

idiom 물론이지, 바로 그거야
You use 'You bet' to say yes in an emphatic way or to emphasize a reply or statement.

Chapters 9 & 10

1. What did Mrs. Jewls want the children to do when they returned from Christmas vacation?
   A. She wanted them to share stories about their time with their families.
   B. She wanted them to write poetry about their favorite present.
   C. She wanted them to learn how to knit and make socks.
   D. She wanted them to eat Baloneos.

2. Why was Mrs. Jewls going away?
   A. She was sick.
   B. She was having a baby.
   C. She was moving to another school.
   D. She was getting tired of Wayside School.

3. How did Joe think that Mrs. Jewls should name her baby?
   A. He thought that a girl should be named Rainbow Sunshine and a boy Bucket Head.
   B. He thought that a girl should be named Bucket Head and a boy Rainbow Sunshine.
   C. He thought that a girl should be named Jet Rocket and a boy Cootie Face.
   D. He thought that a girl should be named Cootie Face and a boy Jet Rocket.

4. Why were the students worried about Mr. Gorf?
   A. They once had a teacher named Mrs. Gorf.
   B. They once had a teacher named Mr. Gorf.
   C. They had heard scary stories about Mr. Gorf.
   D. They were afraid of having a man teacher.

5. How did Eric Ovens feel about Mr. Gorf?
   A. He had met Mr. Gorf and thought he was nice.
   B. He thought that people with the same name could be different.
   C. He thought that names determined if somebody was nice or mean.
   D. He thought that they should make a plan to get rid of Mr. Gorf.

6. Why did the students eat the lunch Miss Mush gave them?
   A. They were trying to be nice to Miss Mush.
   B. They had all forgotten to bring lunches from home.
   C. They thought that Mr. Gorf might have been under the table.
   D. They wanted to have energy for an afternoon in Mr. Gorf's class.

7. Why was Mr. Gorf in the closet?
   A. He was listening to the students.
   B. He accidentally locked himself in that morning.
   C. He was hiding from the students and taking a nap.
   D. He was looking for pencils and paper for the students.

Check Your Reading Speed

1분에 몇 단어를 읽는지 리딩 속도를 측정해 보세요.

$$\frac{869 \text{ words}}{\text{reading time (\quad) sec}} \times 60 = (\quad) \text{ WPM}$$

Build Your Vocabulary

knit*
[nit]

v. (실로 옷 등을) 뜨다; n. 뜨개질한 옷
If you knit something, especially an article of clothing, you make it from wool or a similar thread by using two knitting needles or a machine.

needle**
[ni:dl]

n. 바늘; (주사) 바늘, 침 (knitting needle n. 뜨개질바늘)
Knitting needles are thin sticks that are used for knitting. They are usually made of plastic or metal and have a point at one end.

hunk
[hʌŋk]

n. 큰 덩이
A hunk of something is a large piece of it.

yarn*
[ja:rn]

n. 실, 방적사; 긴 이야기
Yarn is thread used for knitting or making cloth.

wrap**
[ræp]

v. (무엇의 둘레를) 두르다; (포장지 등으로) 싸다, 포장하다; n. 포장지
When you wrap something such as a piece of paper or cloth round another thing, you put it around it.

stare복습
[stɛər]

v. 빤히 쳐다보다, 응시하다; n. 빤히 쳐다보기, 응시
If you stare at someone or something, you look at them for a long time.

clue*
[klu:]

n. (문제 해결의) 실마리; (범행의) 단서
A clue to a problem or mystery is something that helps you to find the answer to it.

invent**
[invént]

v. 발명하다; (사실이 아닌 것을) 지어내다
If you invent something such as a machine or process, you are the first person to think of it or make it.

clear one's throat복습

idiom 목을 가다듬다; 헛기침하다
If you clear your throat, you cough once in order to make it easier to speak or to attract people's attention.

gush*
[gʌʃ]

v. (칭찬·감정을) 마구 쏟아 내다; (액체가) 솟구치다; n. 분출
If someone gushes, they express their admiration or pleasure in an exaggerated way.

ooh and aah

idiom 놀람의 소리를 지르다
If you ooh and aah, you exclaim in wonder or admiration.

sob*
[sab]

v. 흐느끼며 말하다; (흑흑) 흐느끼다; n. 흐느낌
If you sob something, you say it while you are crying.

46

flip out

idiom (너무 화가 나거나 흥분하여) 확 돌아 버리다
If you flip out, you become very angry, excited or enthusiastic about something.

ruler*
[rúːlər]

n. (길이 측정·줄긋기에 쓰는) 자; 통치자, 지배자
A ruler is a long flat piece of wood, metal, or plastic with straight edges marked in centimeters or inches.

declare^{복습}
[diklέər]

v. 분명히 말하다; 선언하다, 공표하다
If you declare that something is true, you say that it is true in a firm, deliberate way.

scissors*
[sízərz]

n. 가위
Scissors are a small cutting tool with two sharp blades that are screwed together.

wipe*
[waip]

v. (먼지·물기 등을 없애기 위해 무엇을) 닦다; n. (행주·걸레를 써서) 닦기
If you wipe something, you rub its surface to remove dirt or liquid from it.

beam^{복습}
[biːm]

v. 활짝 웃다; 비추다; n. 빛줄기; 기둥
If you say that someone is beaming, you mean that they have a big smile on their face because they are happy, pleased, or proud about something.

flight of stairs

idiom 한 줄로 이어진 계단
A flight of stairs is a set of steps or stairs that lead from one level to another without changing direction.

considerate*
[kənsídərət]

a. 사려 깊은, (남을) 배려하는
Someone who is considerate pays attention to the needs, wishes, or feelings of other people.

stomach**
[stʌmək]

n. 위(胃), 복부, 배, 속
You can refer to the front part of your body below your waist as your stomach.

take turns

idiom ~을 교대로 하다
If two or more people take turns to do something, they do it one after the other several times, rather than doing it together.

muse
[mjuːz]

v. 생각에 잠기며 말하다; 사색하다, 골똘히 생각하다
If you muse on something, you think about it, usually saying or writing what you are thinking at the same time.

have a ring to it

idiom 좋은 느낌이 들다; 괜찮게 들리다
If a word or idea has a ring to it, it sounds interesting or attractive.

cootie
[kúːti]

n. 이
Cootie is an informal name for the body louse.

get straight

idiom 분명히 하다; 이해하다
If you get something straight, you understand it clearly and correctly.

palm*
[paːm]

n. 손바닥; 야자 나무; v. 손 안에 감추다
The palm of your hand is the inside part.

exclaim ^{복습}
[ikskléim]

v. 소리치다, 외치다
If you exclaim, you cry out suddenly in surprise, strong emotion, or pain.

dude
[dju:d]

n. 놈, 녀석
A dude is a man.

whine
[hwain]

v. 칭얼거리다, 우는 소리를 하다
If something or someone whines, they make a long, high-pitched noise, especially one which sounds sad or unpleasant.

substitute[*]
[sʌ́bstətjùːt]

n. 대신하는 사람; 대체물; v. 대신하다, 교체되다
(substitute teacher n. 대체 교사)
A substitute teacher is a teacher whose job is to take the place of other teachers at different schools when they are unable to be there.

neat^{**}
[niːt]

a. 뛰어난, 훌륭한; 정돈된, 단정한
If you say that something is neat, you mean that it is very good.

Check Your Reading Speed

1분에 몇 단어를 읽는지 리딩 속도를 측정해 보세요.

$$\frac{948 \text{ words}}{\text{reading time ( ) sec}} \times 60 = (\quad) \text{ WPM}$$

Build Your Vocabulary

mutter[*]
[mʌ́tər]

v. 중얼거리다; 투덜거리다; n. 중얼거림
If you mutter, you speak very quietly so that you cannot easily be heard, often because you are complaining about something.

recess[복습]
[risés]

v. 휴회하다, 쉬다; n. (학교의) 쉬는 시간; (의회·위원회 등의) 휴회 기간
When formal meetings or court cases recess, they stop temporarily.

nod[복습]
[nad]

v. (고개를) 끄덕이다; n. (고개를) 끄덕임
If you nod, you move your head downward and upward to show that you are answering 'yes' to a question, or to show agreement, understanding, or approval.

catch up

idiom (먼저 간 사람을) 따라가다; (정도나 수준이 앞선 것을) 따라잡다
If you catch up to someone or something, you reach them ahead of you by going faster than them.

horrible[복습]
[hɔ́:rəbl]

a. 지긋지긋한, 끔찍한; 소름끼치는; 불쾌한
If you describe something or someone as horrible, you do not like them at all.

hopeful[**]
[hóupfəl]

a. 희망에 찬, 기대하는; 희망을 주는 (hopefully ad. 희망을 갖고)
If you are hopeful, you are fairly confident that something that you want to happen will happen.

on time

idiom 시간을 어기지 않고, 정각에
If you are on time, you are there at the expected time.

dare[*]
[dɛər]

v. 감히 ~하다, ~할 엄두를 내다; 부추기다; n. 모험, 도전
If you do not dare to do something, you do not have enough courage to do it, or you do not want to do it because you fear the consequences.

take a chance

idiom (~을) 운에 맡기다; (모험치고) 해보다
When you take a chance, you try to do something although there is a large risk of danger or failure.

closet[복습]
[klázit]

n. 벽장
A closet is a piece of furniture with doors at the front and shelves inside, which is used for storing things.

attentive
[ətɛ́ntiv]

a. 주의를 기울이는; 배려하는, 신경을 쓰는 (attentively ad. 주의하여)
If you are attentive, you are paying close attention to what is being said or done.

arithmetic[*]
[əríθmətik]

n. 산수, 연산; 산술, 계산
Arithmetic is the part of mathematics that is concerned with the addition, subtraction, multiplication, and division of numbers.

social studies
[sóuʃəl stʌdiz]

n. (학교 교과로서의) 사회
In the United States, social studies is a subject that is taught in schools, and that includes history, geography, sociology, and politics.

spell[복습]
[spel]

v. 철자를 맞게 쓰다, 맞춤법에 맞게 글을 쓰다; (어떤 단어의) 철자를 말하다
(spelling n. 철자)
A spelling is the correct order of the letters in a word.

neat[복습]
[niːt]

a. 정돈된, 단정한; 뛰어난, 훌륭한 (neatly ad. 깔끔하게)
A neat place, thing, or person is tidy and smart, and has everything in the correct place.

line up

idiom 한 줄로 서다
If people line up, they form a line, standing one behind the other or beside each other.

substitute[복습]
[sʌ́bstətjùːt]

n. 대신하는 사람; 대체물; v. 대신하다, 교체되다
(substitute teacher n. 대체 교사)
A substitute teacher is a teacher whose job is to take the place of other teachers at different schools when they are unable to be there.

playground[복습]
[pléigràund]

n. (학교의) 운동장; 놀이터
A playground is a piece of land, at school or in a public area, where children can play.

tough[*]
[tʌf]

a. 힘든, 어려운; 엄한, 냉정한; 강인한, 굳센; (신체적으로) 억센
A tough task or problem is difficult to do or solve.

just in case

idiom (혹시라도) ~할 경우에 대비해서
If you do something in case or just in case a particular thing happens, you do it because that thing might happen.

bush[**]
[buʃ]

n. 관목, 덤불; 우거진 것
A bush is a large plant which is smaller than a tree and has a lot of branches.

twist[**]
[twist]

v. 돌리다; 비틀리다, 일그러지다; n. (고개·몸 등을) 돌리기
If you twist something, you turn it to make a spiral shape, for example by turning the two ends of it in opposite directions.

mustache[*]
[mʌ́stæʃ]

n. 콧수염
A man's mustache is the hair that grows on his upper lip.

lunchtime
[lʌ́nʧtàim]

n. 점심시간
Lunchtime is the period of the day when people have their lunch.

serve[***]
[səːrv]

v. (식당 등에서 음식을) 제공하다; 도움이 되다, 기여하다; n. (테니스 등에서) 서브
When you serve food and drink, you give people food and drink.

practice[복습]
[præktis]

v. 연습하다; (의사·변호사 등으로) 일하다; n. 실행; 연습
If you practice something, you keep doing it regularly in order to be able to do it better.

handwriting[*]
[hǽndràitiŋ]

n. 손으로 쓰기; (개인의) 필적
Your handwriting is your style of writing with a pen or pencil.

terrible[*]
[térəbl]

a. (나쁜 정도가) 극심한; 끔찍한, 소름끼치는; 심한
You use terrible to emphasize the great extent or degree of something.

urge[*]
[əːrdʒ]

n. (강한) 욕구, 충동; v. (~하도록) 충고하다, 설득하려 하다
If you have an urge to do or have something, you have a strong wish to do or have it.

hush[*]
[hʌʃ]

v. ~을 조용히 시키다; n. 침묵, 고요
If you hush someone or if they hush, they stop speaking or making a noise.

folk[**]
[fouk]

n. (pl.) 여러분, 얘들아; (일반적인) 사람들; a. 민속의, 전통적인
You can use folks as a term of address when you are talking to several people.

hop[*]
[hap]

v. 깡충깡충 뛰다; 급히 가다; n. 깡충 뛰기
If you hop, you move along by jumping on one foot.

leap[*]
[liːp]

n. 높이 뛰기, 도약; v. (높이·길게) 뛰다, 뛰어오르다
A leap is a forceful jump or quick movement.

land[***]
[lænd]

v. 내려앉다, 착륙하다; 도착하다; n. 육지, 땅; 지역
When someone or something lands, they come down to the ground after moving through the air or falling.

suck[**]
[sʌk]

v. (무엇을 입에 넣고 계속) 빨다; (액체·공기 등을) 빨아 먹다
If you suck something, you hold it in your mouth and pull at it with the muscles in your cheeks and tongue, for example in order to get liquid out of it.

beg[*]
[beg]

v. 간청하다, 애원하다; 구걸하다
If you beg someone to do something, you ask them very anxiously or eagerly to do it.

get real

idiom 꿈 깨!
If you say 'get real!' to someone, you are telling them that they should try to understand the true facts of a situation and not hope for what is impossible.

get rid of

idiom ~을 처리하다, 없애다
When you get rid of someone or something that is annoying you or that you do not want, you make yourself free of them or throw something away.

accidental[*]
[æksədéntl]

a. 우연한, 돌발적인 (accidentally ad. 우연히, 뜻하지 않게)
An accidental event happens by chance or as the result of an accident, and is not deliberately intended.

lock[복습]
[lak]

v. (자물쇠로) 잠그다; n. 자물쇠
When you lock something such as a door, drawer, or case, you fasten it, usually with a key, so that other people cannot open it.

swallow** [swálou]

v. (음식 등을) 삼키다; 마른침을 삼키다; n. [동물] 제비

If you swallow something, you cause it to go from your mouth down into your stomach.

and all

idiom ~까지; ~을 포함하여

You use and all when you want to emphasize that what you are talking about includes the thing mentioned, especially when this is surprising or unusual.

1. Why were the students not afraid of Mr. Gorf?

    A. He was handsome.

    B. His voice was full of comfort.

    C. His eyes were full of sincerity.

    D. His mustache was full of wisdom.

2. Why did Alison remain silent?

    A. Alison was shy of Mr. Gorf.

    B. Mr. Gorf had stolen her voice first.

    C. Alison was waiting for the right moment to speak.

    D. Alison didn't know the answer to the homework question.

3. How did Mr. Gorf's real voice sound?

    A. A Scottish gentleman

    B. A pineapple milkshake

    C. A cat walking across a piano

    D. A French donkey with a sore throat

4. How was Mr. Gorf related to Mrs. Gorf?

    A. He was her son.

    B. He was her husband.

    C. He was her brother.

    D. He was her father.

5. Why was Mr. Gorf playing Who Am I Now?

   A. He wanted to give the children a chance to get their voices back.

   B. He wanted to take the mothers of the children away from them.

   C. He wanted to make the children angry at each other.

   D. He wanted to steal the mothers of the children.

6. What happened when Mr. Gorf sneezed?

   A. He sounded like a donkey laughing.

   B. He lost his nose and fell out the window.

   C. He spoke in all of the stolen voices at once.

   D. The children got their voices back and his nose flew off his face.

7. How did Miss Mush know to smash a pepper pie in Mr. Gorf's face?

   A. She had noticed that Mr. Gorf never used pepper when he ate.

   B. She had read a book about people who had three nostrils and stole voices.

   C. She thought that either Kathy was nice or Mr. Gorf was a mean teacher who sucked children's voices up his nose.

   D. She thought that Kathy had told her to use pepper to make Mr. Gorf sneeze so that the children's voices would return back to them.

Check Your Reading Speed

1분에 몇 단어를 읽는지 리딩 속도를 측정해 보세요.

$$\frac{850 \text{ words}}{\text{reading time ( ) sec}} \times 60 = (\quad) \text{ WPM}$$

Build Your Vocabulary

closet^{복습}
[klázit]

n. 벽장
A closet is a piece of furniture with doors at the front and shelves inside, which is used for storing things.

comfort**
[kʌ́mfərt]

n. 안락, 편안; 위안; v. 위로하다
Comfort is what you feel when worries or unhappiness stop.

wisdom*
[wízdəm]

n. 지혜, 슬기, 현명함
Wisdom is the ability to use your experience and knowledge in order to make sensible decisions or judgments.

leather**
[léðər]

n. 가죽
Leather is treated animal skin which is used for making shoes, clothes, bags, and furniture.

dusty*
[dʌ́sti]

a. 먼지투성이의
If a room, house, or object is dusty, it is covered with very small pieces of dirt.

comb*
[koum]

v. 빗다; 샅샅이 찾다; n. 빗
When you comb your hair, you tidy it using a comb.

fingernail*
[fíŋgərnèil]

n. 손톱
Your fingernails are the thin hard areas at the end of each of your fingers.

briefcase
[brí:fkeis]

n. 서류 가방
A briefcase is a case used for carrying documents in.

nostril
[nástrəl]

n. 콧구멍
Your nostrils are the two openings at the end of your nose.

rusty*
[rʌ́sti]

a. 녹슨; 예전 같지 않은
A rusty metal object such as a car or a machine is covered with rust, which is a brown substance that forms on iron or steel when it comes into contact with water.

drainpipe
[dréinpàip]

n. (지붕에 연결된) 홈통; 하수관
A drainpipe is a pipe attached to the side of a building, through which rainwater flows from the roof into a drain.

bachelor
[bǽʧələr]

n. 미혼남, 독신남
A bachelor is a man who has never married.

relieve* [rilíːv]
v. 안도하게 하다; (불쾌감·고통 등을) 없애 주다 (relieved a. 안도하는)
If you are relieved, you feel happy because something unpleasant has not happened or is no longer happening.

freight^{복습} [freit]
n. 화물; 화물 운송; v. 화물을 보내다 (freight train n. 화물 열차)
A freight train is a train on which goods are transported.

ladder* [lǽdər]
n. 사다리
A ladder is a piece of equipment used for climbing up something or down from something. It consists of two long pieces of wood, metal, or rope with steps fixed between them.

flare [flɛər]
v. (코를) 벌름거리다; 확 타오르다; n. 확 타오르는 불길
If someone's nostrils flare or if they flare them, their nostrils become wider, often because the person is angry or upset.

cough** [kɔːf]
v. 기침하다; (기침을 하여 무엇을) 토하다; n. 기침
When you cough, you force air out of your throat with a sudden, harsh noise.

giggle* [gigl]
v. 피식 웃다, 킥킥거리다; n. 피식 웃음, 킥킥거림
If someone giggles, they laugh in a childlike way, because they are amused, nervous, or embarrassed.

polka-dot [póulkə-dàt]
a. 물방울무늬의
Polka-dot is one of a series of dots that make a pattern especially on fabric or clothing.

suck^{복습} [sʌk]
v. (액체·공기 등을) 빨아 먹다; (무엇을 입에 넣고 계속) 빨다
If something sucks a liquid, gas, or object in a particular direction, it draws it there with a powerful force.

snort* [snɔːrt]
v. 코웃음을 치다, 콧방귀를 뀌다; n. 코웃음, 콧방귀
When people or animals snort, they breathe air noisily out through their noses. People sometimes snort in order to express disapproval or amusement.

tip^{복습} [tip]
n. (뾰족한) 끝; v. 기울이다, 젖히다
The tip of something long and narrow is the end of it.

squawk [skwɔːk]
v. 꽥꽥거리다, 시끄럽게 떠들다; (크게) 꽥꽥 울다
If a person squawks, they complain loudly, often in a high-pitched, harsh tone.

donkey* [dáŋki]
n. [동물] 당나귀
A donkey is an animal which is like a horse but which is smaller and has longer ears.

sore** [sɔːr]
a. 아픈, 따가운; n. 상처 (sore throat n. 인후염, 후두염)
If part of your body is sore, it causes you pain and discomfort.

accent^{복습} [ǽksent]
n. 말씨, 악센트; 강세; 억양; v. (어떤 부분을) 강조하다
Someone who speaks with a particular accent pronounces the words of a language in a distinctive way that shows which country, region, or social class they come from.

freeze**
[friːz]

v. (두려움 등으로 몸이) 얼어붙다; 얼다; 얼리다; n. 동결; 한파
(frozen a. (몸이) 얼어붙은)
If someone who is moving freezes, they suddenly stop and become completely still and quiet.

scare**
[skɛər]

v. 겁주다, 놀라게 하다 (scared a. 무서워하는, 겁먹은)
If you are scared of someone or something, you are frightened of them.

knock^{복습}
[nak]

n. 문 두드리는 소리;
v. (문 등을) 두드리다; (때리거나 타격을 가해) ~한 상태가 되게 만들다
A knock is a sudden short noise made when someone or something hits a hard surface.

pleasant^{복습}
[plézənt]

a. 상냥한; 쾌적한, 즐거운
Someone who is pleasant is friendly and likeable.

field***
[fiːld]

n. (도서관·실험실 등이 아닌) 현장; 들판, 밭 (field trip n. 현장 학습)
A field trip is a trip made by students or research workers to study something at first hand.

charming*
[ʧáːrmiŋ]

a. 매력적인, 멋진
If you say that something is charming, you mean that it is very pleasant or attractive.

Check Your Reading Speed

1분에 몇 단어를 읽는지 리딩 속도를 측정해 보세요.

$$\frac{993 \text{ words}}{\text{reading time ( ) sec}} \times 60 = (\quad) \text{ WPM}$$

Build Your Vocabulary

interrupt**
[ìntərʌ́pt]

v. (말·행동을) 방해하다; 중단시키다 (interruption n. 가로막음, 방해함)
If you interrupt someone who is speaking, you say or do something that causes them to stop.

slip*
[slip]

v. 살짝 넣다[꺼내다]; 미끄러지다; 빠져 나가다; n. (작은) 실수
If you slip something somewhere, you put it there quickly in a way that does not attract attention.

feel around

idiom ~을 찾아서 더듬다
If you feel around for something, you explore it by the sense of touch, especially when seeking an item.

drawer**
[drɔːr]

n. 서랍
A drawer is part of a desk, chest, or other piece of furniture that is shaped like a box and is designed for putting things in.

donkey^{복습}
[dáŋki]

n. [동물] 당나귀
A donkey is an animal which is like a horse but which is smaller and has longer ears.

sore^{복습}
[sɔːr]

a. 아픈, 따가운; n. 상처 (sore throat n. 인후염, 후두염)
If part of your body is sore, it causes you pain and discomfort.

lap^{복습}
[læp]

n. 무릎; (경주에서 트랙의) 한 바퀴
If you have something on your lap when you are sitting down, it is on top of your legs and near to your body.

yard^{복습}
[jaːrd]

n. (학교의) 운동장; 마당, 뜰; 정원
A yard is a flat area of concrete or stone that is next to a building and often has a wall around it.

tip^{복습}
[tip]

n. (뾰족한) 끝; v. 기울이다, 젖히다
The tip of something long and narrow is the end of it.

giggle^{복습}
[gigl]

n. 피식 웃음, 킥킥거림; v. 피식 웃다, 킥킥거리다
Giggle is a foolish or nervous laugh.

briefcase^{복습}
[bríːfkeis]

n. 서류 가방
A briefcase is a case used for carrying documents in.

remove**
[rimúːv]

v. (어떤 곳에서) 치우다; (옷 등을) 벗다; 없애다
If you remove something from a place, you take it away.

portable*
[pɔ́:rtəbl]

a. 휴대가 쉬운, 휴대용의 (portable phone n. 휴대 전화)
A portable machine or device is designed to be easily carried or moved.

dial*
[dáiəl]

v. 전화를 걸다; n. (시계·계기 등의) 문자반
If you dial or if you dial a number, you turn the dial or press the buttons on a telephone in order to phone someone.

hang up

idiom 전화를 끊다
If you hang up on someone, you end a telephone conversation, often very suddenly, by putting down the part of the telephone that you speak into or switching the telephone off.

toss*
[tɔ:s]

v. (가볍게·아무렇게나) 던지다; n. (고개를) 홱 젖히기
If you toss something somewhere, you throw it there lightly, often in a rather careless way.

sail**
[seil]

v. 미끄러지듯 나아가다; 항해하다; n. 돛; 항해
If a person or thing sails somewhere, they move there smoothly and fairly quickly.

land복습
[lænd]

v. 내려앉다, 착륙하다; 도착하다; n. 육지, 땅; 지역
When someone or something lands, they come down to the ground after moving through the air or falling.

sneer
[sniər]

v. 비웃다, 조롱하다; n. 비웃음, 경멸
If you sneer at someone or something, you express your contempt for them by the expression on your face or by what you say.

clear one's throat복습

idiom 목을 가다듬다; 헛기침하다
If you clear your throat, you cough once in order to make it easier to speak or to attract people's attention.

boot*
[bu:t]

n. (pl.) 목이 긴 신발, 부츠; v. 세게 차다; (컴퓨터를) 부팅하다
Boots are shoes that cover your whole foot and the lower part of your leg.

slosh
[slaʃ]

v. (물·진창 속을) 철벅거리며 걷다; (액체가) 철벅거리다
If you slosh through mud or water, you walk through it in an energetic way, so that the mud or water makes sounds as you walk.

bake복습
[beik]

v. (음식을) 굽다; 매우 뜨겁다
If you bake, you spend some time preparing and mixing together ingredients to make bread, cakes, pies, or other food which is cooked in the oven.

sigh*
[sai]

v. 한숨을 쉬다, 한숨짓다; n. 한숨 (소리)
When you sigh, you let out a deep breath, as a way of expressing feelings such as disappointment, tiredness, or pleasure.

bachelor복습
[bǽʧələr]

n. 미혼남, 독신남
A bachelor is a man who has never married.

and all복습

idiom ~까지; ~을 포함하여
You use and all when you want to emphasize that what you are talking about includes the thing mentioned, especially when this is surprising or unusual.

60

disturb[**]
[distə́:rb]

v. 방해하다; (제자리에 있는 것을) 건드리다
If you disturb someone, you interrupt what they are doing and upset them.

I'll tell you what

idiom 이렇게 하면 어떨까, 있잖아(제안을 하려고 할 때 씀)
You can say 'I'll tell you what' to make a suggestion.

glare[*]
[glɛər]

v. 노려보다; 환하다, 눈부시다; n. 노려봄; 눈부심
If you glare at someone, you look at them with an angry expression on your face.

dare[복습]
[dɛər]

v. 부추기다; 감히 ~하다, ~할 엄두를 내다; n. 모험, 도전
If you dare someone to do something, you challenge them to prove that they are not frightened of doing it.

pepper[**]
[pépər]

n. 후추; v. 후추를 치다
Pepper is a hot-tasting spice which is used to flavor food.

smash[복습]
[smæʃ]

v. 부딪치다, 충돌하다; 박살내다; n. 박살내기
If something smashes or is smashed against something solid, it moves very fast and with great force against it.

sneeze[*]
[sni:z]

v. 재채기하다; n. 재채기
When you sneeze, you suddenly take in your breath and then blow it down your nose noisily without being able to stop yourself, for example because you have a cold.

cackle
[kækl]

v. (불쾌하게) 낄낄 웃다, 키득거리다; (닭이) 꼬꼬댁 울다; n. 낄낄거림
If someone cackles, they laugh in a loud unpleasant way, often at something bad that happens to someone else.

bark[복습]
[ba:rk]

v. (개가) 짖다; n. 나무껍질; (개 등이) 짖는 소리
When a dog barks, it makes a short, loud noise, once or several times.

gross[복습]
[grous]

a. 역겨운; 아주 무례한
If you describe something as gross, you think it is very unpleasant.

panic[*]
[pǽnik]

v. 겁에 질려 어쩔 줄 모르다, 공황 상태에 빠지다; n. 극심한 공포, 공황
If you panic or if someone panics you, you suddenly feel anxious or afraid, and act quickly and without thinking carefully.

bounce[*]
[bauns]

v. 튀다; 튀기다; n. 튐, 튀어 오름
When an object such as a ball bounces or when you bounce it, it moves upward from a surface or away from it immediately after hitting it.

belong[***]
[bilɔ́:ŋ]

v. 제자리에 있다; ~에 속하다, ~의 소유물이다; 소속감을 느끼다
If a person or thing belongs in a particular place or situation, that is where they should be.

exact[복습]
[igzǽkt]

a. 정확한, 정밀한; 꼼꼼한, 빈틈없는 (exactly ad. 정확히, 꼭)
You use exactly before an amount, number, or position to emphasize that it is no more, no less, or no different from what you are stating.

shrug^{복습}
[ʃrʌg]

v. (두 손바닥을 위로 하고) 어깨를 으쓱하다; n. 어깨를 으쓱하기
If you shrug, you raise your shoulders to show that you are not interested in something or that you do not know or care about something.

mutter^{복습}
[mʌ́tər]

v. 중얼거리다; 투덜거리다; n. 중얼거림
If you mutter, you speak very quietly so that you cannot easily be heard, often because you are complaining about something.

apron[*]
[éiprən]

n. 앞치마
An apron is a piece of clothing that you put on over the front of your normal clothes and tie round your waist, especially when you are cooking.

Chapters 13 & 14

1. Why did the new teacher say that she was not from Brazil?
   A. People thought she looked like she was from Brazil.
   B. She had once traveled to Brazil.
   C. She wanted to teach the children about world geography.
   D. She wanted to help with her name, since Brazil rhymes with Drazil.

2. How did Deedee feel about Mrs. Drazil's name?
   A. She thought that it was a silly name.
   B. She thought that she had heard it before.
   C. She thought that something about it sounded nice.
   D. She thought that it didn't really rhyme with Brazil.

3. How did Mrs. Drazil feel about the children telling her to stop talking?
   A. She thought that it was very rude and wouldn't allow it.
   B. She thought that it would help her and the rest of the class to learn.
   C. She thought that it was the only bad thing in class that would get the children sent home.
   D. She thought that the children should stay silent and listen without interrupting her.

4. What did Mrs. Drazil say would happen if the students crossed her?

A. She said that she would always immediately punish students.

B. She said that she would forgive and forget about whatever happened.

C. She said that someday she would get them and they couldn't hide.

D. She said that she would make them write their names in her blue notebook.

5. Why did Mrs. Drazil suddenly turn mean when the children were trying to get the light bulb?

A. They had tried to use her blue notebook.

B. They had almost broken the light bulb on her desk.

C. They had stolen something from Mr. Kidswatter.

D. They were damaging school property.

6. Which of the following was NOT one of the objects that Mrs. Drazil used for her experiment?

A. A light bulb

B. A sack of potatoes

C. A coffeepot

D. A pencil

7. How was the school like the Leaning Tower of Pisa during the experiment?

A. It felt like it was in Italy.

B. The school leaned naturally because it had been built that way.

C. The school leaned when objects were thrown out from the sides.

D. The school leaned a little bit with everyone on the same side of the classroom.

Check Your Reading Speed

1분에 몇 단어를 읽는지 리딩 속도를 측정해 보세요.

$$\frac{857 \text{ words}}{\text{reading time ( ) sec}} \times 60 = (\quad) \text{ WPM}$$

Build Your Vocabulary

stuff*
[stʌf]

v. (빽빽히) 채워 넣다; (재빨리) 쑤셔 넣다; n. 것(들), 물건, 물질
If you stuff a container or space with something, you fill it with something or with a quantity of things until it is full.

stare복습
[stɛər]

v. 빤히 쳐다보다, 응시하다; n. 빤히 쳐다보기, 응시
If you stare at someone or something, you look at them for a long time.

rhyme복습
[raim]

v. (두 단어나 음절이) 운이 맞다; n. 운(음조가 비슷한 글자)
If one word rhymes with another or if two words rhyme, they have a very similar sound.

bosom*
[búzəm]

n. (여자의) 가슴
A woman's breasts are sometimes referred to as her bosom or her bosoms.

brassiere
[brəzíər]

n. (= bra) 브래지어
A brassiere is the same as a bra which is is a piece of underwear that women wear to support their breasts.

laughter*
[lǽftər]

n. 웃음; 웃음소리
Laughter is the sound of people laughing, for example because they are amused or happy.

criminal**
[krímənl]

n. 범인, 범죄자; a. 범죄의
A criminal is a person who regularly commits crimes.

gasp복습
[gæsp]

v. 숨이 턱 막히다, 헉 하고 숨을 쉬다; n. (숨이 막히는 듯) 헉 하는 소리를 냄
When you gasp, you take a short quick breath through your mouth, especially when you are surprised, shocked, or in pain.

weigh**
[wei]

v. 무게가 ~이다; 무게를 달다
If someone or something weighs a particular amount, this amount is how heavy they are.

rip-off
[ríp-ɔːf]

n. 도둑질, 강탈, 사기
If you say that something that you bought was a rip-off, you mean that you were charged too much money or that it was of very poor quality.

count복습
[kaunt]

v. (수를) 세다; 계산에 넣다; n. (하나부터 순서대로 세는) 셈; 계산
(count on one's fingers idiom 손가락으로 세다)
When you count, you say all the numbers one after another up to a particular number.

jail^{복습}
[dʒeil]

n. 교도소, 감옥
A jail is a place where criminals are kept in order to punish them, or where people waiting to be tried are kept.

get carried away

idiom ~에 열중하다; 흥분하다
If you get carried away, you are so excited and enthusiastic about something that you lose control of your feelings and may behave in a silly way or without thinking.

bore*
[bɔ:r]

v. 지루하게 하다 (boring a. 재미없는, 지루한)
Someone or something boring is so dull and uninteresting that they make people tired and impatient.

for real

idiom 정말로, 진심의
If you do something for real, you do something which is genuine or serious, rather than imagined, practised, or talked about.

strict**
[strikt]

a. 엄격한; (규칙 등이) 엄한; 엄밀한
If a parent or other person in authority is strict, they regard many actions as unacceptable and do not allow them.

fingernail^{복습}
[fíŋgərnèil]

n. 손톱
Your fingernails are the thin hard areas at the end of each of your fingers.

tuck*
[tʌk]

v. (끝부분을 단정하게) 밀어넣다; (따뜻하게) 단단히 덮어 주다; n. 주름
If you tuck something somewhere, you put it there so that it is safe, comfortable, or neat.

besides^{복습}
[bisáidz]

ad. 게다가, 뿐만 아니라; prep. ~외에
Besides is used to emphasize an additional point that you are making, especially one that you consider to be important.

sour**
[sauər]

a. 심술궂은; 시큰둥한; (맛이) 신, 시큼한; v. 안 좋아지다
Someone who is sour is bad-tempered and unfriendly.

mutual*
[mjú:ʧuəl]

a. 상호간의, 서로의; 공동의
You use mutual to describe a situation, feeling, or action that is experienced, felt, or done by both of two people mentioned.

cooperate**
[kouápərèit]

v. 협력하다, 협동하다 (cooperation n. 협력, 합동)
Cooperation means the action or process of working together to the same end.

enjoyable*
[indʒɔ́iəbl]

a. 즐거운
Something that is enjoyable gives you pleasure.

cross***
[krɔ:s]

v. 반대하다, 거스르다; 가로지르다; n. 십자 기호
If you cross someone who is likely to get angry, you oppose them or refuse to do what they want.

$$\frac{895 \text{ words}}{\text{reading time ( ) sec}} \times 60 = (\quad) \text{ WPM}$$

Build Your Vocabulary

telescope*
[téləskòup]

n. 망원경
A telescope is a long instrument shaped like a tube. It has lenses inside it that make distant things seem larger and nearer when you look through it.

figure out^{복습}

idiom (생각한 끝에) ~을 이해하다; (양·비용을) 계산하다
If you figure out someone or something, you come to understand them by thinking carefully.

gravity**
[grǽvəti]

n. (지구) 중력
Gravity is the force which causes things to drop to the ground.

conduct**
[kándʌkt]

v. (특정한 활동을) 하다; (열이나 전기를) 전도하다; n. 행동
When you conduct an activity or task, you organize it and carry it out.

experiment***
[ikspérəmənt]

n. (과학적인) 실험; v. (과학적인) 실험을 하다
An experiment is a scientific test which is done in order to discover what happens to something in particular conditions.

lean**
[liːn]

v. 기울다, (몸을) 숙이다; ~에 기대다; a. 군살이 없는, 호리호리한
When you lean in a particular direction, you bend your body in that direction.

bore^{복습}
[bɔːr]

v. 지루하게 하다 (boring a. 재미없는, 지루한)
Someone or something boring is so dull and uninteresting that they make people tired and impatient.

oh my goodness

idiom (놀람을 나타내어) 오! 맙소사!
People sometimes say 'oh my goodness' to express surprise.

nod^{복습}
[nad]

v. (고개를) 끄덕이다; n. (고개를) 끄덕임
If you nod, you move your head downward and upward to show that you are answering 'yes' to a question, or to show agreement, understanding, or approval.

exclaim^{복습}
[ikskléim]

v. 소리치다, 외치다
If you exclaim, you cry out suddenly in surprise, strong emotion, or pain.

rub^{복습}
[rʌb]

v. (손·손수건 등을 대고) 문지르다; (표면이) 쓸리다; n. 문지르기, 비비기
If you rub two things together or if they rub together, they move backward and forward, pressing against each other.

coffeepot*
[kɔ́:fipàt]

n. 커피 주전자
A coffeepot is a tall narrow pot with a spout and a lid, in which coffee is made or served.

sharpen^{복습}
[ʃá:rpən]

v. (날카롭게) 깎다; (느낌·감정이) 더 분명해지다 (sharpener n. ~을 깎는 기구)
A sharpener is a tool or machine used for sharpening pencils or knives.

light bulb
[láit bʌlb]

n. 백열 전구
A light bulb or bulb is the round glass part of an electric light or lamp which light shines from.

sack*
[sæk]

n. (종이) 봉지, 부대
A sack is a large bag made of rough woven material. Sacks are used to carry or store things such as vegetables or coal.

bet^{복습}
[bet]

v. 틀림없다, 분명하다; 돈을 걸다; n. 내기; 짐작
You use expressions such as 'I bet,' 'I'll bet,' and 'you can bet' to indicate that you are sure something is true.

screwdriver
[skrú:dràivər]

n. 나사돌리개, 드라이버
A screwdriver is a tool that is used for turning screws. It consists of a metal rod with a flat or cross-shaped end that fits into the top of the screw.

fluorescent
[fluərésnt]

a. 형광성의; 화사한, 선명한 (fluorescent light n. 형광등)
A fluorescent light shines with a very hard, bright light and is usually in the form of a long strip.

ceiling**
[sí:liŋ]

n. 천장
A ceiling is the horizontal surface that forms the top part or roof inside a room.

dump*
[dʌmp]

v. (아무렇게나) 내려놓다; 버리다; n. (쓰레기) 폐기장
If you dump something somewhere, you put it or unload it there quickly and carelessly.

wastepaper
[wéistpeipər]

n. 휴지 (wastepaper basket n. 휴지통)
Wastepaper is paper discarded after use.

trash^{복습}
[træʃ]

n. 쓰레기; v. 부수다, 엉망으로 만들다; (필요 없는 것을) 버리다
(trash can n. 쓰레기통)
A trash can is a large round container which people put their rubbish in and which is usually kept outside their house.

upside down
[ʌ́psàid dáun]

ad. (아래위가) 거꾸로
If something has been moved upside down, it has been turned round so that the part that is usually lowest is above the part that is usually highest.

dictionary**
[díkʃənèri]

n. 사전
A dictionary is a book in which the words and phrases of a language are listed alphabetically, together with their meanings or their translations in another language.

donate*
[dóuneit]

v. 기부하다, 기증하다; 헌혈하다
If you donate something to a charity or other organization, you give it to them.

grab^{복습}
[græb]

v. (와락·단단히) 붙잡다; ~을 잡으려고 하다; n. 와락 잡아채려고 함
If you grab something, you take it or pick it up suddenly and roughly.

yell^{복습}
[jel]

v. 고함치다, 소리 지르다; n. 고함, 외침
If you yell, you shout loudly, usually because you are excited, angry, or in pain.

tremble[*]
[trembl]

v. 떨다, 떨리다; (가슴이) 떨리다; n. 떨림, 전율
If you tremble, you shake slightly because you are frightened or cold.

lunch box
[lʌ́nʧ bɑ̀ks]

n. 도시락(통)
A lunch box is a small container with a lid. You put food such as sandwiches in it to eat for lunch at work or at school.

tiptoe
[típtòu]

n. 발끝; v. 발끝으로 살금살금 걷다
(stand on one's tiptoes idiom 발끝으로 서다)
Tiptoes are the ends of toes.

pile^{**}
[pail]

n. 쌓아 놓은 것, 더미; v. (물건을 차곡차곡) 쌓다
A pile of things is a quantity of things that have been put neatly somewhere so that each thing is on top of the one below.

collapse^{복습}
[kəlǽps]

v. 붕괴되다, 무너지다; 주저앉다; n. (건물의) 붕괴
If a building or other structure collapses, it falls down very suddenly.

triumphant
[traiʌ́mfənt]

a. 의기양양한; 크게 성공한 (triumphantly ad. 의기양양하여)
Someone who is triumphant has gained a victory or succeeded in something and feels very happy about it.

screw^{**}
[skru:]

v. 나사로 고정시키다; 돌려서 조이다; n. 나사(못)
(unscrew v. (나사를 풀어서) 떼어 내다)
If you unscrew something such as a sign or mirror which is fastened to something by screws, you remove it by taking out the screws.

blackboard^{복습}
[blǽkbɔ̀:rd]

n. 칠판
A blackboard is a dark-colored board that you can write on with chalk.

judge^{***}
[dʒʌdʒ]

n. 심판; 판사; v. 판단하다; (크기·양 등을) 짐작하다
A judge is a person who decides who will be the winner of a competition.

pavement[*]
[péivmənt]

n. 포장도로; 인도, 보도
A pavement is a path with a hard surface, usually by the side of a road.

splatter
[splǽtər]

v. (물·흙탕물 등이) 튀다, 튀기다; 후두둑 떨어지다
If a thick wet substance splatters on something or is splattered on it, it drops or is thrown over it.

explode[*]
[iksplóud]

v. 터지다, 폭발하다; 갑자기 ~하다 (explosion n. 폭발; 폭파)
An explosion is a sudden, violent burst of energy, for example one caused by a bomb.

70

rate[**]
[reit]

n. 속도; 비율; v. 평가하다, 여기다; 등급을 매기다
The rate at which something happens is the speed with which it happens.

resist[**]
[rizíst]

v. 저항하다; 참다, 견디다 (resistance n. (이동·진로를 방해하는) 저항)
Wind or air resistance is a force which slows down a moving object or vehicle.

otherwise[**]
[ʌ́ðərwàiz]

ad. 그렇지 않으면; 그 외에는; ~와는 다르게
You use otherwise after stating a situation or fact, in order to say what the result or consequence would be if this situation or fact was not the case.

raindrop
[réindràp]

n. 빗방울
A raindrop is a single drop of rain.

crumple
[krʌmpl]

v. 구기다; 구겨지다; (얼굴이) 일그러지다
If you crumple something such as paper or cloth, or if it crumples, it is squashed and becomes full of untidy creases and folds.

lick[복습]
[lik]

v. 핥다; 핥아먹다; n. 한 번 핥기, 핥아먹기
When people or animals lick something, they move their tongue across its surface.

Chapters 15 & 16

1. Which of the following was NOT a reason that the children gave for Louis not to worry about Mrs. Drazil?
   A. She was nice and not mean.
   B. Her hair was white and not brown.
   C. Louis was a teacher now too.
   D. Their classroom had no trash can.

2. What did Mrs. Drazil pull out of her blue notebook?
   A. A homework assignment from Louis
   B. A mean note that Louis had written
   C. A lesson plan for her students
   D. A list of classroom rules

3. How did Mrs. Drazil feel about Louis and his mustache?
   A. She felt that he was too old to have a mustache and told him to shave it off.
   B. She felt that it looked like a hairy caterpillar and told him to shave it off.
   C. She felt that it made him look more mature and handsome.
   D. She felt that it was too short and asked him to grow it longer.

4. Why were the girls unable to recognize Louis at first?

   A. He was wearing new glasses.

   B. He had worn a suit to school.

   C. He had shaved off his mustache.

   D. He had shaved the hair off his head.

5. Why did Louis want the children to call him Mr. Louis?

   A. He expected to get married soon.

   B. He expected to be treated with respect.

   C. He expected to impress Mr. Kidswatter.

   D. He expected to be seen as older without his mustache.

6. Why did Louis refuse to pass out balls at recess?

   A. He needed to clean them and fill them with air first.

   B. He needed to make sure he handed them out to children fairly.

   C. He needed to make sure the children knew how to use them.

   D. He needed to count them and organize them first.

7. Why did Louis not let any of the children outside at recess?

   A. He was mopping the stairs.

   B. He was painting the blacktop.

   C. He was mowing the grass.

   D. He was painting the doors.

Check Your Reading Speed

1분에 몇 단어를 읽는지 리딩 속도를 측정해 보세요.

$$\frac{896 \text{ words}}{\text{reading time ( ) sec}} \times 60 = (\quad) \text{ WPM}$$

Build Your Vocabulary

recess ^{복습}
[risés]

n. (학교의) 쉬는 시간; (의회·위원회 등의) 휴회 기간; v. 휴회하다, 쉬다
A recess is a break between classes at a school.

explode ^{복습}
[iksplóud]

v. 갑자기 ~하다; 터지다, 폭발하다 (explosion n. 폭발; 폭파)
If something explodes, it increases suddenly and rapidly in number or intensity.

pile ^{복습}
[pail]

n. 쌓아 놓은 것, 더미; v. (물건을 차곡차곡) 쌓다
A pile of things is a quantity of things that have been put neatly somewhere so that each thing is on top of the one below.

toss ^{복습}
[tɔ:s]

v. (가볍게·아무렇게나) 던지다; n. (고개를) 홱 젖히기
If you toss something somewhere, you throw it there lightly, often in a rather careless way.

charge**
[ʧa:rdʒ]

v. 급히 가다, 달려가다; (요금·값을) 청구하다; n. 요금
If you charge toward someone or something, you move quickly and aggressively toward them.

playground ^{복습}
[pléigràund]

n. (학교의) 운동장; 놀이터
A playground is a piece of land, at school or in a public area, where children can play.

knock ^{복습}
[nak]

v. (때리거나 타격을 가해) ~한 상태가 되게 만들다; (문 등을) 두드리다;
n. 문 두드리는 소리
To knock someone into a particular position or condition means to hit them very hard so that they fall over or become unconscious.

bonk
[ba:ŋk]

v. (~의) 머리를 툭 때리다; n. (~에) 머리를 부딪치기
If you bonk something, you hit it hard on your head.

conk
[kaŋk]

v. 머리를 세게 때리다
If you conk someone, you strike them a blow, especially on the head or nose.

wastepaper ^{복습}
[wéistpeipər]

n. 휴지 (wastepaper basket n. 휴지통)
Wastepaper is paper discarded after use.

call on

idiom (이름을 불러서) 학생에게 시키다; (사람을) 방문하다
If a teacher calls on students in a class, he or she asks them to answer a question or give their opinion.

shudder*
[ʃʌdər]

v. (공포·추위 등으로) 몸을 떨다, 몸서리치다; n. 몸이 떨림, 전율
If you shudder, you shake with fear, horror, or disgust, or because you are cold.

74

substitute^{복습}
[sʌ́bstətjùːt]

n. 대신하는 사람; 대체물; v. 대신하다, 교체되다
(substitute teacher n. 대체 교사)
A substitute teacher is a teacher whose job is to take the place of other teachers at different schools when they are unable to be there.

no way^{복습}

idiom (강한 거절의 의미로) 절대로 안 돼, 싫어; 절대로 안 되다
You can say 'no way' as an emphatic way of saying 'no.'

silly**
[síli]

a. 어리석은, 바보 같은; n. 바보
If you say that someone or something is silly, you mean that they are foolish, childish, or ridiculous.

bulletin board*
[búlitən bɔːrd]

n. 게시판
A bulletin board is a board which is usually attached to a wall in order to display notices giving information about something.

pin**
[pin]

v. (핀 등으로) 고정시키다; 꼼짝 못하게 하다; n. 핀
If you pin something on or to something, you attach it with a pin, a drawing pin, or a safety pin.

arithmetic^{복습}
[əríθmətik]

n. 산수, 연산; 산술, 계산
Arithmetic is the part of mathematics that is concerned with the addition, subtraction, multiplication, and division of numbers.

pale**
[peil]

v. 창백해지다; a. 창백한, 핼쑥한; (색깔이) 옅은
If someone pales, their face becomes a lighter color than usual, usually because they are ill, frightened, or shocked.

freeze^{복습}
[friːz]

v. (froze-frozen) (두려움 등으로 몸이) 얼어붙다; 얼다; 얼리다; n. 동결; 한파
If someone who is moving freezes, they suddenly stop and become completely still and quiet.

flip through

idiom (책장을) 휙휙 넘기다
If you flip through something such as the pages of a book or a pile of papers, you turn over it quickly, or look through it without reading everything.

remove^{복습}
[rimúːv]

v. (어떤 곳에서) 치우다; (옷 등을) 벗다; 없애다
If you remove something from a place, you take it away.

point^{복습}
[pɔint]

n. (사물의 뾰족한) 끝; (말·글에서 제시하는) 의견; 요점; 점수; 점;
v. (손가락 등으로) 가리키다
The point of something such as a pin, needle, or knife is the thin, sharp end of it.

sharpen^{복습}
[ʃáːrpən]

v. (날카롭게) 깎다; (느낌·감정이) 더 분명해지다
If you sharpen an object, you make its edge very thin or you make its end pointed.

trick^{복습}
[trik]

n. 속임수; v. 속이다, 속임수를 쓰다
A trick is an action that is intended to deceive someone.

struggle**
[strʌgl]

v. 투쟁하다, 몸부림치다; 힘겹게 나아가다; n. 투쟁, 분투; 몸부림
If you struggle to do something, you try hard to do it, even though other people or things may be making it difficult for you to succeed.

neat^{복습}
[niːt]

a. 정돈된, 단정한; 뛰어난, 훌륭한 (neatness n. 단정함, 깔끔함)
A neat place, thing, or person is tidy and smart, and has everything in the correct place.

frown^{복습}
[fraun]

v. 얼굴을 찌푸리다; n. 찡그림, 찌푸림
When someone frowns, their eyebrows become drawn together, because they are annoyed or puzzled.

filthy
[filθi]

a. 아주 더러운; 추잡한; 심술이 난
Something that is filthy is very dirty indeed.

dirt**
[dəːrt]

n. 흙; 먼지, 때
You can refer to the earth on the ground as dirt, especially when it is dusty.

stuff^{복습}
[stʌf]

n. 것(들), 물건, 물질; v. (빽빽히) 채워 넣다; (재빨리) 쑤셔 넣다
You can use stuff to refer to things such as a substance, a collection of things, events, or ideas, or the contents of something in a general way without mentioning the thing itself by name.

be at it

idiom (일 등에) 착수해 있다
If you are at something, you are busy doing it.

shave*
[ʃeiv]

v. 면도하다; n. 면도 (shave off idiom (수염을) 밀어 버리다)
If someone shaves off their hairs, they remove them from their face, head, or body.

mustache^{복습}
[mʌ́stæʃ]

n. 콧수염
A man's mustache is the hair that grows on his upper lip.

hairy*
[héəri]

a. 털이 많은, 털투성이의
Someone or something that is hairy is covered with hairs.

caterpillar*
[kǽtərpilər]

n. 애벌레
A caterpillar is a small, worm-like animal that feeds on plants and eventually develops into a butterfly or moth.

crawl**
[krɔːl]

v. 기어가다; 기다, 몹시 느리게 가다; n. 기어가기, 서행
When an insect crawls somewhere, it moves there quite slowly.

rip*
[rip]

v. 떼어 내다; (갑자기·거칠게) 찢다; n. (길게) 찢어진 곳
If you rip something off, you remove it quickly and forcefully.

terrible^{복습}
[térəbl]

a. 끔찍한, 소름끼치는; 심한; (나쁜 정도가) 극심한
A terrible experience or situation is very serious or very unpleasant.

76

Check Your Reading Speed

1분에 몇 단어를 읽는지 리딩 속도를 측정해 보세요.

$$\frac{893 \text{ words}}{\text{reading time ( ) sec}} \times 60 = (\quad) \text{ WPM}$$

Build Your Vocabulary

twirl
[twəːrl]

v. 빙빙 돌리다, 빠르게 돌다; n. 회전
If you twirl something or if it twirls, it turns around and around with a smooth, fairly fast movement.

pajamas^{복습}
[pədʒáːməz]

n. (바지와 상의로 된) 잠옷
A pair of pajamas consists of loose trousers and a loose jacket that people, especially men, wear in bed.

grocery store
[gróusəri stɔːr]

n. 식료품점
A grocery store is a store that sells food and other things used in the home.

smash^{복습}
[smæʃ]

v. 박살내다; 부딪치다, 충돌하다; n. 박살내기
If you smash something or if it smashes, it breaks into many pieces, for example when it is hit or dropped.

bunch^{복습}
[bʌnʧ]

n. (양·수가) 많음; 다발, 송이
A bunch of things is a number of things, especially a large number.

dozen**
[dʌzn]

n. 12개짜리 한 묶음, 다스; 다수, 여러 개
If you have a dozen things, you have twelve of them.

dump^{복습}
[dʌmp]

v. 버리다; (아무렇게나) 내려놓다; n. (쓰레기) 폐기장
If you dump something somewhere, you put it or unload it there quickly and carelessly.

jar**
[dʒaːr]

n. 병; v. 부딪치다, 충격을 주다; 불쾌감을 주다
A jar is a glass container with a lid that is used for storing food.

apricot
[æprəkat]

n. 살구; 살구색
An apricot is a small, soft, round fruit with yellowish-orange flesh and a stone inside.

glop
[glap]

n. (기분 나쁘게) 질척거리는 것
Glop is any gummy shapeless matter. It is usually unpleasant.

barber*
[báːrbər]

n. 이발사 (barber shop n. 이발소)
A barber is a man whose job is cutting men's hair.

icky^{복습}
[íki]

a. (특히 끈적끈적하게) 기분 나쁜
If you describe a substance as icky, you mean that it is disgustingly sticky.

sticky*
[stíki]

a. 끈적거리는, 끈적끈적한, 달라붙는
A sticky substance is soft, or thick and liquid, and can stick to other things.

tear**
[tɛər]

① v. (tore-torn) 구멍을 뚫다; 찢다, 뜯다; n. 찢어진 곳, 구멍 ② n. 눈물
If you tear paper, cloth, or another material, or if it tears, you pull it into two pieces or you pull it so that a hole appears in it.

trip***
[trip]

v. 발을 헛디디다; n. 여행
If you trip when you are walking, you knock your foot against something and fall or nearly fall.

scare^{복습}
[skɛər]

v. 겁주다, 놀라게 하다 (scared a. 무서워하는, 겁먹은)
If you are scared of someone or something, you are frightened of them.

yard^{복습}
[jaːrd]

n. (학교의) 운동장; 마당, 뜰; 정원
A yard is a flat area of concrete or stone that is next to a building and often has a wall around it.

comb^{복습}
[koum]

v. 빗다; 샅샅이 찾다; n. 빗
When you comb your hair, you tidy it using a comb.

tuck^{복습}
[tʌk]

v. (끝부분을 단정하게) 밀어넣다; (따뜻하게) 단단히 덮어 주다; n. 주름
If you tuck something somewhere, you put it there so that it is safe, comfortable, or neat.

shave^{복습}
[ʃeiv]

v. 면도하다; n. 면도 (shave off idiom (수염을) 밀어 버리다)
If someone shaves off their hair, they remove it from their face, head, or body.

blindfold
[bláindfòuld]

v. (눈가리개로) 눈을 가리다; n. 눈가리개 (blindfolded a. 눈을 가린 채)
If someone does something blindfold, they do it while wearing a blindfold.

professional**
[prəféʃənl]

a. 직업의, 전문적인; 전문가의; 능숙한; n. 전문가
Professional people have jobs that require advanced education or training.

supervisor
[súːpərvàizər]

n. 감독관, 관리자
A supervisor is a person who supervises activities or people, especially workers or students.

correct***
[kərékt]

v. 바로잡다, 정정하다; a. 맞는, 정확한; 적절한, 옳은
If you correct someone, you say something which you think is more accurate or appropriate than what they have just said.

pat*
[pæt]

v. 쓰다듬다, 토닥거리다; n. 쓰다듬기, 토닥거리기
If you pat something or someone, you tap them lightly, usually with your hand held flat.

goofy
[gúːfi]

a. 바보 같은, 얼빠진
If you describe someone or something as goofy, you think they are rather silly or ridiculous.

weird^{복습}
[wiərd]

a. 기이한, 기묘한; 기괴한, 섬뜩한
If you describe something or someone as weird, you mean that they are strange.

blacktop
[blǽktap]

n. 아스팔트 도로; (포장에 쓰이는) 아스팔트; v. 아스팔트로 포장하다
Blacktop is a hard black substance which is used as a surface for roads.

complain^{복습}
[kəmpléin]

v. 불평하다, 항의하다
If you complain about a situation, you say that you are not satisfied with it.

all the way^{복습}

idiom 내내, 시종; 완전히
You use all the way to emphasize how long a distance is.

troublemaker
[trʌ́blmèikər]

n. 말썽꾸러기
If you refer to someone as a troublemaker, you mean that they cause unpleasantness, quarrels, or fights.

filthy^{복습}
[fílθi]

a. 아주 더러운; 추잡한; 심술이 난
Something that is filthy is very dirty indeed.

pump[*]
[pʌmp]

v. 펌프로 공기를 넣다; (거세게) 솟구치다; n. 펌프
To pump a liquid or gas in a particular direction means to force it to flow in that direction using a pump.

precise[*]
[prisáis]

a. 정확한, 정밀한; 엄밀한, 꼼꼼한
Something that is precise is exact and accurate in all its details.

specify[*]
[spésəfài]

v. (구체적으로) 명시하다 (specified a. 명시된)
If you specify something, you give information about what is required or should happen in a certain situation.

organization^{**}
[ɔ̀rgənizéiʃən]

n. 조직, 단체; 준비, 구성
An organization is an official group of people, for example a political party, a business, a charity, or a club.

handbook
[hǽndbùk]

n. (직업 교육용 등의) 안내서, 입문서
A handbook is a book that gives you advice and instructions about a particular subject, tool, or machine.

stay off

idiom ~에서 떨어져 있다; 삼가다, 멀리하다
If you stay off something, you keep away from it.

excessive^{**}
[iksésiv]

a. 과도한, 지나친
If you describe the amount or level of something as excessive, you disapprove of it because it is more or higher than is necessary or reasonable.

mutter^{복습}
[mʌ́tər]

v. 중얼거리다; 투덜거리다; n. 중얼거림
If you mutter, you speak very quietly so that you cannot easily be heard, often because you are complaining about something.

make it

idiom 가다; 성공하다, 해내다
If you make it to somewhere, you succeed in reaching there.

jam^{**}
[dʒæm]

v. 가득 채우다; (좁은 곳에 잔뜩) 밀어넣다; n. 잼; 혼잡, 교통 체증
If a lot of people jam a place, or jam into a place, they are pressed tightly together so that they can hardly move.

go too far

idiom 도를 넘다; 이 정도까지 (극단적으로) 하다
If you say that someone goes too far, you mean that they say or do something which is considered too extreme or socially unacceptable.

coming through

idiom 잠깐 지나갈게요
You say 'coming through' when you are trying to get through a crowd of people, as in a passageway or an elevator.

squeeze*
[skwi:z]

v. (억지로) 비집고 들어가다; (꼭) 짜다; n. 짜기, 쥐기
If you squeeze a person or thing somewhere or if they squeeze there, they manage to get through or into a small space.

crawl복습
[krɔːl]

v. 기어가다; 기다, 몹시 느리게 가다; n. 기어가기, 서행
When you crawl, you move forward on your hands and knees.

make one's way

idiom 나아가다, 가다
When you make your way somewhere, you walk or travel there.

slop
[slap]

v. 엎지르다; (액체를) 넘치게 하다; n. 오물
If liquid slops from a container or if you slop liquid somewhere, it comes out over the edge of the container, usually accidentally.

bucket*
[bʌkit]

n. 양동이, 들통
A bucket is a round metal or plastic container with a handle attached to its sides.

demand복습
[dimǽnd]

v. 강력히 묻다, 따지다; 요구하다; n. 요구 (사항)
If you demand something such as information or action, you ask for it in a very forceful way.

land복습
[lænd]

v. 내려앉다, 착륙하다; 도착하다; n. 육지, 땅; 지역
When someone or something lands, they come down to the ground after moving through the air or falling.

plop
[plap]

n. 풍당 (하는 소리); v. 풍당 하고 떨어지다; 털썩 주저앉다
A plop is a soft, gentle sound, like the sound made by something dropping into water without disturbing the surface much.

80

Chapters 17 & 18

1. How was Mrs. Drazil fair to her class?
   A. She let them all go out for recess.
   B. She wanted each child to get the same amount of cookies.
   C. She let the children ask each other for help with homework.
   D. She gave cookies to children who finished their homework.

2. What did Mrs. Drazil say was a goozack?
   A. A door
   B. Their classroom
   C. Mr. Kidswatter
   D. An alien

3. Why had the children decided to get rid of Mrs. Drazil?
   A. She had made them eat Miss Mush's food.
   B. She had made them say a bad word.
   C. She had made Louis shave off his mustache.
   D. She had made them do extra homework.

4. How did the children's plan depend on Sharie?
   A. She had to fall asleep in class.
   B. She had to distract Mrs. Drazil.
   C. She had to get the blue notebook from the desk.
   D. She had to bring Louis up to the classroom.

5. Why did Deedee volunteer for her part in the plan?
    A. She had brought Louis up to meet Drazil in the first place.
    B. She had gotten rid of Mr. Gorf and made them get a new teacher.
    C. She liked being important and doing dangerous work.
    D. She thought that it would be the easiest part of the plan.

6. Why were the children crowding around Deedee at recess?
    A. She was going through the blue notebook.
    B. She was telling the children a story about Louis.
    C. She was passing out the balls to the children.
    D. She was showing the blue notebook to Louis.

7. Which of the following did the children learn from the blue notebook at recess?
    A. Louis had never done anything wrong.
    B. Mrs. Drazil never actually put a trash can on Louis's head.
    C. There were other kids a lot worse than Louis.
    D. Louis once put a rat in Mrs. Drazil's shoe.

Check Your Reading Speed

1분에 몇 단어를 읽는지 리딩 속도를 측정해 보세요.

$$\frac{488\ words}{reading\ time\ (\quad)\ sec} \times 60 = (\quad)\ WPM$$

Build Your Vocabulary

announce**
[ənáuns]

v. 발표하다, 알리다; (공공장소에서) 방송으로 알리다
If you announce something, you tell people about it publicly or officially.

dozen** ^{복습}
[dʌzn]

n. 12개짜리 한 묶음, 다스; 다수, 여러 개
If you have a dozen things, you have twelve of them.

wave**
[weiv]

v. (손·팔을) 흔들다; 손짓하다; n. 파도, 물결; (팔·손·몸을) 흔들기
If you wave or wave your hand, you move your hand from side to side in the air, usually in order to say hello or goodbye to someone.

back and forth ^{복습}
[bæk ən fɔ́:rθ]

ad. 앞뒤로; 좌우로; 여기저기에, 왔다갔다
If someone moves back and forth, they repeatedly move in one direction and then in the opposite direction.

patient**
[péiʃənt]

a. 인내심 있는; n. 환자
If you are patient, you stay calm and do not get annoyed, for example when something takes a long time, or when someone is not doing what you want them to do.

times
[taimz]

prep. ~으로 곱한
You use times in arithmetic to link numbers or amounts that are multiplied together to reach a total.

tear ^{복습}
[tɛər]

① v. (tore-torn) 찢다, 뜯다; 구멍을 뚫다; n. 찢어진 곳, 구멍 ② n. 눈물
If you tear paper, cloth, or another material, or if it tears, you pull it into two pieces or you pull it so that a hole appears in it.

mathematical*
[mæθəmǽtikəl]

a. 수학의, 수리적인
Something that is mathematical involves numbers and calculations.

method**
[méθəd]

n. 방법
A method is a particular way of doing something.

sigh ^{복습}
[sai]

n. 한숨 (소리); v. 한숨을 쉬다, 한숨짓다
A sigh is a long, deep audible exhalation expressing sadness, relief, or tiredness.

be left over

idiom 남다
If food or money is left over, it remains when the rest has been eaten or used up.

exact^{복습}
[igzǽkt]

a. 정확한, 정밀한; 꼼꼼한, 빈틈없는 (exactly ad. 정확히, 꼭)
You use exactly before an amount, number, or position to emphasize that it is no more, no less, or no different from what you are stating.

recipe**
[résəpi]

n. 조리법, 요리법; 방안
A recipe is a list of ingredients and a set of instructions that tell you how to cook something.

pinch*
[pinʧ]

n. 한 자밤, 조금; 꼬집기; v. 꼬집다; 꼭 집다
A pinch of an ingredient such as salt is the amount of it that you can hold between your thumb and your first finger.

gasp^{복습}
[gæsp]

v. 숨이 턱 막히다, 헉 하고 숨을 쉬다; n. (숨이 막히는 듯) 헉 하는 소리를 냄
When you gasp, you take a short quick breath through your mouth, especially when you are surprised, shocked, or in pain.

word***
[wə:rd]

n. 터부시되는 말; 단어, 낱말; v. (특정한) 말을 쓰다
You can use -word after a letter of the alphabet to refer politely or humorously to a word beginning with that letter which people find offensive or are embarrassed to use.

shave^{복습}
[ʃeiv]

v. 면도하다; n. 면도 (shave off idiom (수염을) 밀어 버리다)
If someone shaves off their hair, they remove it from their face, head, or body.

Check Your Reading Speed

1분에 몇 단어를 읽는지 리딩 속도를 측정해 보세요.

$$\frac{602 \text{ words}}{\text{reading time ( ) sec}} \times 60 = (\quad) \text{ WPM}$$

Build Your Vocabulary

depend on
idiom ~에 달려 있다; ~에게 기대다, 의존하다
If you say that one thing depends on another, you mean that the first thing will be affected or determined by the second.

fluffy 복습
[flʌ́fi]
a. 푹신해 보이는, 솜털 같은; 솜털의
If you describe something such as a towel or a toy animal as fluffy, you mean that it is very soft.

yawn*
[jɔːn]
v. 하품하다; n. 하품
If you yawn, you open your mouth very wide and breathe in more air than usual, often when you are tired or when you are not interested in something.

pillow 복습
[pílou]
n. 베개
A pillow is a rectangular cushion which you rest your head on when you are in bed.

wrap 복습
[ræp]
v. (무엇의 둘레를) 두르다; (포장지 등으로) 싸다, 포장하다; n. 포장지
When you wrap something such as a piece of paper or cloth round another thing, you put it around it.

cozy*
[kóuzi]
a. 아늑한; 친밀한, 은밀한
A house or room that is cozy is comfortable and warm.

overcoat 복습
[óuvərkòut]
n. 외투, 오버코트
An overcoat is a thick warm coat that you wear in winter.

snug
[snʌg]
a. 포근한, 아늑한; 꼭 맞는 (snugly ad. 아늑하게, 포근하게)
If you feel snug or are in a snug place, you are very warm and comfortable, especially because you are protected from cold weather.

eyelash
[áilæʃ]
n. 속눈썹
Your eyelashes are the hairs which grow on the edges of your eyelids.

stick out 복습
idiom ~을 내밀다, 튀어나오게 하다
If something is sticking out from a surface or object, it extends up or away from it.

spaceship
[spéisʃip]
n. 우주선
A spaceship is a spacecraft that carries people through space.

86

outer space
[áutər spéis]

n. (대기권 외) 우주 공간
Outer space is the area outside the earth's atmosphere where the other planets and stars are situated.

bend**
[bend]

v. (bent-bent) (몸이나 머리를) 굽히다, 숙이다; (무엇을) 구부리다;
n. 굽이, 굽은 곳
When you bend, you move the top part of your body downward and forward.

volunteer*
[valəntíər]

v. 자원하다, 자진하다; n. 자원 봉사자
If you volunteer to do something, you offer to do it without being forced to do it.

duty**
[djú:ti]

n. 직무, 임무; (도덕적·법률적) 의무
If you say that something is your duty, you believe that you ought to do it because it is your responsibility.

in the first place

idiom 애초에; 우선, 먼저
You use in the first place at the end of a sentence to talk about why something was done or whether it should have been done or not.

sooner or later

idiom 조만간, 머잖아
If you say that something will happen sooner or later, you mean that it will happen at some time in the future, even though it might take a long time.

crawl복습
[krɔ:l]

v. 기어가다; 기다, 몹시 느리게 가다; n. 기어가기, 서행
When you crawl, you move forward on your hands and knees.

drawer복습
[drɔ:r]

n. 서랍
A drawer is part of a desk, chest, or other piece of furniture that is shaped like a box and is designed for putting things in.

remove복습
[rimú:v]

v. (어떤 곳에서) 치우다; (옷 등을) 벗다; 없애다
If you remove something from a place, you take it away.

stare복습
[stɛər]

v. 빤히 쳐다보다, 응시하다; n. 빤히 쳐다보기, 응시
If you stare at someone or something, you look at them for a long time.

mysterious**
[mistíəriəs]

a. 이해하기 힘든, 기이한, 불가사의한 (mysteriously ad. 모호하게; 이상하게)
Someone or something that is mysterious is strange and is not known about or understood.

go through복습

idiom ~을 살펴보다; ~을 검토하다
If you go through something, you look at, check or examine it closely and carefully, especially in order to find something.

pick on

idiom (부당하게) ~을 괴롭히다; ~을 선택하다
If you pick on someone, you treat them badly or unfairly, especially repeatedly.

no wonder

idiom ~하는 것도 당연하다, ~할 만도 하다; (별로) 놀랄 일이 아니다
If you say 'no wonder,' you mean that something is not surprising.

trash^{복습}
[træʃ]

n. 쓰레기; v. 부수다, 엉망으로 만들다; (필요 없는 것을) 버리다
(trash can n. 쓰레기통)
A trash can is a large round container which people put their rubbish in and which is usually kept outside their house.

flip through^{복습}

idiom (책장을) 휙휙 넘기다
If you flip through something such as the pages of a book or a pile of papers, you turn over it quickly, or look through it without reading everything.

lizard
[lízərd]

n. [동물] 도마뱀
A lizard is a reptile with short legs and a long tail.

rub^{복습}
[rʌb]

v. (손·손수건 등을 대고) 문지르다; (표면이) 쓸리다; n. 문지르기, 비비기
If you rub a part of your body, you move your hand or fingers backward and forward over it while pressing firmly.

tummy
[támi]

n. 배
Your tummy is the part of the front of your body below your waist.

assign[*]
[əsáin]

v. (일·책임 등을) 맡기다; 선임하다, 파견하다 (assignment n. 과제, 임무)
An assignment is a task or piece of work that you are given to do, especially as part of your job or studies.

Chapters 19 & 20

1. Why was Miss Zarves so upset?
   A. She knew that she didn't exist.
   B. There was a cow in her classroom.
   C. Her students weren't paying attention to her.
   D. She wanted to find a new school.

2. Why was Miss Zarves called on last in class when she was a little girl?
   A. She sat in the back of the classroom.
   B. She never raised her hand in class.
   C. She always shouted out in class.
   D. She was last alphabetically.

3. How did Mr. Kidswatter react to Miss Zarves coming to her office?
   A. He didn't react at all.
   B. He told her to go away.
   C. He gave her a rubber band ball as a gift.
   D. He asked her for more rubber bands.

4. How did the bald-headed man and the men with black mustaches feel about Miss Zarves?

   A. They felt that she would be happier at a different school.

   B. They could see her and appreciated all her hard work.

   C. They admired her for never leaving the school.

   D. They thought that her students were the best in the school.

5. What was the important announcement made by Mr. Kidswatter?

   A. He was going on vacation to a beach in Jamaica.

   B. There were new rules for using the stairs.

   C. Elevators were being installed.

   D. Escalators were being installed.

6. Why did everyone keep bumping into each other on the stairs every day?

   A. The elevator was broken.

   B. Everyone went up and down on the right.

   C. Everyone went up on the right and down on the left.

   D. Everyone went up on the left and down on the right.

7. How did the elevators at Wayside School operate?

   A. They went up on the right and down on the left.

   B. The elevators changed colors and operated perfectly many times.

   C. The red one only went up and the blue one only went down but they only worked once.

   D. The blue one only went up and the red one only went down but they only worked once.

Check Your Reading Speed

1분에 몇 단어를 읽는지 리딩 속도를 측정해 보세요.

$$\frac{1{,}238 \text{ words}}{\text{reading time ( ) sec}} \times 60 = (\qquad) \text{ WPM}$$

Build Your Vocabulary

story 복습
[stɔ́:ri]

① n. (= storey) (건물의) 층 ② n. 이야기, 소설; 설명
A story of a building is one of its different levels, which is situated above or below other levels.

triangle*
[tráiæŋgl]

n. 삼각형
A triangle is an object, arrangement, or flat shape with three straight sides and three angles.

blackboard 복습
[blǽkbɔ̀:rd]

n. 칠판
A blackboard is a dark-colored board that you can write on with chalk.

square*
[skwɛər]

n. 정사각형; a. 정사각형 모양의; 공정한, 정직한
A square is a shape with four sides that are all the same length and four corners that are all right angles.

pentagon
[péntəgan]

n. 오각형
A pentagon is a shape with five sides.

hexagon
[héksəgən]

n. 6각형
A hexagon is a shape that has six straight sides.

heptagon
[héptəgən]

n. 7각형
A heptagon is a polygon having seven sides.

degree*
[digrí:]

n. (각도·온도의 단위인) 도; 정도; 학위
A degree is a unit of measurement that is used to measure angles, and also longitude and latitude.

talent*
[tǽlənt]

n. 재주, (타고난) 재능; 재능 있는 사람
Talent is the natural ability to do something well.

appreciate*
[əprí:ʃièit]

v. 진가를 알아보다; 고마워하다
If you appreciate something, for example a piece of music or good food, you like it because you recognize its good qualities.

count 복습
[kaunt]

v. (수를) 세다; 계산에 넣다; n. (하나부터 순서대로 세는) 셈; 계산
When you count, you say all the numbers one after another up to a particular number.

moo 복습
[mu:]

n. 음매(소의 울음소리); v. (소가) 음매 하고 울다
When cattle, especially cows, moo, they make the long low sound that cattle typically make.

chalk**
[ʧɔːk]

n. 분필
Chalk is small sticks of soft white rock, used for writing or drawing with.

glare^{복습}
[glɛər]

v. 노려보다; 환하다, 눈부시다; n. 노려봄; 눈부심
If you glare at someone, you look at them with an angry expression on your face.

gape
[geip]

v. (놀라서) 입을 딱 벌리고 바라보다; 벌어지다
If you gape, you look at someone or something in surprise, usually with an open mouth.

octagon
[áktəgan]

n. 8각형
An octagon is a shape that has eight straight sides.

chest**
[ʧest]

n. 가슴, 흉부; (나무로 만든) 상자
Your chest is the top part of the front of your body where your ribs, lungs, and heart are.

pleasant^{복습}
[plézənt]

a. 상냥한; 쾌적한, 즐거운
Someone who is pleasant is friendly and likeable.

disposition**
[dispəzíʃən]

n. 기질, 성격; 성향; 배치
Someone's disposition is the way that they tend to behave or feel.

goldfish
[góuldfiʃ]

n. [동물] 금붕어
Goldfish are small gold or orange fish which are often kept as pets.

have it

idiom (부정문에서) 용인하다, 용납하다
You can say 'I won't have it' to mean that you will not allow or put up with something.

accommodate*
[əkámədèit]

v. (요구 등에) 부응하다, 협조하다; (환경 등에) 맞추다; 공간을 제공하다
If you do something to accommodate someone, you do it with the main purpose of pleasing or satisfying them.

call on^{복습}

idiom (이름을 불러서) 학생에게 시키다; (사람을) 방문하다
If a teacher calls on students in a class, he or she asks them to answer a question or give their opinion.

alphabetical*
[ælfəbétikəl]

a. 알파벳순의 (alphabetically ad. 알파벳순으로)
Alphabetical means arranged according to the normal order of the letters in the alphabet.

dress up^{복습}

idiom 옷을 갖춰 입다; 변장을 하다
If you dress up, you put on clothes that are more formal than the clothes you usually wear.

fancy**
[fǽnsi]

a. 값비싼, 고급의; 장식이 많은; v. 생각하다, 상상하다
If you describe something as fancy, you mean that it is very expensive or of very high quality, and you often dislike it because of this.

tuck^{복습}
[tʌk]

v. (따뜻하게) 단단히 덮어 주다; (끝부분을 단정하게) 밀어넣다; n. 주름
(tuck in idiom ~에게 이불을 잘 덮어 주다)
If you tuck someone in, you cover them, especially a child, comfortably in bed by pulling the covers around them.

tissue* [tíʃuː]

n. 화장지; (세포) 조직
A tissue is a piece of thin soft paper that you use to blow your nose.

sleeve* [sliːv]

n. (옷의) 소매
The sleeves of a coat, shirt, or other item of clothing are the parts that cover your arms.

wipe^{복습} [waip]

v. (먼지·물기 등을 없애기 위해 무엇을) 닦다; n. (행주·걸레를 써서) 닦기
If you wipe something, you rub its surface to remove dirt or liquid from it.

walk all over

idiom 모질게 다루다
If you walk all over someone, you treat them badly, without considering them or their needs.

squeaky [skwíːki]

a. 끼익 하는 소리가 나는
Something that is squeaky makes high-pitched sounds.

wheel** [hwiːl]

n. 바퀴; (자동차 등의) 핸들; v. (바퀴 달린 것을) 밀다, 끌다
The wheels of a vehicle are the circular objects which are fixed underneath it and which enable it to move along the ground.

grease* [griːs]

n. (끈적끈적한) 기름, 윤활유; v. 기름을 바르다
Grease is a thick, oily substance which is put on the moving parts of cars and other machines in order to make them work smoothly.

principal^{복습} [prínsəpəl]

n. 교장; 학장, 총장; a. 주요한, 주된
The principal of a school or college is the person in charge of the school or college.

tease* [tiːz]

v. 놀리다, 장난하다; 괴롭히다; n. 남을 놀리기 좋아하는 사람
To tease someone means to laugh at them or make jokes about them in order to embarrass, annoy, or upset them.

gross^{복습} [grous]

a. 역겨운; 아주 무례한
If you describe something as gross, you think it is very unpleasant.

steady** [stédi]

v. 진정시키다, 가라앉히다; 균형을 잡다; a. 꾸준한; 안정된
If you steady yourself, you control your voice or expression, so that people will think that you are calm and not nervous.

nerve** [nəːrv]

n. (pl.) 긴장, 불안; 신경
You can refer to someone's feelings of anxiety or tension as nerves.

knock^{복습} [nak]

v. (문 등을) 두드리다; (때리거나 타격을 가해) ~한 상태가 되게 만들다; n. 문 두드리는 소리
If you knock on something such as a door or window, you hit it, usually several times, to attract someone's attention.

march*** [maːrʧ]

v. (단호한 태도로 급히) 걸어가다; 행진하다; n. 행군, 행진; 3월
If you say that someone marches somewhere, you mean that they walk there quickly and in a determined way, for example because they are angry.

rubber band [rʌ́bər bænd]

n. 고무줄
A rubber band is a thin circle of very elastic rubber.

drawer^{복습}
[drɔːr]

n. 서랍
A drawer is part of a desk, chest, or other piece of furniture that is shaped like a box and is designed for putting things in.

press**
[pres]

v. (버튼 등을) 누르다; (~에 대고) 누르다; n. 언론; 누르기
If you press a button or switch, you push it with your finger in order to make a machine or device work.

buzzer
[bʌzər]

n. 버저; 사이렌
A buzzer is an electrical device that is used to make a buzzing sound for example, to attract someone's attention.

startle*
[staːrtl]

v. 깜짝 놀라게 하다 (startled a. 놀란)
If something sudden and unexpected startles you, it surprises and frightens you slightly.

bald*
[bɔːld]

a. 대머리의, 머리가 벗겨진
Someone who is bald has little or no hair on the top of their head.

mustache^{복습}
[mʌstæʃ]

n. 콧수염
A man's mustache is the hair that grows on his upper lip.

attaché case
[ətǽʃei kèis]

n. (작은) 서류 가방
An attaché case is a flat case for holding documents.

nod^{복습}
[nad]

v. (고개를) 끄덕이다; n. (고개를) 끄덕임
If you nod, you move your head downward and upward to show that you are answering 'yes' to a question, or to show agreement, understanding, or approval.

touched
[tʌʧt]

a. 감동한; 감정적이 된
If you are touched, you are feeling happy and grateful or you are moved because of something kind that someone has done.

make fun of

idiom ~을 놀리다
If you make fun of someone or something, you laugh at them, tease them, or make jokes about them in a way that causes them to seem ridiculous.

tragedy*
[trǽdʒədi]

n. 비극(적인 사건)
A tragedy is an extremely sad event or situation.

handkerchief**
[hǽŋkərʧif]

n. 손수건
A handkerchief is a small square piece of fabric which you use for blowing your nose.

blow one's nose

idiom 코를 풀다
When you blow your nose, you force air out of it through your nostrils in order to clear it.

Check Your Reading Speed

1분에 몇 단어를 읽는지 리딩 속도를 측정해 보세요.

$$\frac{269 \text{ words}}{\text{reading time ( ) sec}} \times 60 = (\quad) \text{ WPM}$$

Build Your Vocabulary

loudspeaker
[láudspìːkər]

n. 확성기
A loudspeaker is a piece of equipment through which sound comes out.

pause^{복습}
[pɔːz]

n. (말·행동 등의) 멈춤; v. (말·일을 하다가) 잠시 멈추다; 일시 정지시키다
A pause is a short period when you stop doing something before continuing.

announce^{복습}
[ənáuns]

v. 발표하다, 알리다; (공공장소에서) 방송으로 알리다
(announcement n. 발표 소식)
An announcement is a statement made to the public or to the media which gives information about something that has happened or that will happen.

install**
[instɔ́ːl]

v. (장비·가구를) 설치하다
If you install a piece of equipment, you fit it or put it somewhere so that it is ready to be used.

stun*
[stʌn]

v. (놀람·기쁨으로) 어리벙벙하게 하다; 기절시키다
If you are stunned by something, you are extremely shocked or surprised by it and are therefore unable to speak or do anything.

yahoo
[jəhúː]

int. 야호(신이 나서 외치는 소리)
People sometimes shout 'yahoo!' when they are very happy or excited about something.

yell^{복습}
[jel]

v. 고함치다, 소리 지르다; n. 고함, 외침
If you yell, you shout loudly, usually because you are excited, angry, or in pain.

rush^{복습}
[rʌʃ]

v. 급(속)히 움직이다, (너무 급히) 서두르다; n. 혼잡, 분주함
If you rush somewhere, you go there quickly.

chaos*
[kéias]

n. 혼돈; 혼란
Chaos is a state of complete disorder and confusion.

bump*
[bʌmp]

v. 부딪치다; 덜컹거리며 가다; n. 쿵, 탁(부딪치는 소리); (도로의) 튀어나온 부분
If you bump into something or someone, you accidentally hit them while you are moving.

personally*
[pə́ːrsənəli]

ad. 직접, 개인적으로
If you do something personally, you do it yourself rather than letting someone else do it.

coffeepot 복습
[kɔ́ːfipàt]

n. 커피 주전자
A coffeepot is a tall narrow pot with a spout and a lid, in which coffee is made or served.

Chapters 21 & 22

1. Why did Jason get to leave school early?
   A. He had to go to an artist.
   B. He had to go to a dentist.
   C. He had to go to a funeral.
   D. He had to go to home for being bad in class.

2. Why did Jason not tell Dr. Payne that his tooth hurt?
   A. She might think it was a cavity.
   B. She might hurt it even more.
   C. He didn't want to cry.
   D. He couldn't feel any pain in his mouth.

3. Why did Kendall's mother call Dr. Payne?
   A. She refused to pay the bill, because it was too expensive.
   B. She refused to pay the bill, because she already paid it earlier.
   C. She refused to pay the bill, because the wrong tooth had been pulled.
   D. She refused to pay the bill, because she and Dr. Payne were best friends.

4. Why did Jason open his mouth even wider when he saw the diploma?

A. He was shocked that his dentist was married.

B. He was shocked that the diploma was fake.

C. He was shocked that she had only gotten it a few days earlier.

D. He was shocked that his dentist's name had been Jane Smith.

5. Which of the following is NOT something that Jason and Deedee did as they walked in front of Mrs. Drazil's desk?

A. They spelled out Jane Smith's name.

B. They talked about how many cavities Jason had.

C. They said where Dr. Payne's office was located.

D. They mentioned that Dr. Payne's name had been Jane Smith.

6. What did Dr. Payne and her husband love even more than each other?

A. Brussel sprouts

B. Cars

C. Money

D. Animals

7. How did Dr. Payne try to escape from Mrs. Drazil?

A. She tried to escape in her sports car.

B. She tried to escape in a helicopter.

C. She tried to escape in a motorboat.

D. She tried to escape on a motorcycle.

Check Your Reading Speed

1분에 몇 단어를 읽는지 리딩 속도를 측정해 보세요.

$$\frac{535 \text{ words}}{\text{reading time ( ) sec}} \times 60 = (\quad) \text{ WPM}$$

Build Your Vocabulary

dentist*
[déntist]

n. 치과 의사
A dentist is a person who is qualified to examine and treat people's teeth.

appointment**
[əpóintmənt]

n. 약속; 임명, 지명
If you have an appointment with someone, you have arranged to see them at a particular time, usually in connection with their work or for a serious purpose.

meal***
[mi:l]

n. 식사, 끼니
A meal is an occasion when people sit down and eat, usually at a regular time.

snack
[snæk]

n. 간식; v. 간식을 먹다
A snack is something such as a chocolate bar that you eat between meals.

toothbrush*
[tú:θbrʌʃ]

n. 칫솔
A toothbrush is a small brush that you use for cleaning your teeth.

cavity*
[kǽvəti]

n. 충치; 구멍
In dentistry, a cavity is a hole in a tooth, caused by decay.

fingernail^{복습}
[fíŋgərnèil]

n. 손톱
Your fingernails are the thin hard areas at the end of each of your fingers.

stretch**
[streʧ]

v. (길이·폭 등을) 늘이다; (팔·다리의 근육을) 당기다; n. (길게) 펼쳐져 있는 지역
When something soft or elastic stretches or is stretched, it becomes longer or bigger as well as thinner, usually because it is pulled.

cheek**
[ʧi:k]

n. 뺨, 볼
Your cheeks are the sides of your face below your eyes.

vein*
[vein]

n. 혈관, 정맥
Your veins are the thin tubes in your body through which your blood flows toward your heart.

bulge
[bʌldʒ]

v. 툭 튀어 나오다; (~으로) 가득 차다; n. 툭 튀어 나온 것, 불룩한 것
If someone's eyes or veins are bulging, they seem to stick out a lot, often because the person is making a strong physical effort or is experiencing a strong emotion.

100

water***
[wɔ́:tər]

v. 눈물이 나다; (화초 등에) 물을 주다; n. 물
If your eyes water, tears build up in them because they are hurting or because you are upset.

suck^{복습}
[sʌk]

v. (액체·공기 등을) 빨아 먹다; (무엇을 입에 넣고 계속) 빨다
If something sucks a liquid, gas, or object in a particular direction, it draws it there with a powerful force.

tube**
[tju:b]

n. 관; 튜브; 통
A tube is a long hollow object that is usually round, like a pipe.

gag
[gæg]

v. 목이 막히다; (입에) 재갈을 물리다; n. 재갈; 장난
If you gag, you cannot swallow and nearly vomit.

moisture*
[mɔ́istʃər]

n. 습기, 수분
Moisture is tiny drops of water in the air, on a surface, or in the ground.

poke*
[pouk]

v. (손가락 등으로) 쿡 찌르다; 쑥 내밀다; n. 찌르기, 쑤시기
If you poke someone or something, you quickly push them with your finger or with a sharp object.

tsk
[tisk]

int. 쯧 (혀 차는 소리); v. 쯧쯧 혀를 차다
Tsk is a sound used to express disapproval or annoyance.

pointed^{복습}
[pɔ́intid]

a. (끝이) 뾰족한; (말 등이) 날카로운
Something that is pointed has a point at one end.

tool**
[tu:l]

n. 도구, 연장; 수단
A tool is any instrument or simple piece of equipment that you hold in your hands and use to do a particular kind of work.

agony*
[ǽgəni]

n. 극도의 (육체적·정신적) 고통
Agony is great physical or mental pain.

spot**
[spat]

n. (특정한) 곳; (작은) 점; v. 발견하다, 찾다, 알아채다
You can refer to a particular place as a spot.

sweat*
[swet]

n. 땀; 노력; v. 땀을 흘리다; 물기가 스며 나오다
Sweat is the salty colorless liquid which comes through your skin when you are hot, ill, or afraid.

drip*
[drip]

v. (액체를) 뚝뚝 흘리다; 가득 담고 있다; n. (액체가) 뚝뚝 떨어짐; (작은 액체) 방울
When something drips, drops of liquid fall from it.

receptionist
[risépʃənist]

n. (호텔·사무실·병원 등의) 접수 담당자
In an office or hospital, the receptionist is the person whose job is to answer the telephone, arrange appointments, and deal with people when they first arrive.

bill**
[bil]

n. 고지서, 청구서; (식당의) 계산서
A bill is a written statement of money that you owe for goods or services.

exclaim^{복습}
[ikskléim]

v. 소리치다, 외치다
If you exclaim, you cry out suddenly in surprise, strong emotion, or pain.

dare ^{복습}
[dɛər]

v. 감히 ~하다, ~할 엄두를 내다; 부추기다; n. 모험, 도전
You say 'how dare you' when you are very shocked and angry about something that someone has done.

tummy ^{복습}
[támi]

n. 배
Your tummy is the part of the front of your body below your waist.

slam[*]
[slæm]

v. 세게 놓다; 쾅 닫다; n. 탕 하고 닫기; 쾅 하는 소리
If you slam something down, you put it there quickly and with great force.

diploma[*]
[diplóumə]

n. 졸업장; 수료증
A diploma is a qualification which may be awarded to a student by a university or college, or by a high school in the United States.

Check Your Reading Speed

1분에 몇 단어를 읽는지 리딩 속도를 측정해 보세요.

$$\frac{955 \text{ words}}{\text{reading time ( ) sec}} \times 60 = (\quad) \text{ WPM}$$

Build Your Vocabulary

playground^{복습}
[pléigràund]

n. (학교의) 운동장; 놀이터
A playground is a piece of land, at school or in a public area, where children can play.

whistle**
[hwisl]

n. 호각, 호루라기; 휘파람 (소리); v. 휘파람을 불다; 호루라기를 불다
A whistle is a small metal tube which you blow in order to produce a loud sound and attract someone's attention.

blow**
[blou]

v. (blew-blown) (호각·악기 등을) 불다; (바람·입김에) 날리다; n. 세게 때림
When a whistle or horn blows or someone blows it, they make a sound by blowing into it.

professional^{복습}
[prəféʃənl]

a. 직업의, 전문적인; 전문가의; 능숙한; n. 전문가
Professional means relating to a person's work, especially work that requires special training.

supervisor^{복습}
[súːpərvàizər]

n. 감독관, 관리자
A supervisor is a person who supervises activities or people, especially workers or students.

blacktop^{복습}
[blǽktap]

n. 아스팔트 도로; (포장에 쓰이는) 아스팔트; v. 아스팔트로 포장하다
Blacktop is a hard black substance which is used as a surface for roads.

bench**
[bentʃ]

n. 벤치, 긴 의자; v. 착석시키다
A bench is a long seat of wood or metal that two or more people can sit on.

excessive^{복습}
[iksésiv]

a. 과도한, 지나친
If you describe the amount or level of something as excessive, you disapprove of it because it is more or higher than is necessary or reasonable.

dentist^{복습}
[déntist]

n. 치과 의사
A dentist is a person who is qualified to examine and treat people's teeth.

spell^{복습}
[spel]

v. (어떤 단어의) 철자를 말하다; 철자를 맞게 쓰다, 맞춤법에 맞게 글을 쓰다
When you spell a word, you write or speak each letter in the word in the correct order.

drill*
[dril]

v. (드릴로) 구멍을 뚫다; 반복 연습시키다; n. 드릴, 송곳; 반복 연습
When you drill into something or drill a hole in something, you make a hole in it using a drill.

times ^{복습}
[taimz]

prep. ~으로 곱한
You use times in arithmetic to link numbers or amounts that are multiplied together to reach a total.

cavity ^{복습}
[kǽvəti]

n. 충치; 구멍
In dentistry, a cavity is a hole in a tooth, caused by decay.

patient ^{복습}
[péiʃənt]

n. 환자; a. 인내심 있는
A patient is a person who is receiving medical treatment from a doctor or hospital.

fancy ^{복습}
[fǽnsi]

a. 값비싼, 고급의; 장식이 많은; v. 생각하다, 상상하다
If you describe something as fancy, you mean that it is very expensive or of very high quality, and you often dislike it because of this.

beat-up
[bi:t-ʌ́p]

a. 낡아빠진, 닳아빠진
A beat-up car or other object is old and in bad condition.

rearview mirror
[ríərvju: mírər]

n. (자동차의) 백미러
A rearview mirror is a mirror in a vehicle that allows the driver to see what is behind the vehicle.

mansion*
[mǽnʃən]

n. 대저택
A mansion is a very large house.

press ^{복습}
[pres]

v. (버튼 등을) 누르다; (~에 대고) 누르다; n. 언론; 누르기
If you press a button or switch, you push it with your finger in order to make a machine or device work.

iron**
[áiərn]

n. 철, 쇠; 철분; 다리미 (iron gate n. 철문)
Iron is an element which usually takes the form of a hard, dark grey metal. It is used to make steel, and also forms part of many tools, buildings, and vehicles.

wind**
[waind]

① v. (도로·강 등이) 구불구불하다; 감다 (winding a. 구불구불한) ② n. 바람
If a road, river, or line of people winds in a particular direction, it goes in that direction with a lot of bends or twists in it.

driveway
[dráivwèi]

n. (도로에서 집·차고까지의) 진입로
A driveway is a piece of hard ground that leads from the road to the front of a house or other building.

tailgate
[téilgèit]

n. (트럭·왜건 등의) 뒷문; v. (다른 차의 뒤를) 바짝 따라 달리다
A tailgate is a door at the back of a truck or car, that is hinged at the bottom so that it opens downward.

ladder ^{복습}
[lǽdər]

n. 사다리
A ladder is a piece of equipment used for climbing up something or down from something. It consists of two long pieces of wood, metal, or rope with steps fixed between them.

butler
[bʌ́tlər]

n. 집사
A butler is the most important male servant in a wealthy house.

den
[den]

n. 서재, 작업실; (야생 동물이 사는) 굴
Your den is a quiet room in your house where you can go to study, work, or carry on a hobby without being disturbed.

pet^{복습}
[pet]

v. (동물·아이를 다정하게) 어루만지다; n. 애완동물
If you pet a person or animal, you touch them in an affectionate way.

candlelight
[kǽndllait]

n. 촛불
Candlelight is the light that a candle produces.

deck*
[dek]

n. (집에 딸린) 목제 테라스; (배의) 갑판
A deck is a flat wooden area next to a house, where people can sit and relax or eat.

purr
[pəːr]

v. (기분 좋은 듯이) 그르렁거리다; (낮게) 부르릉 하는 소리를 내다
When a cat purrs, it makes a low vibrating sound with its throat because it is contented.

lap^{복습}
[læp]

n. 무릎; (경주에서 트랙의) 한 바퀴
If you have something on your lap when you are sitting down, it is on top of your legs and near to your body.

faithful**
[féiθfəl]

a. 충실한, 충직한 (faithfully ad. 충실히, 충직하게)
Someone who is faithful to a person, organization, idea, or activity remains firm in their belief in them or support for them.

elderly*
[éldərli]

a. 연세가 드신
You use elderly as a polite way of saying that someone is old.

yard^{복습}
[jaːrd]

n. 정원; (학교의) 운동장; 마당, 뜰
A yard is a piece of land next to someone's house, with grass and plants growing in it.

fingernail^{복습}
[fíŋgərnèil]

n. 손톱
Your fingernails are the thin hard areas at the end of each of your fingers.

dig**
[dig]

v. (dug-dug) (손가락 끝·칼 등을) 찔러넣다; (구멍 등을) 파다; n. 쿡 찌르기
If you dig one thing into another or if one thing digs into another, the first thing is pushed hard into the second, or presses hard into it.

left-over
[léft-ouvər]

n. (식사 후에) 남은 음식
You can refer to food that has not been eaten after a meal as left-overs.

get rid of^{복습}

idiom ~을 처리하다, 없애다
When you get rid of someone or something that is annoying you or that you do not want, you make yourself free of them or throw something away.

hot tub
[hát tʌb]

n. 온수 욕조
A hot tub is a very large, round bath which several people can sit in together.

idiot
[ídiət]

n. 바보, 멍청이
If you call someone an idiot, you are showing that you think they are very stupid or have done something very stupid.

railing
[réiliŋ]

n. 난간; 울타리
A fence made from metal bars is called a railing or railings.

get away

idiom 도망치다; ~로부터 벗어나다; 휴가를 가다
If you get away from someone or somewhere, you escape from them or there.

holler
[hálər]

v. 소리지르다, 고함치다
If you holler, you shout loudly.

ankle^{복습}
[ǽŋkl]

n. 발목
Your ankle is the joint where your foot joins your leg.

sprain
[sprein]

v. (팔목·발목을) 삐다
If you sprain a joint such as your ankle or wrist, you accidentally damage it by twisting it or bending it violently.

agony^{복습}
[ǽgəni]

n. 극도의 (육체적·정신적) 고통
Agony is great physical or mental pain.

twist^{복습}
[twist]

v. 비틀리다, 일그러지다; 돌리다; n. (고개·몸 등을) 돌리기
If you twist something, especially a part of your body, or if it twists, it moves into an unusual, uncomfortable, or bent position, for example because of being hit or pushed, or because you are upset.

rub^{복습}
[rʌb]

v. (손·손수건 등을 대고) 문지르다; (표면이) 쓸리다; n. 문지르기, 비비기
If you rub a part of your body, you move your hand or fingers backward and forward over it while pressing firmly.

tummy^{복습}
[tʌ́mi]

n. 배
Your tummy is the part of the front of your body below your waist.

struggle^{복습}
[strʌgl]

v. 힘겹게 나아가다; 투쟁하다, 몸부림치다; n. 투쟁, 분투; 몸부림
If you struggle to move yourself or to move a heavy object, you try to do it, but it is difficult.

suitcase*
[súːtkeis]

n. 여행 가방
A suitcase is a box or bag with a handle and a hard frame in which you carry your clothes when you are travelling.

stash
[stæʃ]

v. (안전한 곳에) 넣어 두다; n. 숨겨 둔 양
If you stash something valuable in a secret place, you store it there to keep it safe.

boathouse
[bóuthaus]

n. (강이나 호숫가의) 보트 창고
A boathouse is a building at the edge of a lake, in which boats are kept.

just in case^{복습}

idiom (혹시라도) ~할 경우에 대비해서
If you do something in case or just in case a particular thing happens, you do it because that thing might happen.

hobble
[habl]

v. 다리를 절다, 절뚝거리다; 방해하다
If you hobble, you walk in an awkward way with small steps, for example because your foot is injured.

grab^{복습}
[græb]

v. (와락·단단히) 붙잡다; ~을 잡으려고 하다; n. 와락 잡아채려고 함
If you grab something, you take it or pick it up suddenly and roughly.

106

limp[*]
[limp]

v. 다리를 절다, 절뚝거리다; a. 기운이 없는, 축 처진
If a person or animal limps, they walk with difficulty or in an uneven way because one of their legs or feet is hurt.

drag[*]
[dræg]

v. (힘들여) 끌다; (몸을 끌듯) 힘들게 움직이다; n. ~에 대한 장애물
If you drag something, you pull it along the ground, often with difficulty.

groan[*]
[groun]

v. 신음 소리를 내다; 끙끙거리다; n. 신음, 끙 하는 소리
If you groan, you make a long, low sound because you are in pain, or because you are upset or unhappy about something.

motorboat
[móutərbòut]

n. 모터보트, 소형 고속정
A motorboat is a boat that is driven by an engine.

aboard^{**}
[əbɔ́ːrd]

ad. (배·기차·비행기 등에) 탄, 탑승한
If you are aboard a ship or plane, you are on it or in it.

sputter^{복습}
[spʌ́tər]

v. (엔진 등이) 털털거리는 소리를 내다; (분노·충격으로) 더듬거리며 말하다
If something such as an engine or a flame sputters, it works or burns in an uneven way and makes a series of soft popping sounds.

rowboat
[róubòut]

n. (노로 젓는) 보트
A rowboat is a small boat that you move through the water by using oars.

echo[*]
[ékou]

v. (소리가) 울리다, 메아리치다; 그대로 따라 하다; n. (소리의) 울림, 메아리
If a sound echoes, it is reflected off a surface and can be heard again after the original sound has stopped.

Chapters 23 & 24

1. What bothered Wendy about her ears?
   A. She thought they were too big.
   B. She thought she had too many.
   C. She thought they were too small.
   D. She thought they were oddly shaped.

2. What was special about Wendy's third ear?
   A. It could hear animal voices.
   B. It was in the back of her head.
   C. It could hear people's thoughts.
   D. It could always hear beautiful music.

3. How did Xavier feel about Wendy's third ear?
   A. He thought it made her disgusting and a freak.
   B. He thought it made her unique and beautiful.
   C. He thought it was like something from a Dickens book.
   D. He thought that she was listening to his private thoughts.

4. Why did Wendy Nogard become a substitute teacher?
   A. She hated children the most.
   B. She loved being around children.
   C. She wanted to brighten up children's lives.
   D. She wanted to children to laugh and have fun.

5. Which of the following was NOT one of the things that Miss Nogard heard the children think in class?

A. Dana had gotten a haircut and worried that it made her look like a boy.

B. D.J. was going horseback riding after school if it didn't rain.

C. Jason was mad at his older brother from making him feel like a loser when compared to him.

D. Calvin had spilled orange juice on his lap and worried that someone would think he had gone to the bathroom in his pants.

6. How did Miss Nogard embarrass Benjamin?

A. She called him a girl instead of a boy.

B. She asked him if he was Justin.

C. She asked him to say his name in front of people.

D. She asked him if he needed to go to the restroom.

7. What did Louis ask if the children were sure about regarding Miss Nogard?

A. He asked if they were sure that she wasn't related at all to Mrs. Gorf.

B. He asked if they were sure that her name was Miss Nogard and not Mrs. Nogard.

C. He asked if they were sure that her name was Miss Nogard and not Miss Dragon.

D. He asked if they were sure that her name was Miss Nogard and not Miss Nogood.

Check Your Reading Speed

1분에 몇 단어를 읽는지 리딩 속도를 측정해 보세요.

$$\frac{1{,}075 \text{ words}}{\text{reading time (\quad) sec}} \times 60 = (\quad) \text{ WPM}$$

Build Your Vocabulary

frizzy
[frízi]

a. (머리카락이) 곱슬곱슬한
Frizzy hair is very tightly curled.

intelligent**
[intélədʒənt]

a. 총명한, 똑똑한
A person or animal that is intelligent has the ability to think, understand, and learn things quickly and well.

evil**
[í:vəl]

a. 사악한, 악랄한; 악마의; 몹시 불쾌한, 지독한; n. 악
If you describe someone as evil, you mean that they are very wicked by nature and take pleasure in doing things that harm other people.

wicked*
[wíkid]

a. 못된, 사악한; 짓궂은; 위험한
You use wicked to describe someone or something that is very bad and deliberately harmful to people.

vase*
[veis]

n. 꽃병
A vase is a jar, usually made of glass or pottery, used for holding cut flowers or as an ornament.

embarrass**
[imbǽrəs]

v. 당황스럽게 하다; 곤란하게 하다 (embarrassed a. 당황스러운)
A person who is embarrassed feels shy, ashamed, or guilty about something.

quantity**
[kwántəti]

n. 양, 수량
A quantity is an amount that you can measure or count.

quality**
[kwáləti]

n. 질(質); 우수함; 특성; a. 고급의, 양질의
The quality of something is how good or bad it is.

bother複습
[báðər]

v. 신경 쓰이게 하다; 귀찮게 하다, 귀찮게 말을 걸다; n. 성가심
If something bothers you, or if you bother about it, it worries, annoys, or upsets you.

guard複습
[ga:rd]

n. 경비 요원; 보초, 감시; v. 지키다, 보호하다
A guard is a specially organized group of people, such as soldiers or policemen, who protect or watch someone or something.

frightful*
[fráitfəl]

a. (나쁜 정도를 강조하여) 끔찍한, 엄망인; 무서운 (frightfully ad. 몹시, 대단히)
Frightful is used to emphasize the extent or degree of something, usually something bad.

shy*
[ʃai]

a. 수줍음을 많이 타는, 수줍어하는
A shy person is nervous and uncomfortable in the company of other people.

110

blush*
[blʌʃ]

v. 얼굴을 붉히다, 얼굴이 빨개지다; n. 얼굴이 붉어짐
When you blush, your face becomes redder than usual because you are ashamed or embarrassed.

lock^{복습}
[lak]

v. (자물쇠로) 잠그다; n. 자물쇠
When you lock something such as a door, drawer, or case, you fasten it, usually with a key, so that other people cannot open it.

nod^{복습}
[nad]

v. (고개를) 끄덕이다; n. (고개를) 끄덕임
If you nod, you move your head downward and upward to show that you are answering 'yes' to a question, or to show agreement, understanding, or approval.

alas*
[əlǽs]

int. 아아(슬픔·유감을 나타내는 소리)
You use alas to say that you think that the facts you are talking about are sad or unfortunate.

besides^{복습}
[bisáidz]

ad. 게다가, 뿐만 아니라; prep. ~외에
Besides is used to emphasize an additional point that you are making, especially one that you consider to be important.

bore^{복습}
[bɔːr]

v. 지루하게 하다 (boring a. 재미없는, 지루한)
Someone or something boring is so dull and uninteresting that they make people tired and impatient.

move on^{복습}

idiom (새로운 일·주제로) 넘어가다
To move on to something means to start doing or discussing something new.

blurt
[bləːrt]

v. 불쑥 말하다
If someone blurts something, they say it suddenly, after trying hard to keep quiet or to keep it secret.

stare^{복습}
[stɛər]

v. 빤히 쳐다보다, 응시하다; n. 빤히 쳐다보기, 응시
If you stare at someone or something, you look at them for a long time.

hardly^{복습}
[háːrdli]

ad. 거의 ~할 수가 없다; 거의 ~아니다; 막 ~하자마자
When you say you can hardly do something, you are emphasizing that it is very difficult for you to do it.

emotion**
[imóuʃən]

n. 감정; 정서
An emotion is a feeling such as happiness, love, fear, anger, or hatred, which can be caused by the situation that you are in or the people you are with.

bury^{복습}
[béri]

v. (감정·실수 등을) 감추다; (보이지 않게) 묻다
If you bury your feelings or memories, you hide or try to forget them.

pour**
[pɔːr]

v. 마구 쏟아지다; 붓다, 따르다 (pour out idiom (감정·말이) 쏟아져 나오다)
When feelings or words pour out, or someone pours them out, they are expressed, usually after they have been kept hidden for some time.

check out

idiom (도서관 등에서) 대출받다; (흥미로운 것을) 살펴보다
If you check out something such as a book or a video, you borrow it from a library.

pet^{복습}
[pet]

n. 애완동물; v. (동물·아이를 다정하게) 어루만지다 (pet store n. 애완동물 가게)
A pet is an animal that you keep in your home to give you company and pleasure.

nibble
[nibl]

v. 조금씩 깨물다; 약간 관심을 보이다; n. (조금 베어 문) 한 입
If you nibble something, you bite it very gently.

stroke^{복습}
[strouk]

v. 쓰다듬다, 어루만지다; 달래다; n. 치기, 때리기; (손으로) 쓰다듬기
If you stroke someone or something, you move your hand slowly and gently over them.

bump^{복습}
[bʌmp]

v. 부딪치다; 덜컹거리며 가다; n. 쿵, 탁(부딪치는 소리); (도로의) 튀어나온 부분
If you bump into something or someone, you accidentally hit them while you are moving.

part^{***}
[pa:rt]

v. (두 사물·부분이) 갈라지다; (~와) 헤어지다; n. 일부, 약간; 부분
If you part your hair in the middle or at one side, you make it lie in two different directions so that there is a straight line running from the front of your head to the back.

gross^{복습}
[grous]

a. 역겨운; 아주 무례한
If you describe something as gross, you think it is very unpleasant.

disgust[*]
[disgʌ́st]

v. 혐오감을 유발하다, 역겹게 만들다; n. 혐오감, 역겨움, 넌더리
(disgusting a. 역겨운, 구역질나는)
If you say that something is disgusting, you are criticizing it because it is extremely unpleasant.

stand^{***}
[stænd]

v. 참다, 견디다; 서다, 서 있다; n. 태도, 의견
If you cannot stand something, you cannot bear it or tolerate it.

trick^{복습}
[trik]

v. 속이다, 속임수를 쓰다; n. 속임수
If someone tricks you, they deceive you, often in order to make you do something.

freak
[fri:k]

n. 괴짜, 괴물; a. 아주 기이한; v. 기겁을 하다
If you refer to someone as a freak, you mean that they are physically abnormal in some way.

engagement[*]
[ingéidʒmənt]

n. 약혼; (업무상·공적인) 약속
An engagement is an agreement that two people have made with each other to get married.

get over

idiom ~을 극복하다
If you get over something, you deal with or gain control of it.

go out with

idiom ~와 데이트를 하다, 사귀다
If you go out with someone, you spend time with them and have a romantic or sexual relationship with them.

bitter^{**}
[bítər]

a. 쓰라린, 비통한; 격렬한
If someone is bitter after a disappointing experience or after being treated unfairly, they continue to feel angry about it.

rotten[*]
[ratn]

a. 형편없는, 끔찍한; 썩은, 부패한
If you feel rotten, you feel bad, either because you are ill or because you are sorry about something.

112

substitute ^{복습}
[sʌ́bstətjùːt]

n. 대신하는 사람; 대체물; v. 대신하다, 교체되다
(substitute teacher n. 대체 교사)

A substitute teacher is a teacher whose job is to take the place of other teachers at different schools when they are unable to be there.

Check Your Reading Speed

1분에 몇 단어를 읽는지 리딩 속도를 측정해 보세요.

$$\frac{1,038 \text{ words}}{\text{reading time ( ) sec}} \times 60 = (\quad) \text{ WPM}$$

Build Your Vocabulary

story복습
[stɔ́:ri]

① n. (= storey) (건물의) 층 ② n. 이야기, 소설; 설명
A story of a building is one of its different levels, which is situated above or below other levels.

chipper복습
[ʧípər]

a. 기운찬, 쾌활한; v. 기운을 내다
Chipper means cheerful and lively.

glum
[glʌm]

a. 침울한
Someone who is glum is sad and quiet because they are disappointed or unhappy about something.

blah
[blɑ:]

a. 기분이 좀 안 좋은; 재미없는; n. 어쩌고저쩌고
Someone who is blah is without energy or enthusiasm.

spill복습
[spil]

v. 흘리다, 쏟다; n. 유출; 흘린 액체
If a liquid spills or if you spill it, it accidentally flows over the edge of a container.

lap복습
[læp]

n. 무릎; (경주에서 트랙의) 한 바퀴
If you have something on your lap when you are sitting down, it is on top of your legs and near to your body.

sensitive**
[sénsətiv]

a. 예민한, 민감한; 세심한; 감성 있는
If you are sensitive about something, you are easily worried and offended when people talk about it.

compare**
[kəmpéər]

v. 비교하다; 비유하다
When you compare things, you consider them and discover the differences or similarities between them.

loser*
[lú:zər]

n. 실패자; (경쟁에서) 패자
If you refer to someone as a loser, you have a low opinion of them because you think they are always unsuccessful.

itch*
[iʧ]

n. 가려움, 근지러움; v. 가렵다; (몹시 ~하고 싶어 몸이) 근질거리다
An itch is an uncomfortable or unpleasant feeling on your skin or body that makes you want to scratch.

stuff복습
[stʌf]

n. 것(들), 물건, 물질; v. (빽빽히) 채워 넣다; (재빨리) 쑤셔 넣다
You can use stuff to refer to things such as a substance, a collection of things, events, or ideas, or the contents of something in a general way without mentioning the thing itself by name.

horseback riding
[hɔ́:rsbæk raidiŋ]

n. 승마
Horseback riding is the activity of riding a horse, especially for enjoyment or as a form of exercise.

clap[*]
[klæp]

v. 박수를 치다, 손뼉을 치다; n. 박수
When you clap, you hit your hands together to show appreciation or attract attention.

work on

idiom ~에 노력을 들이다, 착수하다
If you work on something, you are busy with a particular activity, project, or a piece of research.

mouth[***]
[mauθ]

v. 입 모양으로만 말하다; n. 입; 입구
If you mouth something, you form words with your lips without making any sound.

embarrass[복습]
[imbǽrəs]

v. 당황스럽게 하다; 곤란하게 하다 (embarrassed a. 당황스러운)
A person who is embarrassed feels shy, ashamed, or guilty about something.

adorable
[ədɔ́:rəbl]

a. 사랑스러운
If you say that someone or something is adorable, you are emphasizing that they are very attractive and you feel great affection for them.

mutter[복습]
[mʌ́tər]

v. 중얼거리다; 투덜거리다; n. 중얼거림
If you mutter, you speak very quietly so that you cannot easily be heard, often because you are complaining about something.

bury[복습]
[béri]

v. (보이지 않게) 묻다; (감정·실수 등을) 감추다
If you bury your head or face in something, you press your head or face against it, often because you are unhappy.

call on[복습]

idiom (이름을 불러서) 학생에게 시키다; (사람을) 방문하다
If a teacher calls on students in a class, he or she asks them to answer a question or give their opinion.

out of nowhere

idiom 난데없이; 어딘선지 모르게
If you say that something or someone appears from nowhere or out of nowhere, you mean that they appear suddenly and unexpectedly.

steady[복습]
[stédi]

v. 진정시키다, 가라앉히다; 균형을 잡다; a. 꾸준한; 안정된
If you steady yourself, you control your voice or expression, so that people will think that you are calm and not nervous.

muscle[**]
[mʌsl]

n. 근육
A muscle is a piece of tissue inside your body which connects two bones and which you use when you make a movement.

tighten[*]
[taitn]

v. (더) 팽팽해지다; 조여지다; 더 엄격하게 하다
If a part of your body tightens, the muscles in it become tense and stiff, for example because you are angry or afraid.

concentrate[**]
[kánsəntrèit]

v. (정신을) 집중하다, 전념하다; n. 농축물
If you concentrate on something, you give all your attention to it.

beg^{복습}
[beg]

v. 간청하다, 애원하다; 구걸하다
If you beg someone to do something, you ask them very anxiously or eagerly to do it.

pardon^{★★}
[pɑ:rdn]

int. 뭐라구요; 미안해요; n. 용서; v. ~를 용서하다
(I beg your pardon idiom 뭐라고요, 다시 한번 말씀해 주세요)
You say 'I beg your pardon?' when you want someone to repeat what they have just said because you have not heard or understood it.

sigh^{복습}
[sai]

v. 한숨을 쉬다, 한숨짓다; n. 한숨 (소리)
When you sigh, you let out a deep breath, as a way of expressing feelings such as disappointment, tiredness, or pleasure.

distract[★]
[distrǽkt]

v. (주의를) 딴 데로 돌리다, 집중이 안 되게 하다 (distracted a. (정신이) 산만해진)
If you are distracted, you are not concentrating on something because you are worried or are thinking about something else.

press^{복습}
[pres]

v. (~에 대고) 누르다; (버튼 등을) 누르다; n. 언론; 누르기
If you press something somewhere, you push it firmly against something else.

ashamed^{★★}
[əʃéimd]

a. (~여서) 부끄러운, 창피한
If someone is ashamed, they feel embarrassed or guilty because of something they do or they have done, or because of their appearance.

exceptional[★]
[iksépʃənl]

a. 이례적일 정도로 우수한, 특출한
You use exceptional to describe someone or something that has a particular quality, usually a good quality, to an unusually high degree.

stink^{복습}
[stiŋk]

v. (고약한) 냄새가 나다; 아무 쓸모없다; n. 악취
To stink means to smell extremely unpleasant.

accidental^{복습}
[æksədéntl]

a. 우연한, 돌발적인 (accidentally ad. 우연히, 뜻하지 않게)
An accidental event happens by chance or as the result of an accident, and is not deliberately intended.

on purpose

idiom 고의로, 일부러
(accidentally-on-purpose idiom 우연을 가장하여 고의로)
If you do something on purpose, you do it intentionally.

miserable[★]
[mízərəbl]

a. 비참한; 우울하게 만드는; 성질 나쁜
If you are miserable, you are very unhappy.

hum[★]
[hʌm]

v. 콧노래를 부르다, (노래를) 흥얼거리다; 웅웅거리다; n. 웅웅거리는 소리
When you hum a tune, you sing it with your lips closed.

scratch^{복습}
[skrætʃ]

v. (가려운 데를) 긁다; 할퀴다; n. 긁힌 자국
If you scratch yourself, you rub your fingernails against your skin because it is itching.

nephew[★]
[néfju:]

n. 조카 (아들)
Someone's nephew is the son of their sister or brother.

thunder[★]
[θʌ́ndər]

v. 천둥이 치다; 우르릉거리다; n. 천둥
When it thunders, a loud noise comes from the sky after a flash of lightning.

116

lightning*
[láitniŋ]

n. 번개; a. 번개같이, 아주 빨리
Lightning is the very bright flashes of light in the sky that happen during thunderstorms.

spook
[spuːk]

v. (사람·동물을) 겁먹게 하다; n. 유령, 귀신
If people are spooked, something has scared them or made them nervous.

terrible^{복습}
[térəbl]

a. (나쁜 정도가) 극심한; 끔찍한, 소름끼치는; 심한 (terribly ad. 몹시, 극심하게)
You use terrible to emphasize the great extent or degree of something.

cast***
[kæst]

n. 깁스 (붕대); v. (시선·미소 등을) 던지다; (그림자를) 드리우다
A cast is the same as a plaster cast which is used to protect a broken bone by keeping part of the body stiff.

positive**
[pázətiv]

a. 긍정적인; 확신하는
If you are positive about things, you are hopeful and confident, and think of the good aspects of a situation rather than the bad ones.

attitude**
[ǽtitjuːd]

n. 태도, 자세; 반항적인 태도
Your attitude to something is the way that you think and feel about it, especially when this shows in the way you behave.

frown^{복습}
[fraun]

v. 얼굴을 찌푸리다; n. 찡그림, 찌푸림
When someone frowns, their eyebrows become drawn together, because they are annoyed or puzzled.

rub^{복습}
[rʌb]

v. (손·손수건 등을 대고) 문지르다; (표면이) 쓸리다; n. 문지르기, 비비기
If you rub a part of your body, you move your hand or fingers backward and forward over it while pressing firmly.

mustache^{복습}
[mʌ́stæʃ]

n. 콧수염
A man's mustache is the hair that grows on his upper lip.

raw**
[rɔː]

a. 피부가 벗겨져 쓰라린; 익히지 않은; 가공되지 않은
If a part of your body is raw, it is red and painful, perhaps because the skin has come off or has been burnt.

shrug^{복습}
[ʃrʌg]

v. (두 손바닥을 위로 하고) 어깨를 으쓱하다; n. 어깨를 으쓱하기
If you shrug, you raise your shoulders to show that you are not interested in something or that you do not know or care about something.

Chapters 25 & 26

1. What was Maurecia guilty of doing?
   A. Pulling Leslie's pigtails
   B. Writing her name in the dictionary
   C. Stealing a dictionary from class
   D. Tearing a page in the dictionary

2. Why did Maurecia have to read the dictionary page aloud to the class?
   A. Each student had to read a page in front of class.
   B. Nobody would ever be able to use that page again.
   C. The class was having a spelling test choosing random words.
   D. Maurecia was helping her class get inspiration for poetry.

3. How did Maurecia think that Miss Nogard knew about the torn page?
   A. She thought that someone in class had seen her and told.
   B. She thought that Miss Nogard could read her secret thoughts.
   C. She thought that Miss Nogard was looking up how to spell 'journey' earlier.
   D. She thought that Mrs. Jewls had told Miss Nogard about the accident.

4. How did Mac feel about show-and-tell?

   A. He felt that it was his favorite subject.

   B. He hated being in front of the class.

   C. He only liked it when others did the showing and telling.

   D. He thought that it was silly and only for younger children.

5. Why was Mac holding a shoelace in front of class?

   A. He wanted someone to show him how to tie his laces.

   B. He was showing the students how to tie special knots.

   C. He wanted someone to help him spell 'shoelace' on the blackboard.

   D. He volunteered for show-and-tell before he realized he hadn't brought anything.

6. How were the students changing after Miss Nogard took over?

   A. They were getting grumpier and grumpier.

   B. They were getting healthier and healthier.

   C. They were studying harder and harder.

   D. They were getting more interested in what others had to say.

7. How did Mac make the shoelace more interesting?

   A. He put it back on his shoe.

   B. He told a story about shoelace.

   C. He tied it in a bow.

   D. He threw it out the window.

Check Your Reading Speed

1분에 몇 단어를 읽는지 리딩 속도를 측정해 보세요.

$$\frac{737 \text{ words}}{\text{reading time ( ) sec}} \times 60 = (\quad) \text{ WPM}$$

Build Your Vocabulary

workbook
[wə́:rkbùk]

n. 연습 문제집
A workbook is a book to help you learn a particular subject which has questions in it with spaces for the answers.

reader*
[rí:dər]

n. (읽기 능력 향상을 돕도록 쉽게 만든) 읽기 교재; 읽는 사람
A reader is a book to help children to learn to read, or to help people to learn a foreign language.

compute*
[kəmpjú:t]

v. 계산하다, 산출하다
To compute a quantity or number means to calculate it.

stamp**
[stæmp]

v. (도장·스탬프 등을) 찍다; (발을) 구르다; n. 우표; 도장
If you stamp a mark or word on an object, you press the mark or word onto the object using a stamp or other device.

cheerful***
[ʧíərfəl]

a. 발랄한, 쾌활한 (cheerfully ad. 기분 좋게, 쾌활하게)
Someone who is cheerful is happy and shows this in their behavior.

patient복습
[péiʃənt]

a. 인내심 있는; n. 환자 (patiently ad. 끈기 있게, 참을성 있게)
If you are patient, you stay calm and do not get annoyed, for example when something takes a long time, or when someone is not doing what you want them to do.

guilty**
[gílti]

a. (잘못된 일에 대해) 책임이 있는; 죄책감이 드는
If someone is guilty of doing something wrong, they have done that thing.

dictionary복습
[díkʃənèri]

n. 사전
A dictionary is a book in which the words and phrases of a language are listed alphabetically, together with their meanings or their translations in another language.

tear복습
[tɛər]

① v. (tore-torn) 찢다, 뜯다; 구멍을 뚫다; n. 찢어진 곳, 구멍 ② n. 눈물
If you tear paper, cloth, or another material, or if it tears, you pull it into two pieces or you pull it so that a hole appears in it.

journey**
[dʒə́:rni]

n. 여행, 여정
When you make a journey, you travel from one place to another.

journal*
[dʒə́:rnl]

n. 일기; 신문, 학술지
A journal is an account which you write of your daily activities.

rip복습
[rip]

v. (갑자기·거칠게) 찢다; 떼어 내다; n. (길게) 찢어진 곳
When something rips or when you rip it, you tear it forcefully with your hands or with a tool such as a knife.

nod^{복습}
[nad]

v. (고개를) 끄덕이다; n. (고개를) 끄덕임
If you nod, you move your head downward and upward to show that you are answering 'yes' to a question, or to show agreement, understanding, or approval.

figure out^{복습}

idiom (생각한 끝에) ~을 이해하다; (양·비용을) 계산하다
If you figure out someone or something, you come to understand them by thinking carefully.

no way^{복습}

idiom 절대로 안 되다; (강한 거절의 의미로) 절대로 안 돼, 싫어
If you say there's no way that something will happen, you are emphasizing that you think it will definitely not happen.

innocent[*]
[ínəsənt]

a. 악의 없는; 아무 잘못이 없는, 무죄인, 결백한; 순결한, 순진한
(innocently ad. 천진난만하게)
An innocent question, remark, or comment is not intended to offend or upset people, even if it does so.

crash^{**}
[kræʃ]

v. 부딪치다, 박살나다; 충돌하다; n. (자동차·항공기) 사고; 요란한 소리
If something crashes somewhere, it moves and hits something else violently, making a loud noise.

numb[*]
[nʌm]

a. 멍한; (신체 부위가) 감각이 없는; v. (신체 부위에) 감각이 없게 만들다
(numbly ad. 멍하게)
If you are numb with shock, fear, or grief, you are so shocked, frightened, or upset that you cannot think clearly or feel any emotion.

flip through^{복습}

idiom (책장을) 휙휙 넘기다
If you flip through something such as the pages of a book or a pile of papers, you turn over it quickly, or look through it without reading everything.

take it^{복습}

idiom (비난·고통 등을) 견디다, 참다; 이해하다
If you say that you can take it, you mean that you are able to bear or tolerate something difficult or unpleasant such as stress, criticism or pain.

vandalize
[vǽndəlàiz]

v. 공공 기물을 파손하다
If something such as a building or part of a building is vandalized by someone, it is damaged on purpose.

horrible^{복습}
[hɔ́:rəbl]

a. 지긋지긋한, 끔찍한; 소름끼치는; 불쾌한
If you describe something or someone as horrible, you do not like them at all.

belong^{복습}
[bilɔ́:ŋ]

v. ~에 속하다, ~의 소유물이다; 제자리에 있다; 소속감을 느끼다
If something belongs to you, you own it.

struggle^{복습}
[strʌgl]

v. 힘겹게 나아가다; 투쟁하다, 몸부림치다; n. 투쟁, 분투; 몸부림
If you struggle to do something, you try hard to do it, even though other people or things may be making it difficult for you to succeed.

journalism^{**}
[dʒɔ́:rnəlìzm]

n. 저널리즘, 언론계
Journalism is the job of collecting news and writing about it for newspapers, magazines, television, or radio.

judicious
[dʒuːdíʃəs]

a. 신중한, 판단력 있는
If you describe an action or decision as judicious, you approve of it because you think that it shows good judgment and sense.

speak up

idiom 더 크게 말하다
If you tell someone to speak up, you ask them to speak louder.

pay attention

idiom 관심을 갖다
If you pay attention to someone, you watch them, listen to them, or take notice of them.

complain^{복습}
[kəmpléin]

v. 불평하다, 항의하다
If you complain about a situation, you say that you are not satisfied with it.

punish***
[pʌ́niʃ]

v. 처벌하다, 벌주다; (특정한 형벌·형에) 처하다
To punish someone means to make them suffer in some way because they have done something wrong.

memorize*
[méməràiz]

v. 암기하다
If you memorize something, you learn it so that you can remember it exactly.

gripe
[graip]

v. 불평하다, 투덜거리다; n. 불만, 불평
If you say that someone is griping, you mean they are annoying you because they keep on complaining about something.

tattle
[tætl]

v. 고자질하다
To tattle means to tell a parent or a teacher about something bad or wrong that another child has done.

no-good
[nóu-gud]

a. (사람이) 못된; 쓸모 없는
If you describe someone as no-good, you feel strong dislike and disrespect for them.

double-cross
[dʌbl-krɔ́ːs]

v. 배반하다, 배신하다
If someone you trust double-crosses you, they do something which harms you instead of doing something they had promised to do.

122

Check Your Reading Speed

1분에 몇 단어를 읽는지 리딩 속도를 측정해 보세요.

$$\frac{765 \text{ words}}{\text{reading time (} \quad \text{) sec}} \times 60 = (\quad) \text{ WPM}$$

Build Your Vocabulary

shoelace
[ʃúːleis]

n. 신발끈
Shoelaces are long, narrow pieces of material like pieces of string that you use to fasten your shoes.

fool^{복습}
[fuːl]

n. 바보; v. 속이다, 기만하다
If you call someone a fool, you are indicating that you think they are not at all sensible and show a lack of good judgment.

subject**
[sʌ́bdʒikt]

n. 학과, 과목; (논의 등의) 주제
A subject is an area of knowledge or study, especially one that you study at school, college, or university.

garbage*
[gáːrbidʒ]

n. 쓰레기; 쓰레기장 (garbage can n. 쓰레기통)
A garbage can is a container that you put rubbish into.

gushy
[gʌ́ʃi]

a. 지나치게 감상적인; 쏟아져 나오는
If you describe something as gushy, you mean that it is displaying excessive admiration or sentimentality.

slime
[slaim]

n. (더럽고) 끈적끈적한 물질, 점액
Slime is a thick, wet substance which covers a surface or comes from the bodies of animals such as snails.

groan^{복습}
[groun]

v. 신음 소리를 내다; 끙끙거리다; n. 신음, 끙 하는 소리
If you groan something, you say it in a low, unhappy voice.

end up

idiom 결국 (어떤 처지에) 처하게 되다
If you end up doing something or end up in a particular state, you reach or come to a particular place or situation that you did not expect or intend to be in.

dangle
[dǽŋgl]

v. (달랑) 매달리다; (무엇을) 매달리게 들다
If something dangles from somewhere or if you dangle it somewhere, it hangs or swings loosely.

worm^{복습}
[wəːrm]

n. 벌레; v. 꿈틀거리며 나아가다
A worm is a small animal with a long thin body, no bones and no legs.

sneaker^{복습}
[sníːkər]

n. (pl.) 고무창을 댄 운동화
Sneakers are casual shoes with rubber soles.

bow*
[bou]

① n. (리본 등의) 나비매듭; 활 ② v. (허리를 굽혀) 절하다; (고개를) 숙이다
A bow is a knot with two loops and two loose ends that is used in tying shoelaces and ribbons.

boo
[buː]

v. (우우하고) 야유하다; n. 야유 (소리)
If you boo a speaker or performer, you shout 'boo' or make other loud sounds to indicate that you do not like them, their opinions, or their performance.

grumpy
[grʌ́mpi]

a. 성격이 나쁜
If you say that someone is grumpy, you mean that they are bad-tempered and miserable.

take over

idiom (~로부터) (~을) 인계받다, (기업 등을) 인수하다
If you take over something, you take responsibility for it after someone else has finished or you do it instead of them.

stink^{복습}
[stiŋk]

v. (고약한) 냄새가 나다; 아무 쓸모없다; n. 악취
To stink means to smell extremely unpleasant.

invent^{복습}
[invént]

v. 발명하다; (사실이 아닌 것을) 지어내다
If you invent something such as a machine or process, you are the first person to think of it or make it.

race
[reis]

v. 경주하다, 경쟁하다; 급히 가다; n. 경주; 인종, 종족
If you race, you take part in a race.

impress^{복습}
[imprés]

v. 깊은 인상을 주다, 감동을 주다; (마음·기억 등에) 강하게 남다
(impressed a. 인상 깊게 생각하는)
If something impresses you, you feel great admiration for it.

shrug^{복습}
[ʃrʌg]

v. (두 손바닥을 위로 하고) 어깨를 으쓱하다; n. 어깨를 으쓱하기
If you shrug, you raise your shoulders to show that you are not interested in something or that you do not know or care about something.

stub
[stʌb]

v. (~에) 발가락이 차이다
If you stub your toe, you hurt it by accidentally kicking something.

blister^{복습}
[blístər]

n. 물집, 수포; v. 물집이 생기다
A blister is a painful swelling on the surface of your skin. Blisters contain a clear liquid and are usually caused by heat or by something repeatedly rubbing your skin.

bleed*
[bliːd]

v. 피를 흘리다, 출혈하다 (bleeding a. 피투성이의)
When you bleed, you lose blood from your body as a result of injury or illness.

pus
[pʌs]

n. 고름
Pus is a thick yellowish liquid that forms in wounds when they are infected.

ooze
[uːz]

v. (걸쭉한 액체가) 흐르다; (특징·자질 등을) 발산하다; n. (액체가) 스며 나오는 것
When a thick or sticky liquid oozes from something or when something oozes it, the liquid flows slowly and in small quantities.

gross^{복습}
[grous]

a. 역겨운; 아주 무례한
If you describe something as gross, you think it is very unpleasant.

wide-eyed
[wáid-aid]

a. 눈을 크게 뜬, 깜짝 놀란
If you describe someone as wide-eyed, you mean that they are having their eyes wide open as a result of surprise or fear.

pay attention^{복습}

idiom 관심을 갖다
If you pay attention to someone, you watch them, listen to them, or take notice of them.

trail*
[treil]

n. 자국, 흔적; 시골길, 산길; v. 뒤쫓다, 추적하다; 끌다
A trail is a series of marks or other signs of movement or other activities left by someone or something.

bloody*
[blʌ́di]

a. 피투성이의
You can describe someone or something as bloody if they are covered in a lot of blood.

footprint
[fútprìnt]

n. 발자국
A footprint is a mark in the shape of a foot that a person or animal makes in or on a surface.

nail**
[neil]

v. 못으로 박다; n. 못
If you nail something somewhere, you fix it there using one or more nails.

exclaim^{복습}
[ikskléim]

v. 소리치다, 외치다
If you exclaim, you cry out suddenly in surprise, strong emotion, or pain.

glue^{복습}
[glu:]

v. (접착제로) 붙이다; n. 접착제
If you glue one object to another, you stick them together using glue.

peel*
[pi:l]

v. 벗겨지다; (과일·채소 등의) 껍질을 벗기다; n. (과일·채소의 두꺼운) 껍질
If you peel off something that has been sticking to a surface or if it peels off, it comes away from the surface.

layer*
[léiər]

n. 막, 층, 겹; v. 층층이 쌓다
A layer of a material or substance is a quantity or piece of it that covers a surface or that is between two other things.

shriek*
[ʃri:k]

v. 꽥 소리를 지르다; (날카롭게) 비명을 지르다; n. 비명
If you shriek something, you shout it in a loud, high-pitched voice.

championship*

n. 선수권, 챔피언 지위; (pl.) 선수권 대회
The championship refers to the title or status of being a sports champion.

get off

idiom 떠나다, 출발하다
If you get off, you leave a place or start a journey.

trip^{복습}
[trip]

v. 발을 헛디디다; n. 여행
If you trip when you are walking, you knock your foot against something and fall or nearly fall.

applaud*
[əplɔ́:d]

v. 박수를 치다; 갈채를 보내다
When a group of people applaud, they clap their hands in order to show approval, for example when they have enjoyed a play or concert.

1. Which of the following was NOT true about the game that the Erics were playing?

   A. It was called way-high-up ball.

   B. They had invented it themselves.

   C. You only got points for throwing the ball.

   D. It wasn't allowed after the Erics broke a window.

2. What did Louis ask the Erics to do?

   A. He asked if he could play.

   B. He asked them to stop playing it.

   C. He asked them to go get Miss Nogard.

   D. He asked them to let other children play with them.

3. Why did the children want to see Louis throw the ball?

   A. They wanted Louis to distract Miss Nogard.

   B. They wanted to see an adult play a game for children.

   C. They wanted to see Louis break a window.

   D. They wanted to see how high he could throw it.

4. What did the children try to get Louis to do about Miss Nogard?

   A. They wanted him to take her out on a date.

   B. They wanted him to make Miss Nogard be nicer to them.

   C. They wanted him to help them get rid of Miss Nogard.

   D. They wanted him to invite her to play way-high-up ball.

5. How did Miss Nogard know all about Louis?

   A. She was just listening to the children's thoughts.

   B. She was just listening to what the children told her.

   C. She was listening to the children's thoughts and what they told her.

   D. She was listening to Louis's thoughts and what he told her.

6. What had Miss Nogard become an expert at doing ever since Xavier?

   A. She had become an expert at reading minds.

   B. She had become an expert at breaking hearts.

   C. She had become an expert at making children happy.

   D. She had become an expert at teaching children.

7. How did Mr. Kidswatter feel about Louis?

   A. He felt that Louis was like a son to him.

   B. He felt that Louis was his best friend.

   C. He felt that Louis was like a brother to him.

   D. He felt that Louis was a weird teacher.

Check Your Reading Speed

1분에 몇 단어를 읽는지 리딩 속도를 측정해 보세요.

$$\frac{981 \text{ words}}{\text{reading time ( ) sec}} \times 60 = (\quad) \text{ WPM}$$

Build Your Vocabulary

way***
[wei]

ad. 아주 멀리; 큰 차이로, 훨씬; n. 방법, 방식; (어떤 곳에 이르는) 길
You can use way to emphasize, for example, that something is a great distance away or is very much below or above a particular level or amount.

make up^{복습}

idiom (이야기 등을) 만들어 내다; (~와) 화해하다
If you make up something, you invent it, often in order to trick someone.

rubber**
[rʌ́bər]

n. 고무
Rubber is a strong, waterproof, elastic substance made from the juice of a tropical tree or produced chemically.

bounce^{복습}
[bauns]

v. 튀다; 튀기다; n. 튐, 튀어 오름
When an object such as a ball bounces or when you bounce it, it moves upward from a surface or away from it immediately after hitting it.

story^{복습}
[stɔ́:ri]

① n. (= storey) (건물의) 층 ② n. 이야기, 소설; 설명
A story of a building is one of its levels, which is situated above or below other levels.

shove*
[ʃʌv]

v. (거칠게) 떠밀다; 아무렇게나 놓다; n. 힘껏 밀침
If you shove someone or something, you push them with a quick, violent movement.

elbow**
[élbou]

v. (팔꿈치로) 밀치다; n. 팔꿈치
If you elbow people aside or elbow your way somewhere, you push people with your elbows in order to move somewhere.

fingertip
[fíŋgərtip]

n. 손가락 끝
Your fingertips are the ends of your fingers.

stick out^{복습}

idiom ~을 내밀다, 튀어나오게 하다
If something is sticking out from a surface or object, it extends up or away from it.

whistle^{복습}
[hwisl]

v. 휘파람을 불다; 호루라기를 불다; n. 휘파람 (소리); 호각, 호루라기
When someone whistles, they make a sound by forcing their breath out between their lips or their teeth.

bang*
[bæŋ]

v. 쾅 하고 치다; 쾅 하고 닫다; 쿵 하고 찧다; n. 쾅 (하는 소리)
If you bang on something or if you bang it, you hit it hard, making a loud noise.

stare^{복습}
[stɛər]

v. 빤히 쳐다보다, 응시하다; n. 빤히 쳐다보기, 응시
If you stare at someone or something, you look at them for a long time.

hairy^{복습}
[héəri]

a. 털이 많은, 털투성이의
Someone or something that is hairy is covered with hairs.

belong^{복습}
[bilɔ́:ŋ]

v. ~에 속하다, ~의 소유물이다; 제자리에 있다; 소속감을 느끼다
You say that something belongs to a particular person when you are guessing, discovering, or explaining that it was produced by or is part of that person.

yard^{복습}
[ja:rd]

n. (학교의) 운동장; 마당, 뜰; 정원
A yard is a flat area of concrete or stone that is next to a building and often has a wall around it.

grip**
[grip]

v. 꽉 잡다, 움켜잡다; n. 꽉 붙잡음; 통제, 지배
If you grip something, you take hold of it with your hand and continue to hold it firmly.

soar*
[sɔ:r]

v. (허공으로) 솟구치다; 급증하다
If something such as a bird soars into the air, it goes quickly up into the air.

rebound
[ribáund]

n. (공이) 다시 튀어나옴; v. (공 등이) 다시 튀어나오다
In basketball, a rebound is a shot which someone catches after it has hit the board behind the basket.

playground^{복습}
[pléigràund]

n. (학교의) 운동장; 놀이터
A playground is a piece of land, at school or in a public area, where children can play.

scramble*
[skrǽmbl]

n. 쟁탈전을 벌이기; (힘들게) 기어가기; v. 재빨리 움직이다; 서로 밀치다
A scramble is the act of moving or acting quickly to do, find, or get something.

come up with

idiom (해답·돈 등을) 찾아내다
If you come up with something, you find or produce something that someone needs.

urge^{복습}
[ə:rdʒ]

v. (~하도록) 충고하다, 설득하려 하다; n. (강한) 욕구, 충동
If you urge someone to do something, you try hard to persuade them to do it.

sly*
[slai]

a. 다 알고 있다는 듯한; 교활한, 음흉한 (slyly ad. 다 알고 있다는 듯이)
A sly look, expression, or remark shows that you know something that other people do not know or that was meant to be a secret.

glance*
[glæns]

v. 흘깃 보다; 대충 훑어보다; n. 흘깃 봄
If you glance at something or someone, you look at them very quickly and then look away again immediately.

hurl*
[hə:rl]

v. (거칠게) 던지다; 비난을 퍼붓다
If you hurl something, you throw it violently and with a lot of force.

might*
[mait]

n. (강력한) 힘, 권력; 세력
Might is power or strength.

halfway*
[hǽfwèi]

ad. (거리·시간상으로) 중간에, 가운데쯤에
Halfway means in the middle of a place or between two points, at an equal distance from each of them.

wobble
[wabl]

v. (불안정하게) 흔들리다; 뒤뚱거리며 가다; n. 흔들림, 떨림
If something or someone wobbles, they make small movements from side to side, for example because they are unsteady.

flow***
[flou]

v. (액체·기체·전류가) 흐르다; 술술 나오다; 넘쳐나다; n. 흐름
If a liquid, gas, or electrical current flows somewhere, it moves there steadily and continuously.

nudge
[nʌdʒ]

v. (팔꿈치로 살짝) 쿡 찌르다; 살살 밀다; n. (살짝) 쿡 찌르기
If you nudge someone, you push them gently, usually with your elbow, in order to draw their attention to something.

giggle^{복습}
[gigl]

v. 피식 웃다, 킥킥거리다; n. 피식 웃음, 킥킥거림
If someone giggles, they laugh in a childlike way, because they are amused, nervous, or embarrassed.

ask out

idiom ~에게 데이트를 신청하다
If you ask someone out, you invite them to go out with you, especially when you would like a romantic relationship with them.

gushy^{복습}
[gʌ́ʃi]

a. 지나치게 감상적인; 쏟아져 나오는
If you describe something as gushy, you mean that it is displaying excessive admiration or sentimentality.

stuff^{복습}
[stʌf]

n. 것(들), 물건, 물질; v. (빽빽히) 채워 넣다; (재빨리) 쑤셔 넣다
You can use stuff to refer to things such as a substance, a collection of things, events, or ideas, or the contents of something in a general way without mentioning the thing itself by name.

scary^{복습}
[skéəri]

a. 무서운, 겁나는
Something that is scary is rather frightening.

scare^{복습}
[skɛər]

v. 겁주다, 놀라게 하다 (scared a. 무서워하는, 겁먹은)
If you are scared of someone or something, you are frightened of them.

Check Your Reading Speed

1분에 몇 단어를 읽는지 리딩 속도를 측정해 보세요.

$$\frac{659 \text{ words}}{\text{reading time ( ) sec}} \times 60 = (\quad) \text{ WPM}$$

Build Your Vocabulary

buzz* [bʌz]
v. 웅성대다; 부산스럽다; 윙윙거리다; n. 윙윙거리는 소리
If your head is buzzing with questions or ideas, you are thinking about a lot of things, often in a confused way.

yard^{복습} [jaːrd]
n. (학교의) 운동장; 마당, 뜰; 정원
A yard is a flat area of concrete or stone that is next to a building and often has a wall around it.

mustache^{복습} [mʌ́stæʃ]
n. 콧수염
A man's mustache is the hair that grows on his upper lip.

tickle* [tikl]
v. 간질이다; (손가락으로) 간지럼을 태우다; n. 간지럽히기; 간지러움
If something tickles you or tickles, it causes an irritating feeling by lightly touching a part of your body.

gasp^{복습} [gæsp]
v. 숨이 턱 막히다, 헉 하고 숨을 쉬다; n. (숨이 막히는 듯) 헉 하는 소리를 냄
When you gasp, you take a short quick breath through your mouth, especially when you are surprised, shocked, or in pain.

expert* [ékspəːrt]
n. 전문가; a. 전문가의, 전문적인; 숙련된
An expert is a person who is very skilled at doing something or who knows a lot about a particular subject.

shatter* [ʃǽtər]
v. 산산조각 내다; 산산이 부서지다; 엄청난 충격을 주다
If something shatters your dreams, hopes, or beliefs, it completely destroys them.

incapable* [inkéipəbl]
a. ~을 할 수 없는, ~하지 못하는; 무능한
Someone who is incapable of doing something is unable to do it.

clog [klag]
v. 막다; 막히다
When something clogs a hole or place, it blocks it so that nothing can pass through.

bitter^{복습} [bítər]
a. 쓰라린, 비통한; 격렬한 (bitterness n. 신랄함; 비통함)
If someone is bitter after a disappointing experience or after being treated unfairly, they continue to feel angry about it.

besides^{복습} [bisáidz]
ad. 게다가, 뿐만 아니라; prep. ~외에
Besides is used to emphasize an additional point that you are making, especially one that you consider to be important.

pang [pæŋ]
n. 마음의 고통, 비통; (육체상의) 격통
A pang is a sudden strong feeling or emotion, for example of sadness or pain.

puppy[*]
[pʌ́pi]

n. 강아지
A puppy is a young dog.

recess[복습]
[risés]

n. (학교의) 쉬는 시간; (의회·위원회 등의) 휴회 기간; v. 휴회하다, 쉬다
A recess is a break between classes at a school.

kickball
[kíkbɔːl]

n. 발야구
Kickball is an informal game combining elements of baseball and soccer, in which a soccer ball is thrown to a person who kicks it and proceeds to run the bases.

weird[복습]
[wiərd]

a. 기이한, 기묘한; 기괴한, 섬뜩한
If you describe something or someone as weird, you mean that they are strange.

terrible[복습]
[térəbl]

a. (나쁜 정도가) 극심한; 끔찍한, 소름끼치는; 심한 (terribly ad. 몹시, 극심하게)
You use terrible to emphasize the great extent or degree of something.

bounce[복습]
[bauns]

v. 튀다; 튀기다; n. 튐, 튀어 오름
When an object such as a ball bounces or when you bounce it, it moves upward from a surface or away from it immediately after hitting it.

disease[**]
[dizíːz]

n. 질병, 병, 질환
A disease is an illness which affects people, animals, or plants, for example one which is caused by bacteria or infection.

spell[복습]
[spel]

v. (어떤 단어의) 철자를 말하다; 철자를 맞게 쓰다, 맞춤법에 맞게 글을 쓰다
When you spell a word, you write or speak each letter in the word in the correct order.

bunch[복습]
[bʌnʧ]

n. 다발, 송이; (양·수가) 많음
A bunch of flowers is a number of flowers with their stalks held or tied together.

field[복습]
[fiːld]

n. 들판, 밭; (도서관·실험실 등이 아닌) 현장
A field is an area of grass, for example in a park or on a farm.

wildflower
[wáildflàuər]

n. 들꽃, 야생초
Wildflowers are flowers which grow naturally in the countryside, rather than being grown by people in gardens.

wink[복습]
[wiŋk]

v. 윙크하다; (빛이) 깜박거리다; a. 윙크
When you wink at someone, you look toward them and close one eye very briefly, usually as a signal that something is a joke or a secret.

vase[복습]
[veis]

n. 꽃병
A vase is a jar, usually made of glass or pottery, used for holding cut flowers or as an ornament.

freeze[복습]
[friːz]

v. (froze-frozen) (두려움 등으로 몸이) 얼어붙다; 얼다; 얼리다; n. 동결; 한파
If someone who is moving freezes, they suddenly stop and become completely still and quiet.

132

rattle^{복습}
[rǽtl]

v. 덜거덕거리다; 당황하게 하다; n. 덜커덕거리는 소리
When something rattles or when you rattle it, it makes short sharp knocking sounds because it is being shaken or it keeps hitting against something hard.

shaky
[ʃéiki]

a. 떨리는, 휘청거리는; 불안한; 불안정한
If your body or your voice is shaky, you cannot control it properly and it shakes, for example because you are ill or nervous.

petal
[pétəl]

n. 꽃잎
The petals of a flower are the thin colored or white parts which together form the flower.

thrust[*]
[θrʌst]

v. (거칠게) 밀다; 찌르다; n. 찌르기; 추진력
If you thrust something or someone somewhere, you push or move them there quickly with a lot of force.

infest
[infést]

v. (곤충·쥐 등이) 들끓다, 우글거리다
When creatures such as insects or rats infest plants or a place, they are present in large numbers and cause damage.

mutter^{복습}
[mʌ́tər]

v. 중얼거리다; 투덜거리다; n. 중얼거림
If you mutter, you speak very quietly so that you cannot easily be heard, often because you are complaining about something.

magnificent[*]
[mægnífəsnt]

a. 훌륭한, 참으로 아름다운, 감명 깊은
If you say that something or someone is magnificent, you mean that you think they are extremely good, beautiful, or impressive.

Chapters 29 & 30

1. Why did Miss Nogard say that there would not be homework that night at first?

   A. The children said they had had no trouble with the previous homework.

   B. The children had all turned in their homework on time.

   C. The children would be going on a field trip instead.

   D. The children had been working hard and deserved a break from homework.

2. How did Miss Nogard call on students to give answers to the homework questions?

   A. She listened to their thoughts and called on the person with the wrong answer.

   B. She listened to their thoughts and called on the person with the right answer.

   C. She listened to their thoughts and called on the person who was the loudest.

   D. She called on the person who just shouted out answers without raising their hands first.

3. Why did Miss Nogard assign homework after all?

   A. She wasn't able to finish her lesson in class.

   B. She said that they hadn't understood it.

   C. She said that she always wanted to give them homework.

   D. Only some of the students had gotten any of the correct answers.

4. How did all the children feel about everyone else?

   A. They felt that everyone else was smart.

   B. They felt that everyone else was stupid.

   C. They felt that everyone else could help them with their homework.

   D. They felt that everyone else never did their homework at all.

5. Why did Miss Nogard listen to Mavis's thoughts?

   A. She wanted to see if Mavis was scared of her.

   B. She was curious about how Mavis felt about the class.

   C. She always liked listening to the thoughts of babies.

   D. She was curious about the kind of thoughts that babies had.

6. How did listening to Mavis's thoughts dissolve the bitterness in Miss Nogard?

   A. Mavis's thoughts were just baby sounds which were hard to understand.

   B. Mavis's thoughts were only about Mrs. Jewls and happiness.

   C. Babies don't think in words and Miss Nogard heard pure love.

   D. Babies only think in sounds that break people's hearts.

7. How did Miss Nogard know that Louis was telling the truth about his feelings for her?

   A. He kissed her.

   B. She read Louis's mind.

   C. She could see it in his eyes.

   D. The children had already told her that she liked him.

Check Your Reading Speed

1분에 몇 단어를 읽는지 리딩 속도를 측정해 보세요.

$$\frac{572 \text{ words}}{\text{reading time (\quad) sec}} \times 60 = (\quad) \text{ WPM}$$

Build Your Vocabulary

go over	idiom ~을 점검하다; 거듭 살피다 If you go over something, you examine or check the details of it.
stomach^{복습} [stʌ́mək]	n. 위(胃), 복부, 배, 속 You can refer to the front part of your body below your waist as your stomach.
flip* [flip]	v. 홱 뒤집(히)다; (손가락으로) 툭 던지다; n. 톡 던지기 If something flips over, or if you flip it over or into a different position, it moves or is moved into a different position.
fumble [fʌmbl]	v. (손으로) 더듬거리다; (말을) 더듬거리다 If you fumble for something or fumble with something, you try and reach for it or hold it in a clumsy way.
flip through^{복습}	idiom (책장을) 휙휙 넘기다 If you flip through something such as the pages of a book or a pile of papers, you turn over it quickly, or look through it without reading everything.
handful* [hǽndfùl]	n. 몇 안 되는 수; 줌, 움큼 A handful of people or things is a small number of them.
cucumber [kjú:kʌmbər]	n. 오이 A cucumber is a long thin vegetable with a hard green skin and wet transparent flesh. It is eaten raw in salads.
call on^{복습}	idiom (이름을 불러서) 학생에게 시키다; (사람을) 방문하다 If a teacher calls on students in a class, he or she asks them to answer a question or give their opinion.
squirm [skwəːrm]	v. (몸을) 꼼지락대다; 몹시 당혹해 하다 If you squirm, you move your body from side to side, usually because you are nervous or uncomfortable.
goat* [gout]	n. [동물] 염소 A goat is a farm animal or a wild animal that is about the size of a sheep, with horns and beard on their chin.
hopeful^{복습} [hóupfəl]	a. 희망에 찬, 기대하는; 희망을 주는 (hopefully ad. 희망을 갖고) If you are hopeful, you are fairly confident that something that you want to happen will happen.

idiot[복습]
[ídiət]

n. 바보, 멍청이
If you call someone an idiot, you are showing that you think they are very stupid or have done something very stupid.

go through[복습]

idiom ~을 살펴보다; ~을 검토하다
If you go through something, you look at, check or examine it closely and carefully, especially in order to find something.

assign[복습]
[əsáin]

v. (일·책임 등을) 맡기다; 선임하다, 파견하다 (assignment n. 과제, 임무)
An assignment is a task or piece of work that you are given to do, especially as part of your job or studies.

correct[복습]
[kərékt]

a. 맞는, 정확한; 적절한, 옳은; v. 바로잡다, 정정하다
If something is correct, it is in accordance with the facts and has no mistakes.

obvious**
[ábviəs]

a. 분명한, 명백한; 확실한; 너무 빤한 (obviously ad. 분명히, 명백히)
You use obviously to indicate that something is easily noticed, seen, or recognized.

groan[복습]
[groun]

v. 신음 소리를 내다; 끙끙거리다; n. 신음, 끙 하는 소리
If you groan, you make a long, low sound because you are in pain, or because you are upset or unhappy about something.

blame**
[bleim]

v. ~을 탓하다, ~때문으로 보다; n. 책임; 탓
If you blame a person or thing for something bad, you believe or say that they are responsible for it or that they caused it.

Check Your Reading Speed

1분에 몇 단어를 읽는지 리딩 속도를 측정해 보세요.

$$\frac{1{,}118 \text{ words}}{\text{reading time ( ) sec}} \times 60 = (\quad) \text{ WPM}$$

Build Your Vocabulary

hairy 복습
[héəri]
a. 털이 많은, 털투성이의
Someone or something that is hairy is covered with hairs.

paw*
[pɔː]
n. (사람의) 손; (동물의 발톱이 달린) 발; v. 발로 긁다; (함부로) 건드리다
You can describe someone's hand as their paw, especially if it is very large or if they are very clumsy.

bald 복습
[bɔːld]
a. 대머리의, 머리가 벗겨진
Someone who is bald has little or no hair on the top of their head.

diaper
[dáiəpər]
n. 기저귀
A diaper is a piece of soft towel or paper, which you fasten round a baby's bottom in order to soak up its urine and faeces.

assortment
[əsɔ́ːrtmənt]
n. (같은 종류의 여러 가지) 모음, 종합
An assortment is a group of similar things that are of different sizes or colors or have different qualities.

baby bottle
[béibi batl]
n. 젖병
A baby bottle is a plastic bottle with a special rubber top through which a baby can suck milk or other liquids.

exclaim 복습
[ikskléim]
v. 소리치다, 외치다
If you exclaim, you cry out suddenly in surprise, strong emotion, or pain.

blanket*
[blǽŋkit]
n. 담요; v. (완전히) 뒤덮다
A blanket is a large square or rectangular piece of thick cloth, especially one which you put on a bed to keep you warm.

squeal 복습
[skwiːl]
v. 꽤액 하는 소리를 내다; n. 끼익 하는 소리
If someone or something squeals, they make a long, high-pitched sound.

check out 복습
idiom (흥미로운 것을) 살펴보다; (도서관 등에서) 대출받다
If you check out someone or something, you look at them because they seem interesting or attractive.

take turns 복습
idiom ~을 교대로 하다
If two or more people take turns to do something, they do it one after the other several times, rather than doing it together.

tap*
[tæp]
v. (가볍게) 톡톡 두드리다; 박자를 맞추다; n. 수도꼭지; (가볍게) 두드리기
If you tap something, you hit it with a quick light blow or a series of quick light blows.

138

tickle ^{복습}
[tikl]

v. (손가락으로) 간지럼을 태우다; 간질이다; n. 간지럽히기; 간지러움
When you tickle someone, you move your fingers lightly over a sensitive part of their body, often in order to make them laugh.

coo
[ku:]

v. 달콤하게 속삭이다; (비둘기가) 울다
When someone coos, they speak in a very soft, quiet voice which is intended to sound attractive.

substitute ^{복습}
[sʌ́bstətjùːt]

n. 대신하는 사람; 대체물; v. 대신하다, 교체되다
(substitute teacher n. 대체 교사)
A substitute teacher is a teacher whose job is to take the place of other teachers at different schools when they are unable to be there.

interrupt ^{복습}
[ìntərʌ́pt]

v. (말·행동을) 방해하다; 중단시키다
If you interrupt someone who is speaking, you say or do something that causes them to stop.

adorable ^{복습}
[ədɔ́ːrəbl]

a. 사랑스러운
If you say that someone or something is adorable, you are emphasizing that they are very attractive and you feel great affection for them.

accidental ^{복습}
[æksədéntl]

a. 우연한, 돌발적인 (accidentally ad. 우연히, 뜻하지 않게)
An accidental event happens by chance or as the result of an accident, and is not deliberately intended.

sway ^{복습}
[swei]

v. (전후·좌우로 천천히) 흔들리다; (마음을) 동요시키다; n. 흔들림
When people or things sway, they lean or swing slowly from one side to the other.

rubber band ^{복습}
[rʌ́bər bænd]

n. 고무줄
A rubber band is a thin circle of very elastic rubber.

trip ^{복습}
[trip]

v. 발을 헛디디다; n. 여행
If you trip when you are walking, you knock your foot against something and fall or nearly fall.

awful ^{복습}
[ɔ́ːfəl]

a. 끔찍한, 지독한; (정도가) 대단한
If you say that someone or something is awful, you dislike that person or thing or you think that they are not very good.

curious ^{**}
[kjúəriəs]

a. 궁금한; 호기심이 많은; 별난
If you are curious about something, you are interested in it and want to know more about it.

gasp ^{복습}
[gæsp]

v. 숨이 턱 막히다, 헉 하고 숨을 쉬다; n. (숨이 막히는 듯) 헉 하는 소리를 냄
When you gasp, you take a short quick breath through your mouth, especially when you are surprised, shocked, or in pain.

wobble ^{복습}
[wabl]

v. (불안정하게) 흔들리다; 뒤뚱거리며 가다; n. 흔들림, 떨림
If something or someone wobbles, they make small movements from side to side, for example because they are unsteady.

balance ^{**}
[bǽləns]

n. (몸의) 균형; 평형; v. 균형을 유지하다
Balance is the ability to remain steady when you are standing up.

grab 복습
[græb]

v. (와락·단단히) 붙잡다; ~을 잡으려고 하다; n. 와락 잡아채려고 함
If you grab something, you take it or pick it up suddenly and roughly.

just in time

idiom 겨우 시간에 맞춰; 마침 좋은 때에
If something occurs just in time, it happens at the last possible moment.

tender*
[téndər]

a. 상냥한, 다정한; 연한 (tenderly ad. 상냥하게, 친절하게)
Someone or something that is tender expresses gentle and caring feelings.

faint*
[feint]

v. 실신하다; a. (빛·소리·냄새 등이) 희미한
If you faint, you lose consciousness for a short time, especially because you are hungry, or because of pain, heat, or shock.

exact 복습
[igzǽkt]

a. 정확한, 정밀한; 꼼꼼한, 빈틈없는 (exactly ad. 정확히, 꼭)
You use exactly before an amount, number, or position to emphasize that it is no more, no less, or no different from what you are stating.

dissolve*
[dizálv]

v. 사라지다, 흩어지다; 녹다, 용해되다
If something such as a problem or feeling dissolves or is dissolved, it becomes weaker and disappears.

bitter 복습
[bítər]

a. 쓰라린, 비통한; 격렬한 (bitterness n. 신랄함; 비통함)
If someone is bitter after a disappointing experience or after being treated unfairly, they continue to feel angry about it.

cake**
[keik]

v. 두껍게 바르다; (마르면서) 딱딱해지다; n. 케이크
To cake something means to cover it with an outer layer that becomes hard as it dries.

steady 복습
[stédi]

v. 진정시키다, 가라앉히다; 균형을 잡다; a. 꾸준한; 안정된
If you steady yourself, you control your voice or expression, so that people will think that you are calm and not nervous.

well behaved
[wel bihéivd]

a. 품행이 바른, 예의 바른
If you describe someone, especially a child, as well behaved, you mean that they behave in a way that adults generally like and think is correct.

fluff
[flʌf]

v. 부풀리다; n. 보풀; 솜털
If you fluff something, you make it appear fuller and softer by shaking or brushing it.

obstetrician
[àbstitríʃən]

n. 산부인과 전문의
An obstetrician is a doctor who is specially trained to deal with pregnant women and with women who are giving birth.

pediatrician
[pìːdiətríʃən]

n. 소아과 의사
A pediatrician is a doctor who specializes in treating sick children.

podiatrist
[pədáiətrist]

n. 발 전문가, 족부의사
A podiatrist is a person whose job is to treat and care for people's feet.

bore^{복습}
[bɔːr]

v. 지루하게 하다 (boring a. 재미없는, 지루한)
Someone or something boring is so dull and uninteresting that they make people tired and impatient.

blackboard^{복습}
[blǽkbɔ̀ːrd]

n. 칠판
A blackboard is a dark-colored board that you can write on with chalk.

discipline^{복습}
[dísəplin]

n. 규율, 훈육; 단련법, 수련법
Discipline is the practice of making people obey rules or standards of behavior, and punishing them when they do not.

ask out^{복습}

idiom ~에게 데이트를 신청하다
If you ask someone out, you invite them to go out with you, especially when you would like a romantic relationship with them.

way to go

idiom 잘 했어!
You can say way to go to tell someone that you are pleased about something they have done.

urge^{복습}
[əːrdʒ]

v. (~하도록) 충고하다, 설득하려 하다; n. (강한) 욕구, 충동
If you urge someone to do something, you try hard to persuade them to do it.

bend^{복습}
[bend]

v. (bent-bent) (몸이나 머리를) 굽히다, 숙이다; (무엇을) 구부리다;
n. 굽이, 굽은 곳
When you bend, you move the top part of your body downward and forward.

part^{복습}
[paːrt]

v. (두 사물·부분이) 갈라지다; (~와) 헤어지다; n. 일부, 약간; 부분
If you part your hair in the middle or at one side, you make it lie in two different directions so that there is a straight line running from the front of your head to the back.

go out with^{복습}

idiom ~와 데이트를 하다, 사귀다
If you go out with someone, you spend time with them and have a romantic or sexual relationship with them.

pause^{복습}
[pɔːz]

v. (말·일을 하다가) 잠시 멈추다; 일시 정지시키다; n. (말·행동 등의) 멈춤
If you pause while you are doing something, you stop for a short period and then continue.

assure^{복습}
[əʃúər]

v. 장담하다, 확언하다; 확인하다
If you assure someone that something is true or will happen, you tell them that it is definitely true or will definitely happen, often in order to make them less worried.

eyebrow^{복습}
[áibràu]

n. 눈썹
Your eyebrows are the lines of hair which grow above your eyes.

mustache^{복습}
[mʌ́stæʃ]

n. 콧수염
A man's mustache is the hair that grows on his upper lip.

수고하셨습니다!

드디어 끝까지 다 읽으셨군요! 축하드립니다! 여러분은 이 책을 통해 총 24,003 개의 단어를 읽으셨고, 800개 이상의 어휘와 표현들을 익히셨습니다. 이 책에는 다른 원서를 읽을 때도 빈번히 만날 수 있는 어휘들이 있습니다. 이 책을 읽었던 경험은 비슷한 수준의 다른 원서들을 읽을 때 큰 도움이 될 것입니다.

이제 자신의 상황에 맞게 원서를 반복해서 읽거나, 오디오북을 들어 볼 수 있습니다. 혹은 비슷한 수준의 다른 원서를 찾아 읽는 것도 좋습니다. 일단 원서를 완독한 뒤에 어떻게 계속 영어 공부를 이어갈 수 있을지, 다음에 제시되는 Tip을 꼼꼼히 살펴보고 각자 상황에 맞게 적용해 보세요!

리딩(Reading)을 확실히 다지길 원한다면? 반복해서 읽자!

리딩 실력을 탄탄하게 다지길 원한다면, 같은 원서를 2~3번 반복해서 읽을 것을 권합니다. 같은 책을 여러 번 읽으면 지루할 것 같지만, 꼭 그렇지도 않습니다. 반복해서 읽을 때 처음과 주안점을 다르게 두면, 전혀 다른 느낌으로 재미있게 읽을 수 있습니다.

처음 원서를 읽을 때는 생소한 단어들과 스토리로 인해 읽고 이해하기가 매우 힘듭니다. 전체 맥락을 잡고 읽어도 약간 버거운 느낌이지요. 하지만 반복해서 읽기 시작하면 달라집니다. 내용은 일단 파악해 둔 상황이기 때문에 문장 구조나 어휘의 활용에 더 집중하게 되고, 조금 더 깊이 있게 읽을 수 있게 됩니다. 좋은 표현과 문장을 수집하고 메모할 만한 여유도 생기게 되지요. 어휘도 많이 익숙해졌기 때문에 리딩 속도도 탄력이 붙습니다. 처음 읽을 때는 '내용'에서 재미를 느꼈다면, 반복해서 읽을 때는 '영어'에서 재미를 느끼게 되는 것입니다.

따라서 리딩 실력을 더욱 확고하게 다지고자 한다면, 같은 책을 2~3회 정도 반복해서 읽을 것을 권해드립니다.

리스닝(Listening)이 문제라면? 오디오북을 귀로 읽자!

많은 영어 학습자들이 '리스닝이 안 돼서 문제'라고 한탄합니다. 그리고 리스닝 실력을 늘리는 방법으로, 무슨 뜻인지 몰라도 반복해 듣는 '무작정 듣기'를 선택합니다. 하지만 뜻도 모르면서 무작정 듣는 것은 엄청난 인내력이 필요합니다. 그래서 대부분 며칠 시도하다가 포기해 버리고 말지요.

따라서 모르는 내용을 무작정 듣는 것보다는 어느 정도 알고 있는 내용을 반복해서 듣는 것이 더 효과적인 듣기 방법입니다. 그리고 이런 방식의 듣기에 활용할 수 있는 가장 좋은 교재가 오디오북입니다.

리스닝 실력을 향상하길 원한다면, 이 책에서 제공하는 오디오북을 이용해서 듣는 연습을 해 보세요. 활용법은 간단합니다. 일단 책을 한 번 완독했다면, 오디오북을 통해 다시 들어 보세요. MP3에 넣어 시간이 날 때 틈틈이 듣는 것도 좋고, 책상에 앉아 눈으로는 텍스트를 보며 귀로 읽는 것도 좋습니다. 이미 읽었던 내용이라 이해하기가 훨씬 수월하고, 애매했던 발음들도 자연스럽게 교정하게 됩니다. 또 성우의 목소리 연기를 듣다 보면 내용이 더욱 생동감 있게 다가와 이해도가 높아지는 효과도 거둘 수 있습니다.

반대로 듣기에 자신 있는 사람이라면, 책을 읽기 전에 처음부터 오디오북을 먼저 듣는 것도 좋은 방법입니다! 귀를 통해 책을 쭉 읽어 보고, 이후에 다시 눈으로 책을 읽으면서 잘 들리지 않았던 부분을 보충하는 것이지요.

중요한 것은 내용을 따라가면서, 내용에 푹 빠져서 반복해 들어야 한다는 것입니다. 이렇게 연습을 반복해서 눈으로 읽지 않은 책이라도 '귀를 통해' 읽을 수 있을 정도가 되면, 리스닝으로 고생하는 일은 거의 없을 것입니다.

이 책은 저자 루이스 새커가 직접 읽은 오디오북을 기본 제공하고 있습니다. (미국 현지 판매가 $21.56) 오디오북들은 MP3 파일로 제공되니 MP3 기기나 컴퓨터에 옮겨서 사용하시면 됩니다. 혹 오디오북에 이상이 있을 경우 helper@longtailbooks.co.kr로 메일을 주시면 안내를 받으실 수 있습니다.

스피킹(Speaking)이 고민이라면? 소리 내어 읽어 보자!

스피킹 역시 많은 학습자들이 고민하는 부분입니다. 스피킹이 고민이라면, 원서를 큰 소리로 읽는 낭독 훈련(Voice Reading)을 해 보세요!
'소리 내서 읽는 것이 말하기에 정말로 도움이 될까?'라고 의아한 생각이 들 수도 있습니다. 하지만, 인간의 두뇌 입장에서 봤을 때, 성대 구조를 활용해서 '발화'한다는 점에서는 소리 내서 읽기와 말하기는 큰 차이가 없다고 합니다. 소리 내서 읽는 것은 '타인의 생각'을 전달하고, 직접 말하는 것은 '자신의 생각'을 전달한다는 차이가 있을 뿐, 머릿속에서 문장을 처리하고 조음기관(혀와 성대 등)을 움직여 의미를 만든다는 점에서 같은 과정인 것이지요. 따라서 소리 내서 읽는 연습을 꾸준히 하는 것은 스피킹 연습에 큰 도움이 됩니다.
소리 내어 읽기를 하는 방법도 간단합니다. 일단 오디오북을 들으면서 성우의 목소리를 최대한 따라 하며 같이 읽어보세요. 발음 뿐 아니라, 억양, 어조, 느낌까지 완벽히 따라 한다고 생각하면서 소리 내어 읽습니다. 따라 읽는 것이 조금 익숙해지면, 옆의 누군가에게 이 책을 읽어 준다는 생각으로 소리 내서 계속 읽어 나갑니다. 한 번 눈과 귀로 읽었던 책이라 보다 수월하게 진행할 수 있고, 자연스럽게 어휘와 표현을 복습하는 효과도 거두게 됩니다. 또 이렇게 소리 내어 읽는 것을 녹음해서 들어 보면 스스로에게 좋은 피드백이 됩니다.
최근 말하기가 강조되면서 소리 내어 읽기가 크게 각광을 받고 있긴 하지만, 그렇다고 소리 내어 읽기가 무조건 좋은 것만은 아닙니다. 책을 소리 내어 읽다 보면, 무의식적으로 속으로 발음을 하는 습관을 가지게 되어 리딩 속도 자체는 오히려 크게 떨어지는 현상이 발생할 수 있습니다. 따라서 빠른 리딩 속도가 중요한 수험생이나 고학력 학습자들에겐 소리 내어 읽기가 적절하지 않은 방법입니다. 효과가 좋다는 말만 믿고 무턱대고 따라 하기보다는 자신의 필요에 맞게 우선순위를 가지고 원서를 활용하는 것이 좋습니다.

라이팅(Writing)까지 욕심이 난다면? 영어로 요약해 보자!

최근엔 라이팅에도 욕심을 내는 학습자들이 많이 있습니다. 원서를 라이팅 연습에 직접적으로 활용하기에는 한계가 있지만, 역시 적절히 활용하면 유용한 자료가 될 수 있습니다.

특히 책을 읽고 그 내용을 요약하는 연습은 큰 도움이 됩니다. 요약 훈련의 방식도 간단합니다. 원서를 읽고 그날 읽은 분량만큼 혹은 책을 다 읽고 전체 내용을 기반으로, 책 내용을 한번 요약하고 나의 느낌을 영어로 적어 보는 것입니다.

이때 그 책에 나왔던 단어와 표현을 최대한 활용해서 요약하는 것이 중요합니다. 영어 표현력은 결국 얼마나 다양한 어휘로 많은 표현을 해 보았느냐가 좌우하게 됩니다. 이런 면에서 내가 읽은 책을, 그 책에 나온 문장과 어휘로 다시 표현해 보는 것은 매우 효율적인 방법입니다. 책에 나온 어휘와 표현을 단순히 읽고 무슨 말인지 아는 정도가 아니라, 실제로 직접 활용해서 쓸 수 있을 만큼 확실하게 익히게 되는 것이지요. 여기에 첨삭까지 받을 수 있는 방법이 있다면 금상첨화입니다.

또한 이런 '표현하기' 연습은 스피킹 훈련에도 그대로 적용할 수 있습니다. 책을 읽고 그 내용을 3분 안에 다른 사람에게 영어로 말하는 연습을 해 보세요. 순발력과 표현력을 기르는 좋은 훈련이 됩니다.

꾸준히 원서를 읽고 싶다면? 뉴베리 수상작을 계속 읽어 보자!

뉴베리 상은 세계 최대 권위의 아동 문학상인 만큼 수상작들은 확실히 검증받은 책이라고 할 수 있습니다. 특히 '쉬운 어휘로 쓰인 깊이 있는 문장'으로 영어 학습자들에게 큰 호응을 얻고 있습니다. 이런 '검증받은 원서'를 꾸준히 읽는 것도 영어 실력 향상에 큰 도움이 됩니다.

아래에 수준별로 제시된 뉴베리 수상작 목록을 보며 적절한 책들을 찾아 계속 읽어 보세요. 혹은 꼭 수상작이 아니더라도 마음에 드는 작가의 다른 책들을 읽어 보는 것도 아주 좋은 방법입니다.

• 영어 초보자도 쉽게 읽을 만한 아주 쉬운 수준. 소리 내어 읽기에도 아주 적합.
Sarah Plain and Tall*(Medal, 8,331단어), The Hundred Penny Box(Honor, 5,878단어), The Hundred Dresses*(Honor, 7,329단어), My Father's Dragon (Honor, 7,682단어), 26 Fairmount Avenue(Honor, 6,737단어)

• 중·고등학생 정도 영어 학습자라면 쉽게 읽을 수 있는 수준. 소리 내어 읽기에도 비교적 적합한 편.

Because of Winn-Dixie★(Honor, 22,123단어), What Jamie Saw(Honor, 17,203단어), Charlotte's Web(Honor, 31,938단어), Dear Mr. Henshaw(Medal, 18,145단어), Missing May(Medal, 17,509단어)

• 대학생 정도 영어 학습자라면 무난한 수준. 소리 내어 읽기에 적합하지 않음.

Number The Stars★(Medal, 27,197단어), A Single Shard(Medal, 33,726단어), The Tale of Despereaux★(Medal, 32,375단어), Hatchet★(Medal, 42,328단어), Bridge to Terabithia(Medal, 32,888단어), A Fine White Dust(Honor, 19,022단어), Jennifer, Hecate, Macbeth, William McKinley and Me, Elizabeth(Honor, 23,266단어)

• 원서 완독 경험을 가진 학습자에게 적절한 수준. 소리 내어 읽기에 적합하지 않음.

The Giver★(Medal, 43,617단어), From the Mixed-Up Files of Mrs. Basil E. Frankweiler(Medal, 30,906단어), The View from Saturday(Medal, 42,685단어), Holes★(Medal, 47,079단어), Criss Cross(Medal, 48,221단어), Walk Two Moons(Medal, 59,400단어), The Graveyard Book(Medal, 67,380단어)

뉴베리 수상작과 뉴베리 수상 작가의 좋은 작품을 엄선한 「뉴베리 컬렉션」에도 위 목록에 있는 도서 중 상당수가 포함될 예정입니다!

★「뉴베리 컬렉션」으로 이미 출간된 도서

어떤 책들이 출간되었는지 확인하려면, 지금 인터넷 서점에서 뉴베리 컬렉션을 검색해 보세요.

웨이사이드 스쿨 시리즈를 동영상 강의로 만나 보세요!

지금 영서당(yseodang.com)에서 웨이사이드 스쿨 시리즈를 동영상 강의로 만날 수 있습니다. 또한 뉴베리 수상작과 다양한 영어 원서 강의가 진행되고 있습니다. 지금 사이트를 방문해서 무료 샘플 강의를 들어 보세요!

'스피드 리딩 카페'를 통해 원서 읽기 습관을 길러 보세요!

일상에서 영어를 한마디도 쓰지 않는 비영어권 국가에서 살고 있는 우리가 영어 환경에 가장 쉽고, 편하고, 저렴하게 노출되는 방법은, 바로 '영어원서 읽기'입니다. 언제 어디서든 원서를 붙잡고 읽기만 하면 곧바로 영어를 접하는 환경이 만들어지기 때문이지요. 하루에 20분씩만 꾸준히 읽는다면, 1년에 무려 120시간 동안 영어에 노출될 수 있습니다. 이런 이유 때문에 '영어를 좀 한다'는 사람들은 다들 영어원서 읽기를 추천하는 것이지요.

하지만 원서 읽기가 좋다는 것을 알아도 막상 꾸준히 하기가 힘듭니다. 그럴 때는 13만 명 이상의 회원을 보유한 국내 최대 원서 읽기 동호회 〈스피드 리딩 카페〉(cafe.naver.com/readingtc)를 방문해 보세요.

원서별로 정리된 무료 PDF 단어장과 수준별 추천 원서 목록 등 유용한 자료는 물론, 뉴베리 수상작을 포함한 다양한 원서의 리뷰와 정보를 무료로 확인할 수 있습니다. 특히 함께 모여서 원서를 읽는 '북클럽'은 중간에 포기하지 않고 원서 읽기 습관을 기르는 데 큰 도움이 될 것입니다!

Chapters 1 & 2

1. A   Louis was afraid he'd cry if he talked to them.

2. B   Some days it seemed hopeless. The worst part was the smell. He often had to run and stick his head out a window to get a breath of fresh air. But whenever he felt like quitting, he thought about those poor kids, stuck in those horrible schools, and he just worked harder.

3. D   Well, almost ready. There was one little problem. Suddenly, from somewhere inside the building, or maybe just inside his head, Louis heard a loud "moo."

4. C   But Todd didn't answer. He just kept running until he reached the school building. Then he kissed Wayside School. Out of all the schools, Todd had been sent to the very worst one. It was awful!

5. A   One by one the other children staggered into the classroom, huffing and puffing. They were all out of shape.

6. B   "Civilization!" declared Mac. ... Rondi raised her hand. "Evaporation," she said. ... Dana raised her hand. "I learned about exaggeration," she said. "It was all my teacher ever talked about. We had like ten thousand tests on it, and the teacher would kill you if you didn't spell it right."

7. C   Just then Mr. Kidswatter's voice came over the P.A. system. "Good morning, boys and girls." Mr. Kidswatter was the principal. He paused a moment because he thought every kid in school was saying "Good morning, Mr. Kidswatter" back to him.

Chapters 3 & 4

1. B   Mrs. Jewls told everyone to pick a color and write a poem about it.

2. C   Joe raised his hand. "I don't know what rhymes with red," he said. Mrs. Jewls gave him a few suggestions. "Bed, led, wed. Think of words that end in 'e-d.' "

3. D   But after making a big stink over it with Rondi, she couldn't switch colors now.

4. B   Actually his name was Doctor Pickell, with the accent on the second syllable.

148

But that wasn't why everyone called him Dr. Pickle. Dr. Pickle was a psychiatrist. He had thick eyebrows and wore tiny glasses. He had a small beard on the tip of his pointed chin. A psychiatrist is a doctor who doesn't cure people with sick bodies. He cures people with sick minds.

5. C   Dr. Pickle held up a gold chain. At the end of the chain was a green stone that was almost transparent, but not quite. It looked like a pickle. Hence, his name.

6. D   "But when you put the cigarette in your mouth," said Dr. Pickle, "it will feel just like a worm. A wiggling, slimy worm." "A - yucky - icky - worm," repeated the woman.

7. D   Eventually Dr. Pickle was caught, and he was no longer allowed to practice psychiatry. So he had to find another job. He became a counselor at an elementary school.

Chapters 5 & 6

1. B   Paul's father was a security guard at a museum. The museum had a very famous painting. It was painted by Leonardo da Vinci. It was called the *Mona Lisa*.

2. A   Paul reached out, grabbed, and yanked! "Yaaaaaaaahhhhhhhh!" screamed Leslie. Mrs. Jewls sent Paul to the counselor's office.

3. C   "I am going to count to five," said the counselor. "And then you will wake up. You will return to your classroom. You will take your seat behind Leslie. You will want to pull one of her pigtails. But when you reach for it, it will turn into a rattlesnake." "Leslie's - pigtails - are - rattlesnakes," said Paul.

4. C   "What's under my desk?" asked Paul. "I'll get it," said Eric Fry. He reached under Paul's desk, picked up the pencil, and handed it to Leslie. She thanked him and everyone returned to work.

5. A   Mrs. Jewls held up two fingers. All the animals became quiet.

6. B   Mrs. Jewls moved on to Ron. "Ron, I see you have a cat." "Dog," said Ron, as he stroked the cat on his lap. Mrs. Jewls shrugged. "Okay," she said. "He's my dog," said D.J. "Ron has your dog?" asked Mrs. Jewls. "Ron has a cat," said D.J. "That's what I thought," said Mrs. Jewls. "But what—" "What's a dog," said Jenny. Mrs. Jewls covered her ears and shook her head. "Let's start all over again," said Mrs. Jewls. She got a new piece of poster board from the supply closet.

7. C   "How do you know what I'll eat, Calvin?" asked Mrs. Jewls, a little annoyed. "I like eating crackers with cheese on top." "Oh, gross!" said Myron.

Chapters 7 & 8

1. A   He walked into his office. Except his office door was closed. He smashed into it, spilling coffee all over his green suit.

2. B   "Who closed my door?" he demanded. "Why didn't you just open it?" asked Mrs. Day. "It's always open in the morning," said Mr. Kidswatter. "How was I supposed to know it was closed this time?"

3. C   "I have made a new rule!" declared Mr. Kidswatter. "You may no longer say that word. You know what word I mean—but don't say it! Instead, I have made up a new word for you: 'Goozack.' Open the goozack. Shut the goozack. Lock the goozack. Don't you think that's a better word? I do. From now on, that other word is a bad word. I have made my decision."

4. A   "My dad locked his keys in the car," Todd explained. "We had to use a coat hanger to unlock the door." Everyone gasped. Mrs. Jewls made Todd write his name on the blackboard under the word DISCIPLINE.

5. C   "Wrong!" said Kathy. "I get lots of presents. My parents buy them for me. They have lots of money. They buy me anything I want." She bit off the head of a reindeer cookie. "The only thing that matters is how rich your parents are. If they have lots of money, then you'll get lots of good presents. If they're poor, then you'll just get a few crummy presents."

6. D   *Outside the window Snowflakes were falling. . . . Inside the window Mrs. Jewls was stalling. . . .*

7. D   "That's easy," said Mrs. Jewls. "You just have to be nice to other people. Whenever you give someone a present or sing a holiday song, you're helping Santa Claus. To me, that's what Christmas is all about. Helping Santa Claus!"

Chapters 9 & 10

1. C   "Today we are going to learn how to knit," said Mrs. Jewls. She showed the class how it was done. "See, you stick this needle through here, then wrap this around this like this, stick this through this, pull this like this, and then you stick this here. Any questions?" Everyone stared at her. "Good," said Mrs. Jewls. "I want everybody to make socks. Okay, get started."

2. B   "No, I'm not sick," said Mrs. Jewls. "In fact, I'm better than I've ever been." She beamed. "I'm going to have a baby!" Everyone gasped.

3. D   "If he's a boy, you should name him Jet Rocket!" said Joe. "Jet Rocket Jewls," mused Mrs. Jewls. "That has a nice ring to it. And what if she's a girl?" "Cootie Face," said Joe.

4. A   Before Mrs. Jewls ever came to Wayside School, the children had a teacher named Mrs. Gorf. She wasn't very nice.

5. B   "Mr. Gorf might be a good teacher," said Eric Bacon. "Just because he has the same last name as Mrs. Gorf doesn't mean he'll be horrible." "That's right," said Eric Ovens. "People with the same name can be different."

6. C   After recess the children returned to class and worked until lunchtime. At lunch they ate all the food Miss Mush served them. Their manners were perfect. Mr. Gorf might have been hiding under the table.

7. B   Myron went to the back of the room and opened the closet door. A man stepped out. "Thank you," he said. "I accidentally locked myself in here this morning, and I've been waiting for someone to open the door."

Chapters 11 & 12

1. B   And, surprising as it may seem, the children weren't afraid. It was his voice. His voice was full of comfort and wisdom, like an old leather chair in a dusty library. It didn't matter what he said. It felt good just to listen to him.

2. C   Mr. Gorf's middle nostril had snorted all of their voices. Except for Allison. She remained silent. She knew she'd only get one chance to speak, and she had to wait for just the right moment.

3. D   "This is my voice!" he squawked. If a donkey could talk, and if the donkey had a sore throat, and if it spoke with a French accent—that was what Mr. Gorf's voice sounded like.

4. A   But what he said next was even more horrible than his voice. "Mrs. Gorf was my mommy."

5. B   Mr. Gorf laughed. He picked up the airplane and unfolded it. "Help," he sneered. "No one can help you now! You took my mommy away from me. And I'm going to take your mommies away from you!"

6. D   Mr. Gorf turned around. His face was covered with a thick pepper cream. He sneezed. Calvin laughed. "Hey, my voice is back!" said Calvin. "Wait a second. This isn't my voice. I sound like Bebe! … "AAAACHOOOO!!!!!!" Mr. Gorf sneezed so hard his nose flew off his face. He screamed like a donkey, then ran noseless out of the room.

7. C   "I wasn't exactly sure," explained Miss Mush. "But when I came up the first time, I heard Kathy say 'Have a nice day.' So, either Kathy had decided to be nice to me, or Mr. Gorf was a mean teacher who sucked children's voices up his nose." She shrugged. "I just didn't think Kathy would be nice."

Chapters 13 & 14

1. D   "No," explained Mrs. Drazil. "It was just a little joke. Brazil rhymes with Drazil. I thought it might help you remember my name."

2. B   But not Deedee. She had heard of Mrs. Drazil somewhere. She was sure of it. And whatever she had heard, she was sure it wasn't good.

3. B   "For real?" asked Todd. "You want us to tell you to stop talking?" "And we won't get in trouble?" asked Bebe. "No, of course not," said Mrs. Drazil. "You'll be helping me and the rest of your class. You're not going to learn anything if you're bored."

4. C   Her face turned sour again. "But if you cross me, you will be very, very sorry." She ran her fingers over her blue notebook. "Oh, maybe not today, maybe not tomorrow, but *someday I will get you!* You can run, but you can't hide."

5. A   Leslie brought the class dictionary. Jenny and Dana donated their math books. Sharie grabbed Mrs. Drazil's old blue notebook. "Put that down!" yelled Mrs. Drazil. "Right now!" Sharie dropped the notebook. Mrs. Drazil's kindly old face had suddenly turned mean. "Don't ever touch that again!" Mrs. Drazil ordered.

6. D   Mrs. Drazil wrote "Coffeepot," "Sack of Potatoes," "Pencil Sharpener," and "Light Bulb" on the blackboard.

7. D   Everyone else crowded around to watch. With everyone on the same side of the classroom, the school leaned a little bit, just like the Leaning Tower of Pisa.

Chapters 15 & 16

1. D   "It's okay," said Jenny. "It can't be the same teacher. Our teacher is nice." "And her hair isn't brown," said Jason. "It's white." Louis relaxed a little bit. "You want to come up and meet her?" asked Deedee. "No way!" said Louis. "Oh, you're so silly, Louis," said Deedee. "She's not the same teacher. And besides, you're a teacher now too."

2. A   "The notebook!" whispered Louis. Mrs. Drazil opened it and flipped through the pages. "Here we are," she said. She removed a piece of paper and handed it to Louis. "Is this your homework?" she asked.

3. B   "I don't want excuses," said Mrs. Drazil. "I want clean fingernails. And while you're at it, shave off that mustache. It looks like a hairy caterpillar crawling across your face!" "Not my mustache," said Louis. "Unless you want me to rip it off for you," said Mrs. Drazil.

4. C   Maurecia looked at the stranger. He did sort of look like Louis. Except his hair was combed. His shirt was tucked in. He was wearing a tie. And there was skin between his nose and mouth. He had shaved off his mustache.

5. B   "That's Mr. Louis to you," said Louis. "I'm a teacher, and I expect to be treated

with respect."

6. A   "I do," said Louis. "Before I can let you play with them, I have to clean them and pump them up with the precise amount of air as specified by POOPS."

7. B   "Hey, what's going on?" shouted Joy. "Louis won't let anyone outside," somebody shouted back. "He's painting the blacktop!"

Chapters 17 & 18

1. B   "We have to divide them evenly," said Mrs. Drazil. "How many cookies should each child get, so that every child gets the same amount?"

2. C   "Jason, would you please open the door?" she said. Everyone gasped. "What's the matter?" she asked. "You said the D-word!" said Dana. "Door?" asked Mrs. Drazil. Everyone gasped again. "You're supposed to call it a goozack," explained Dana. "Who said so?" asked Mrs. Drazil. "Mr. Kidswatter," said Dana. "Mr. Kidswatter is a goozack," said Mrs. Drazil.

3. C   But she made Louis shave off his mustache. And so she had to go.

4. B   Her eyes closed. Then they opened wide. "Whazzat?!" she shouted. "Sharie?" said Mrs. Drazil. "Look!" shouted Sharie, pointing out the window. "It's a— Hurry!" Her long eyelashes stuck straight out.

5. A   Deedee was part of the plan too. She had a dangerous mission. She had volunteered for it. She felt it was her duty, since she was the one who had brought Louis up to meet Mrs. Drazil in the first place.

6. A   At recess everyone crowded around Deedee as she went through the blue notebook.

7. C   But Deedee had already turned the page. "There are other kids a lot worse than Louis," she said, flipping through the pages.

Chapters 19 & 20

1. B   Miss Zarves sighed. "I know," she said. "And I can't teach with a cow in my classroom!" No one had ever seen Miss Zarves so upset. She usually had a pleasant disposition.

2. D   "And she always did things alphabetically, so I was always last, if there was time for me at all.

3. A   "If you don't answer me right now," said Miss Zarves, "I'm walking out the door and never coming back!" Mr. K. pressed the buzzer on his phone. "Miss Night, you need to order more rubber bands." "That's it!" said Miss Zarves. "I'm leaving. Good-bye. I quit!"

4. B   "Can you see me?" she asked. "Yes, of course," said the bald man. "And we appreciate all your hard work."

5. C   "I have a very important announcement," said Mr. K. "Elevators have been installed in Wayside School!"

6. C   "I don't want the same kind of chaos that we have on the stairs every day. I don't know how many times I have to tell you. When you go up the stairs, stay to the right. When you come down the stairs, stay to the left. But still, everyone keeps bumping into each other."

7. D   "There are two elevators. One is blue. One is red. When you want to go up, you take the blue elevator. When you want to go down, you take the red elevator. It's that simple. It can't go wrong! The blue one only goes up. And the red one only goes down. "By the way, has anyone seen my coffeepot?" And so, at last, Wayside School got elevators. A blue one and a red one. They each worked perfectly one time—and never could be used again.

Chapters 21 & 22

1. B   The good news: Jason got to leave school early. The bad news: He had a dentist appointment.

2. A   Jason shook his head. If he told her it hurt, she might think it was a cavity. If she couldn't find it herself, he certainly wasn't going to tell her about it.

3. C   "Kendall's mother is on the phone," said the receptionist. "She refuses to pay her bill." "What?!" exclaimed Dr. Payne. "How dare—" "She says you pulled the wrong tooth."

4. D   Jason looked at the diploma hanging on the wall. Before his dentist got married, her name was Jane Smith. His big mouth opened wider.

5. B   "Her name is Dr. Payne," said Jason. "But that hasn't always been her name." "It hasn't?" asked Deedee. "Oh, no," said Jason. "Before she was married, her name was Jane Smith." "Jane Smith?" asked Deedee. "Is that spelled J-A-N-E S-M-I-T-H?" "Yes, that's how you spell Jane Smith," said Jason. "But like I said, that's not her name anymore. Her name is Dr. Payne. She works at the dentist office at 124 Garden Street."

6. C   "Hi, darling, how was your day?" he asked. "I made fifteen hundred dollars," said Jane. They hugged and kissed. They loved each other, but they loved money even more.

7. C   She had a suitcase stashed in the boathouse, just in case this ever happened. She hobbled to it, grabbed it, then limped down to the lake, dragging her suitcase behind her. Mrs. Drazil hurried down the steps on the side of the deck. Jane groaned as she threw her

suitcase into a motorboat. Then she pulled herself aboard and started the engine.

Chapters 23 & 24

1. B   Actually, the third ear wasn't ugly. In fact, it looked just like her other two. It was quantity, not quality, that bothered her.

2. C   Because there was something else about her ear I haven't told you yet. The one on top of her head, I mean. It didn't hear normal sounds. It heard people's brains.

3. A   "I love you," said Xavier. "That's all that matters to me." That was what he said. But this is what he was thinking. *Oh, gross! You're disgusting! I never want to touch you again! I can't even stand to look at you! You tricked me, you freak! You monster!*

4. A   Whenever she heard someone thinking happy thoughts, she would listen closely and then do and say just the right thing to make the person feel rotten. She hated children the most. Every time she passed a playground, she heard them laughing and having fun. So she became a substitute teacher.

5. B   Jenny was going horseback riding after school, if it didn't rain. She had never gone horseback riding before. She hoped she wouldn't fall off the horse.

6. C   *Just don't ask me my name,* thought Benjamin. *I never can say my name in front of people.* He took a breath to steady himself. "Well, we've been reading—" "First tell me your name," Miss Nogard said sweetly.

7. B   "Miss Nogard," said Bebe as she scratched the back of her leg raw. "Are you sure?" asked Louis. "Huh?" asked Bebe. "I mean," said Louis, "are you sure it's Miss Nogard? Not Mrs. Nogard?"

Chapters 25 & 26

1. D   Miss Nogard waited patiently. Everyone was guilty of something. *I didn't do anything, did I?* thought Maurecia. *I've been good, I think. Unless she found out about that dictionary page I accidentally tore. No, she couldn't know about that! It happened before she even got here. And I don't think anybody saw me do it.*

2. B   Maurecia had to stand in front of the class and tell them she was sorry. Then, since nobody would ever be able to use that page again, she had to read it aloud to the class.

3. A   But there was only one way Miss Nogard could have known about the torn page, she realized. Somebody in the class must have seen her tear it and then tattled on her.

4. A   Mac's favorite subject in the whole world was show-and-tell. He loved it. Especially when he was the one doing the showing and telling.

5. D   Then he remembered something. *I didn't bring anything for show-and-tell!* Miss Nogard heard him. Before he could lower his hand, she called on him. And that was how he ended up with his shoelace dangling from his hand like a dead worm.

6. A   The kids in Mrs. Jewls's class never used to be so mean, but they'd been getting grumpier and grumpier ever since Miss Nogard took over.

7. B   He tried to think of some way to make a shoelace interesting. "Uh, shoelaces are real important," he said. "There was once this guy. He was a real fast runner. His name was Howard. Howard Speed! He was the fastest runner in the world! But this was back before shoelaces were invented. And so, every time Howard raced, he ran right out of his shoes!"

Chapters 27 & 28

1. C   They shoved and elbowed each other out of the way as they waited for it to come down. At the last second, Eric Fry jumped and caught it. He got three points. Eric Ovens also got three points since he was the thrower.

2. A   All three fought for position as they waited for it to come down, but at the last second, a hairy arm reached above them and caught it. The arm belonged to Louis, the yard teacher. "Can I play?" asked Louis. His mustache had grown back completely.

3. D   "No, you throw it," said Louis. "But you can throw it so much higher," said Eric B. "We want to see how high you can throw it, Louis," said Leslie.

4. A   "You should ask her out on a date," said Eric Fry. "No, I don't think that's a very good idea," said Louis. "Why not?" asked Eric Ovens. "I think you two would make a real cute couple."

5. C   Of course Miss Nogard knew all about Louis. The children's brains were buzzing about him. *Louis likes Miss Nogard,* thought Stephen. *Louis is in love with Miss Nogard,* thought Todd. *Louis wants to marry Miss Nogard,* thought Sharie. But even if she couldn't listen to their brains, she would have found out anyway. "Louis, the yard teacher, is madly in love with you," said Jenny.

6. B   Ever since Xavier broke her heart, she'd become an expert at breaking other people's. She listened to men's brains and knew just what to say to make them fall in love with her.

7. A   "No one's ever brought me flowers before," said Mr. Kidswatter. "You may not believe this, Louis, but I don't have many friends." He put his hand on Louis's shoulder. "You're like a son to me," he said.

156

Chapters 29 & 30

1. A   "Did anyone have any trouble with the homework?" asked Miss Nogard. They all shook their heads. Ron shook his head too. *Homework?* he thought. *What homework?* "Good," said Miss Nogard. "Well, in that case, there won't be any homework tonight."

2. A   *Seven lima beans,* thought Jason. *Seven lima beans,* thought Rondi. *Six cucumbers,* thought Deedee. *Seven lima beans,* thought Stephen. Miss Nogard called on Deedee.

3. B   "I'm very disappointed," she said when they were finished. "You obviously didn't understand it. So I'm afraid I'm going to have to assign homework tonight after all.

4. B   It was the same all around the room. Nobody missed more than two problems. Everyone thought everyone else was stupid!

5. D   She was just about to step on it, when suddenly she became very curious about the kind of thoughts babies had. She had never listened to a baby's brain before. Miss Nogard held Mavis close to her heart and listened. . . .

6. C   It is impossible to describe, in words, exactly what Miss Nogard heard when she listened to Mavis's brain. Babies don't think in words. Miss Nogard heard pure love. And trust. And faith. With no words to get in the way. It was a love so strong that it dissolved away all the bitterness that had been caked around her heart.

7. C   Miss Nogard didn't have to read Louis's mind to know he was telling the truth. She could see it in his eyes. His eyes were like the moon.

WAYSIDE SCHOOL GETS A LITTE STRANGER

1판 1쇄 2015년 4월 1일
2판 1쇄 2021년 5월 10일
2판 2쇄 2022년 7월 25일

지은이 Louis Sachar
기획 이수영
책임편집 김보경 정소이
콘텐츠제작및감수 롱테일북스 편집부
저작권 김보경
마케팅 김보미 정경훈

펴낸이 이수영
펴낸곳 롱테일북스
출판등록 제2015-000191호
주소 04033 서울특별시 마포구 양화로 113, 3층(서교동, 순흥빌딩)
전자메일 helper@longtailbooks.co.kr
(학원·학교에서 본 도서를 교재로 사용하길 원하시는 경우
전자메일로 문의주시면 자세한 안내를 받으실 수 있습니다.)

ISBN 979-11-91343-03-8 14740